The Cambridge Introduction to
W. B. Yeats

This introduction to one of the twentieth century's most important
writers examines Yeats's poems, plays, and stories in relation to
biographical, literary, and historical contexts. Yeats wrote with passion
and eloquence about personal disappointments, Ireland's troubled
history, and the modern era's loss of faith in traditional beliefs about art,
religion, empire, social class, gender, and sex. His works uniquely reflect
the gradual transition from Victorian aestheticism to the modernism of
Pound, Eliot, and Joyce. This is the first introductory study to consider
his work in all genres in light of the latest biographies, new editions of
his letters and manuscripts, and recent accounts by feminist and
postcolonial critics. While using this introduction, students will have
access to the world of current Yeats scholarship as well as to the essential
facts about his life and literary career and suggestions for further
reading.

DAVID HOLDEMAN is Professor of English at the University of
North Texas.

Cambridge Introductions to Literature

This series is designed to introduce students to key topics and authors.
Accessible and lively, these introductions will also appeal to readers who
want to broaden their understanding of the books and authors they enjoy.

- Ideal for students, teachers, and lecturers
- Concise, yet packed with essential information
- Key suggestions for further reading

Titles in this series:

Eric Bulson *The Cambridge Introduction to James Joyce*

John Xiros Cooper *The Cambridge Introduction to T. S. Eliot*

Janette Dillon *The Cambridge Introduction to Early English Theatre*

Jane Goldman *The Cambridge Introduction to Virginia Woolf*

David Holdeman *The Cambridge Introduction to W. B. Yeats*

Ronan McDonald *The Cambridge Introduction to Samuel Beckett*

John Peters *The Cambridge Introduction to Joseph Conrad*

Martin Scofield *The Cambridge Introduction to the American Short Story*

Peter Thomson *The Cambridge Introduction to English Theatre, 1660–1900*

Janet Todd *The Cambridge Introduction to Jane Austen*

The Cambridge Introduction to
W. B. Yeats

DAVID HOLDEMAN

Professor of English, The University of North Texas

 CAMBRIDGE
UNIVERSITY PRESS

CAMBRIDGE UNIVERSITY PRESS
Cambridge, New York, Melbourne, Madrid, Cape Town, Singapore, São Paulo

CAMBRIDGE UNIVERSITY PRESS
The Edinburgh Building, Cambridge CB2 2RU, UK
Published in the United States of America by Cambridge University Press, New York

www.cambridge.org
Information on this title: www.cambridge.org/9780521547376

First published 2006

Printed in the United Kingdom at the University Press, Cambridge

A catalogue record for this publication is available from the British Library

Library of Congress Cataloguing in Publication data

ISBN-13 978-0-521-83855-9 hardback
ISBN-10 0-521-83855-x hardback
ISBN-13 978-0-521-54737-6 paperback
ISBN-10 0-521-54737-7 paperback

For Sam and Sarah

Contents

Preface   *page* ix
Acknowledgments   xi
List of abbreviations   xii

Chapter 1 Early Yeats   1

Childhood   1
Early religious and political views   4
"Crossways"   7
Maud Gonne, gender, and *The Countess Cathleen*   12
"The Rose"   17
The Secret Rose and *The Wind Among the Reeds*   22
The fading of the Rose   33

Chapter 2 Middle Yeats   36

The Irish National Theatre   36
Early plays: *Cathleen ni Houlihan, On Baile's
    Strand,* and *The King's Threshold*   41
Drama's influence on Yeats's verse style: *In the Seven Woods*   46
Revisions, masks, and *The Green Helmet and Other Poems*   51
Responsibilities   58
Ireland's "Troubles"   63

Chapter 3 Late Yeats   66

Lunar visions: *The Wild Swans at Coole*   66
Four Plays for Dancers and *Michael Robartes and the Dancer*   70
The Tower   78
The Winding Stair and Other Poems   92

Blueshirts, eugenics, "lust and rage": Yeats's final works   101
Death   113

Chapter 4 Yeats's critics   115

Bibliographies, scholarly editions, and biographies   115
Critical studies   118

Notes   127
Guide to further reading   134
Index   137

Preface

William Butler Yeats ranks among the most widely admired and intensively studied writers of the twentieth century. He attracts such avid interest because, as T. S. Eliot famously suggested, his history is also the history of his time. Beginning as a late-Victorian aesthete and ending as an influential contemporary of Eliot and other modernists, Yeats set the pace for two generations of important writers. Along the way he responded with passion and eloquence to the political and cultural upheavals associated with Ireland's struggle for independence and with the decline (in Ireland and elsewhere) of traditional beliefs about art, religion, empire, social class, gender, and sex. But the same things that make Yeats captivating also make him difficult to study and to teach: few first-time readers know enough about his life and times to do justice to his poems, plays, and other writings. *The Cambridge Introduction to W. B. Yeats* aims to assist such readers by providing introductory tours of the poet's most important works in all genres and by exploring their biographical, historical, and literary contexts. As the first new introduction to appear in more than a decade, it offers an up-to-date account that draws extensively on recent biographies, fresh editions of the letters and manuscripts, and path-breaking studies by critics influenced by feminism and postcolonial theory.

In keeping with the premise that Yeats became an interesting and difficult figure largely because of the way his life, his times, and his works gradually shaped and reshaped each other, this book adopts a chronological structure. Chapter 1 relates the poems and stories of the late 1880s and 1890s to the poet's early passions for occult spirituality, Irish nationalism, and the beautiful nationalist agitator, Maud Gonne. Chapter 2 focuses on the years between 1900 and 1915, when he rejected many of the Romantic idealizations of his early works, founded an Irish national theatre, and developed sparer, proto-modernist modes of both dramatic and lyric writing. Chapter 3 surveys the famous late phase that began with the onset of the Irish "Troubles" of 1916–23 and continued until his death in 1939. Chapter 4 offers a brief sketch of the major critical approaches that have developed between 1939 and the present day.

The first three chapters feature numerous accounts of particular, exemplary works: these accounts attempt to provide starting points for further thought rather than definitive interpretations. They also attempt to nurture the enthusiasm of first-time readers without descending into uncritical celebration. Many of Yeats's attitudes – about class, for example – deserve to be interrogated carefully, even by beginners. But most readers will never become sufficiently interested in the poet to think critically about him unless they are first encouraged to enjoy and appreciate his work. By and large, Yeats elicits admiration not because he worked out systems of thought and belief his admirers would wish to share. Instead, he teaches us and moves us mainly by virtue of his astonishing capacity for feeling and expressing both the universal contradictions that come with being alive and those particular contradictions that came along during the crucial period of his lifetime. His poems and plays do not make statements and ask us to agree or disagree. They transport us to the midst of vital, turbulent currents of thinking, feeling, believing, and doubting. They let us glimpse what it was like to be in love with someone like Gonne. They take us on spiritual quests that alternate moments of triumphant supernatural vision with long stretches of intervening darkness. They dramatize the political debates Yeats staged with himself and others as he watched the ideal Ireland he envisioned in early life lose out to middle-class materialism and to the "terrible beauty" of the Easter Rising and its aftermath. Learning to read Yeats is not only a matter of understanding his beliefs, of seeing how his views were shaped by his life and times and how they in turn shaped his works. It is also, more fundamentally and more excitingly, a matter of opening oneself up imaginatively, of experiencing for oneself the powerful currents of thought and feeling his works set free.

Acknowledgments

My thinking about Yeats is deeply indebted to all of the scholars and critics mentioned in Chapter 4, especially Richard Ellmann, Thomas Parkinson, Elizabeth Butler Cullingford, and R. F. Foster. I am equally indebted to the teachers who first nurtured my interest in the poet: Lewis Miller, Brian Caraher, Donald Gray, and above all George Bornstein. My students have also taught me much, and I am particularly grateful to Deng-Huei Lee, David Tomkins, and Amanda Tucker. Among my colleagues at the University of North Texas, Jenny Adams commented astutely on an early draft, Jack Peters shared useful advice, and James T. F. Tanner enabled the hiring of an assistant, Tammy Walker, to whom I also offer thanks. My greatest debts are to my family. My wife, Karen DeVinney, heartened my spirits and improved my writing. My mother-in-law, Donna DeVinney, read and praised preliminary drafts. My children, Samuel DeVinney Holdeman and Sarah Ruth Holdeman, spent two hot Texas summers playing outside or upstairs while I worked: with much love, I dedicate this book to them.

Abbreviations

Unless otherwise specified, quotations from Yeats's works come from the first two editions listed below. Where further clarification is necessary, parenthetical citations appear. These employ the following abbreviations:

P   *The Collected Works of W. B. Yeats, Volume I: The Poems, Revised*, ed. Richard J. Finneran (Macmillan, 1989).

Pl   *The Collected Works of W. B. Yeats, Volume II: The Plays*, ed. David R. Clark and Rosalind E. Clark (Scribner, 2001).

A   *The Collected Works of W. B. Yeats, Volume III: Autobiographies*, ed. William H. O'Donnell and Douglas N. Archibald (Scribner, 1999).

LE   *The Collected Works of W. B. Yeats, Volume V: Later Essays*, ed. William H. O'Donnell (Scribner, 1994).

SR   *The Secret Rose, Stories by W. B. Yeats: A Variorum Edition*, ed. Warwick Gould, Phillip L. Marcus, and Michael J. Sidnell (Macmillan, 1992).

VP   *The Variorum Edition of the Poems of W. B. Yeats*, ed. Peter Allt and Russell K. Alspach (rev. 3rd printing, Macmillan, 1966).

VPl *The Variorum Edition of the Plays of W. B. Yeats*, ed. Russell K. Alspach (Macmillan, 1966).

Chapter 1

Early Yeats

Childhood   *1*
Early religious and political views   *4*
"Crossways"   *7*
Maud Gonne, gender, and *The Countess Cathleen*   *12*
"The Rose"   *17*
The Secret Rose and *The Wind Among the Reeds*   *22*
The fading of the Rose   *33*

A conviction that the world was now but a bundle of fragments possessed
me without ceasing.

> *Four Years: 1887–1891*, Book I of *The Trembling of the Veil* (1922)

At the age of fifty, Yeats surprised his family by revealing that he remembered
"little of childhood but its pain" (A 45). This confession may also surprise
new readers of his early works, where his sorrowful, otherworldly longings
sometimes seem more literary than real. But the young poet's pain was only
too real. It arose from his keen perception of the fractured state both of the
world around him and of his own inner being, a perception that made life
appear incoherent and therefore empty of meaning and value. In response, he
devoted his art to the never-ending effort to forge his fragmented self and
surroundings into unity, with outcomes by turns triumphant and failed,
admirable and problematic. This chapter outlines his early life and work
through the end of the 1890s.

Childhood

Yeats's youthful anxieties originated in the tensions that troubled his family
and in the social and political divides of late-nineteenth-century Irish life. In
1867, less than two years after the poet's birth in suburban Dublin on June 13,
1865, his father abandoned a promising law career and enrolled in a London
art school with the intention of becoming a painter. Influenced by such

scientific and rationalist thinkers as Charles Darwin and John Stuart Mill, John Butler Yeats had already exchanged Christian belief for skeptical, agnostic views that compensated for religion by playing up the importance of art. Such radical breaks with convention eventually fostered W. B. Yeats's development, not least by bringing him into contact with London's intellectual and artistic circles. But they also opened a deep rift between his parents, placed him at times in impoverished circumstances, and weakened his ties to his forefathers' faith. As a child who divided his time between London and visits to family back home, he grew sharply conscious of the conflicts that alienated colonial Ireland from imperial Britain and that, within Ireland, divided Protestant descendants of British settlers from their usually less powerful and poorer Catholic neighbors.

Yeats's mother, Susan Mary (née Pollexfen) Yeats, came from a prosperous Protestant family. His father's background was even more impeccable: John Butler Yeats hailed from a long line of well-off merchants, government officials, landowners, and Church of Ireland clergymen. When Susan Yeats married in 1863, she had every expectation that her handsome young university-educated husband would become a prominent Dublin lawyer and provide a comfortable Irish life. She certainly had no desire to live among artistic bohemians, and disliked the eccentric friends her husband made in London. She also disliked living in England, and resented the financial hardships and loss of social position that attended her husband's altered choice of an unprofitable and (to her mind) vaguely disreputable career. Over the course of her eldest son's youth she gradually retreated into a speechless and bedridden state, brought on by depression and by a series of strokes that hastened her death in 1900 at the age of fifty-eight. Although the patriarchal structure of Victorian life and her own poor health obliged her to suffer in silence, her brooding presence imprinted her children with a profound sense of loss associated not only with the missing harmony that might have characterized a happier family's life but also with their exile from Ireland and their diminished class status.

John Butler Yeats might have minimized his family's hardships had he been better able to translate his considerable artistic talents into finished, saleable paintings. Had he lived in an earlier era, however, he might never have needed to worry about his fortunes. These were declining even before he left the law for art. His own father had made a number of unsuccessful investments, and at the time of his marriage his only income came from some house property in Dublin and some modest farms in County Kildare. Although this sustained him in comfort in 1863, it soon shrank drastically. By 1880 his property was earning next to nothing, and by 1888 it had all been sold, the proceeds consumed by debts. These were the years when the organization known as the Land League was encouraging poor and mostly Catholic tenant farmers all over Ireland to protest their lot by taking concerted action against their usually Protestant landlords. Tenants withheld rents, ostracized landlords, and sometimes engaged in violent intimidation. Though many landlords responded by evicting their tenants, the Land War (as it came to be called) eventually led to legislative concessions that limited rents and provided funds to assist tenants in purchasing the land they worked. The Yeatses were one of many Protestant landowning families whose status was diminished by this process. Such diminishment – in the form of unpaid bills and somewhat shabby residences – amplified their household tensions and indelibly marked the attitudes of the boy who would later write such poems as "Upon a House shaken by the Land Agitation."

While the deprivations imposed by the Land War and by his family's break with convention forced Yeats to live out part of his boyhood in dingy urban exile, they also sent him to Sligo, the western Irish seaport home of the Pollexfens. After his father's departure for London, lack of money repeatedly obliged the rest of the family to take refuge with Susan Yeats's parents. Yeats's brother Jack – eventually one of the most distinguished Irish painters of the twentieth century – passed most of his childhood in Sligo. Yeats and his other siblings spent less time there, but nevertheless grew accustomed to staying in their grandparents' house for months on end, especially during their earliest years and their summers. That house, Merville, was an impressive one, a roomy mansion on sixty acres at the edge of town where, in addition to their grandparents, the young Yeatses mixed with a large complement of aunts, uncles, and servants. Although the Pollexfens were seen as socially inferior to Sligo's landed gentry, their wealth was considerable and, for the time being, secure, deriving from mid-sized manufacturing and shipping interests unaffected by the Land War. Merville exposed the Yeats children to solid material comforts and – more importantly – some of the most breathtaking countryside in Ireland. East of Sligo the waters of Lough Gill lapped the shores of many small islands such as the one later immortalized as "The Lake Isle of Innisfree." In the north, waterfalls cascaded down the slopes of Ben Bulben, under which stood the fine church at Drumcliff, where Yeats's great-grandfather had been Rector, and where the poet himself would be buried. To the west lay the cairn-topped summit of Knocknarea, the fishing village of Rosses Point, and, after that, the sea.

Both Yeats's earlier and later works make it clear that these places solaced him in deep and lasting ways. And yet his Sligo sojourns did not wholly allay his anxieties. For every restoring voyage west there was another painful return to London, and such oscillation made him wonder if he truly belonged in either place. In London he was the shy, day-dreaming son of a disconsolate mother and an (apparently) unsuccessful father; at school he was placed near the bottom of his class in most subjects and was derided by his classmates for being unathletic and Irish. In Sligo, he communed with soul-restoring beauty but could not escape some awareness of the fact that his Anglo-Irish family's connections to that beauty were less time-honored than those of the Catholic servants and laborers they employed, whose ties went back for centuries, and whose disadvantaged position reflected their ancestors' displacement by British settlers. A more immediate source of anxiety was the atmosphere at Merville. The Pollexfens were a moody, taciturn family. Chief among them was Yeats's grandfather, William Pollexfen, a "silent and fierce old man" who had run away to sea as a boy and, having made his own fortune by acting boldly, had little patience for those more timid or reflective than he (P 101). His grandson's later poems and *Autobiographies* celebrate the heroism he evinced by performing such deeds as diving off the deck of a ship to examine its damaged rudder. But to the sensitive child he was a forbidding figure who presided over a strictly governed household filled with unspoken frustrations.

Eventually, in 1881, in the throes of financial crisis, John Butler Yeats decided that his homeland might produce more art commissions than England had, and returned his family to Ireland, where they stayed for six years before uprooting back to London. They spent the first part of this homecoming at Howth, a scenic coastal village near Dublin. Though by no means reconciled to her life's unexpected turns, Susan Yeats liked Howth and enjoyed exchanging ghost stories and folk tales with the local fishermen's wives. Her husband and eldest son commuted daily by train to Dublin, where the former had a studio and the latter attended, first, Erasmus Smith High School, and then, beginning in 1884, the Metropolitan School of Art. It was during this period that the teen-aged Yeats began to formulate tentative responses to the conflicts that unsettled his country, his family, and his psyche. That he initially opted for art school is testament to his father's early influence. But by 1886 he had abandoned painting and was gathering his nerve to make his own way as a writer.

Early religious and political views

Spiritual impulses were among the first to stir Yeats into writing. His childhood coincided with a time when growing numbers of people were disavowing orthodox Christianity, largely because the stunning discoveries of nineteenth-century science – about the earth's age, the existence of now-extinct species, human evolution, and so on – had made it difficult to accept the Bible and other traditional religious authorities at face value. His father's skepticism was uncommon (especially in Ireland) but by no means unparalleled. Yeats found his father's forcefully expressed views difficult to ignore, but also possessed an unquenchable desire for some form of spiritual wholeness capable of easing the world- and self-splintering tensions he felt so keenly. His father's influence and the narrow conventionality he encountered in both Protestantism and Catholicism combined to make him averse to mainstream religious institutions and their official orthodoxies. But he could not share his father's agnosticism and by late adolescence had already rejected both conventional Christianity and scientific materialism. Insisting on intuitive spiritual truths inaccessible to his father's outlook, he embarked on a lifelong search for the secret, symbolically expressed wisdom he believed the world's various orthodox and unorthodox religious traditions might have in common. At the High School and then during his art school years he made friends with like-minded young men, including George Russell, subsequently to become the visionary poet and artist "AE". Soon he began to join and organize hermetical societies, and when the faddish mélange of eastern and western mystical lore known as Theosophy swept Dublin's occult circles in 1885, he immersed himself eagerly. Later, after his family's return to London in 1887, he sought out the Theosophists' leader, the notorious Madame Blavatsky, and continued his study of Buddhist and Hindu traditions as filtered by her and her followers. Although he always preserved some of his father's skepticism, he also experimented with magic and attended séances, experiencing great shock on one occasion when a spirit actually seemed to possess him for several moments. These experiences eventually affected not only the substance of Yeats's works but also, more fundamentally, what he perceived them to be: for him, there was a tantalizing similarity between the aesthetic wholeness created by a poem and the harmonizing supernatural powers of a magical spell. Poems used symbols to evoke mysterious forces that promised to fit life's broken fragments into a deeper hidden unity.

The urge to connect his broken life to a greater unity soon also led Yeats to write in sympathy with those whose visions of a united Ireland demanded reduced or severed ties to Britain. This commitment is often credited to John O'Leary, the bookish former revolutionary who became the young poet's political mentor in 1885. O'Leary urged his protégé to foster a coherent national culture by emulating Thomas Davis and other poets associated with the Young Ireland movement, who had come to fame in the 1840s by writing popular, patriotic verse about Ireland in the English language. O'Leary's influence was crucial, but Yeats's father also molded his politics. Unlike most members of Protestant families, and despite his losses during the Land War, John Butler Yeats did not embrace Unionism: that set of political and social convictions centering on the preservation of Ireland's political union with Great Britain and of the privileged status conferred by that union on the descendants of the colonists who had crossed the Irish Sea during the centuries-old effort to merge Catholic Ireland with Protestant Britain's empire. He did not, however, approve the aggressive tactics of the Land League or of Charles Stewart Parnell, the leader of the Irish Party in the British Parliament. Before being driven from power by a sex scandal in 1890, Parnell used his control over both the Land League and the Irish Party to maneuver the British Parliament to the verge of granting Home Rule, which would have given Ireland its own partly autonomous legislature. John Butler Yeats supported Home Rule, but believed that pursuing it by threatening means violated the code of an Irish Protestant gentleman. Though his son would later experiment with more radical political ideas, he remained conditioned by his father's instincts about Home Rule and Irish Protestant gentility. His early poems typically offer chivalric allegories that meditate on the complexities of Irish politics and avoid direct calls for real-world insurrections.

Yeats's politics were also conditioned by his meditations on the contrast between London's deprivations and Sligo's more attractive physical and cultural landscapes. By the late 1880s his hatred for the city of his exile had less to do with mere poverty or the humiliation of being singled out as Irish than with the new understanding of London and, more generally, England that he had derived from England's own most radical artists and intellectuals. In addition to being the center of a global empire that included Ireland, England was also the cradle of the industrial revolution and of capitalism, the home of factory-filled, slum-ridden, bustling, wealthy cities. Its association with the enslaving, soul-deadening consequences of empire, mass production, and *laissez-faire* social policies had long been decried by a vibrant counter-cultural tradition stretching from such Romantic poets as Blake and Shelley forward to the critic John Ruskin and to the so-called Pre-Raphaelite group of artists, whose emphasis on individual imagination and preference for preindustrial modes of life and art had inspired John Butler Yeats's artistic aspirations. Steeping himself in this tradition, and in particular in the aesthetic and political doctrines of William Morris, Yeats associated England with everything he loathed about the modern world: with imperialism, with vulgar, godless materialism, with urban ugliness and squalor. Ireland, by contrast, appeared an unspoiled, beautiful place where people lived according to age-old traditions and held on to magical, time-honored beliefs. Ireland's remote western regions held special importance, not only because of Yeats's ties to Sligo but also because of the west's comparative isolation from the British influences that had more powerfully affected the populous and accessible east. Although the west had been ravaged by the famines of the 1840s (and thus marked by the catastrophic effects of British neglect), many of its people still spoke Irish, and many more preserved distinctively Irish stories and values. By his early twenties Yeats was searching for the answers to his spiritual and political questions in the folk beliefs of Ireland's western country people and in the heroic myths of the whole island's ancient Gaelic culture. These traditions, he felt, preserved satisfying ways of life and eternal spiritual truths that had been forgotten in modernized places like England and that were threatened, even in Ireland, by the encroachment of British culture. The British sometimes justified their empire in Ireland and elsewhere by describing those over whom they held sway as savages. In texts ranging from novels to political cartoons, they stereotyped the Irish as irrational, effeminate, and drunken: in other words, as unfit to govern themselves. During his early years, Yeats sought to counter such stereotypes by presenting Ireland – and especially its ancient and rural aspects – as full of beauty, wisdom, and passionate heroism. He thus also laid a foundation for building his own satisfying identity.

"Crossways"

Depending on the edition, Yeats's collected *Poems* begins either with a series of lyrics grouped under the heading of "Crossways" or with a long poem called "The Wanderings of Oisin" (pronounced "AW-sheen").[1] Either way, it commences with material mostly drawn from the poet's first major book, *The Wanderings of Oisin and Other Poems* (1889). Yeats assembled "Crossways" in 1895 for his first collected edition, and though it makes an accessible point of entry to his poetry, readers should understand that it offers a much-revised distillation of the book that appeared in 1889. The desire to construct an oeuvre that brought himself and his world into unity made Yeats an inveterate reviser. As such, he created pitfalls for those who study his compositions without awareness of their textual histories. He also created opportunities for us to strengthen our grasp of his works by comparing earlier and later versions.[2]

"Crossways" opens with "The Song of the Happy Shepherd," a lyric that predates Yeats's decision to focus his writing on Ireland, and that instead reflects his teen-aged immersion in the pastoral and Romantic traditions of English poetry. Though few would rank it among his most accomplished works, it manifests crucial early inclinations. Its speaker is an idealized poet-shepherd of the type that conventionally appears in pastoral poetry, the traditions of which extend back to the ancient Greeks. Belying the title's description of him as "Happy," the shepherd laments the death of these age-old traditions, extinguished in a world that has exchanged nourishing dreams for the "painted toy" of "Grey Truth" (presumably, the spiritless truth of scientific materialism). To a world made "sick" by this situation, he defiantly announces that of all the "changing things" constituting temporal, material experience, "Words alone are certain good." This resonant statement calls to mind Yeats's interest in magic, in symbolic words capable of summoning supernatural realities. But it also suggests the long-standing predilection of Romantic poets for proclaiming the primacy of mind or word over matter; one thinks of Blake's pronouncement that "Mental Things are Alone Real" or the implication of Shelley's "Mont Blanc" that the physical world would be nothing "If to the human mind's imaginings / Silence and solitude were vacancy[.]"[3] Though interested in Theosophy and other similar creeds, Yeats tells us in his *Autobiographies* that, even at this stage of his life, he believed most fundamentally "that whatever the great poets had affirmed in their finest moments was the nearest we could come to an authoritative religion" (A 97). Something deep within him always insisted on his right to imagine the truth for himself, unfettered by others' perceptions. An unmistakable hint of such boldness rings out here, even amid the derivative echoes.

Some of the shepherd's claims for poetic words are asserted so fervently, however, that they seem to betray anxiety. His blustering dismissal of the "warring kings," for example, suggests that, to some extent, his swagger masks the uncertainties of an instinctively timid poet who is far from sure that his preference for "endless reverie" really does make him superior to those who pursue heroic deeds. This uncertainty indicates the nascent presence of a quality that would eventually grow into one of Yeats's greatest strengths: his willingness to explore his doubts, even as he asserts his beliefs. Here, these doubts come across most obviously in what the shepherd tells us about the shell and then about the "hapless faun." The "twisted, echo-harbouring shell" – surely an emblem of poetry itself – responds with solipsistic "guile" to the stories people bring to it, offering comfort only for "a little while" before its echoing words "fade" and "die." Such language greatly undercuts the ensuing repetition of the claim that "words alone are certain good." The faun's evocation is similarly vexed; the only thing certain here is that the faun is dead and buried: that his ghost will be revived by the shepherd's "glad singing" depends upon a dream, possibly an illusory, narcotic one, given the reference to "poppies on the brow." Can dream-inspired words transform the world of the living and reanimate the world of the dead? The poem hopes so, but the more one reads it the less confident its hopes come to seem.

Yeats explores his uncertainties further in subsequent "Crossways" poems, such as "The Sad Shepherd" and the several poems inspired by classical Indian literature that follow. "The Indian upon God" considers whether any deity merely mirrors a narcissistic self, while a similarly narcissistic "parrot . . . / Raging at his own image in the enamelled sea" presides over the paradise promised by "The Indian to his Love." The possibility that poetic words might encourage a self-deceiving solipsism was taken up by an even greater number of poems in the original 1889 book; it represented an obvious nightmare for a young poet who feared nothing more than being trapped inside a fragmented inner being, isolated from cultural and spiritual unities. In 1889, however, the Indian lyrics came before rather than after "The Song of the Happy Shepherd," which there was followed by "The Madness of King Goll," an equally revealing early poem that also earned a prominent place in "Crossways." "King Goll" calls attention to the Happy Shepherd's uncertainties by dramatizing a warring king who has given up dusty deeds only to find that poetic dreams foster "inhuman" desires for things beyond the reach of mere mortals. The poem also illustrates another important facet of Yeats's early work: its interest in pre-Christian Ireland's heroic myths, something emphasized in the 1889 collection by the imposing presence of its lengthy title poem. Yeats based "The Wanderings of Oisin" on an old Irish legend known through comparatively recent English translations. It centers on a warrior much like King Goll whose decision to abandon the mortal world of his fighting companions similarly ends in disaster. Following a beautiful supernatural woman called Niamh (pronounced "NEE-iv"), Oisin crosses western seas to otherworldly islands inhabited by immortals; there he devotes a hundred years each to dancing, fighting, and resting before yielding to the impulse to revisit his former companions. He returns to find them long dead, their heroic, pagan way of life tamed by the Christian orthodoxies of the recently arrived Saint Patrick. Touching the earth, Oisin breaks the spell that has preserved his youth and is suddenly withered by the weight of his 300-year absence. Urged by the saint to repent and convert, he defiantly vows to rejoin the warriors of old, even if he must do so in hell.

Both "The Wanderings of Oisin" and "The Madness of King Goll" exemplify the youthful poet's emerging commitment to Irish cultural nationalism: they associate Ireland with traditions of heroism and beauty and so contest the demeaning stereotypes sometimes used by the British to justify their rule. Traces of a more radical nationalism also show up in "Oisin." When the hero answers the saint by pledging loyalty to the Fenians, he invokes a name that Yeats's readers would have associated not only with Oisin's band of ancient warriors but also with the nineteenth-century forerunners of the Irish Republican Army. But the milder implications that predominate in "Oisin" and "King Goll" typify Yeats's earliest treatments of Irish heroic materials, distinguishing them from the more strident poems O'Leary had suggested as models. If one compares either "Oisin" or "King Goll" to such famous earlier poetic celebrations of Irish national heroes as James Mangan's translation of "O'Hussey's Ode to the Maguire" or Thomas Davis's "Lament for the Death of Owen Roe O'Neill," one notices a number of differences that make Yeats's poems more complex.[4] Yeats focuses on mythic heroes from an age that had faded centuries before the modern struggle between Ireland and Britain began; Mangan and Davis celebrate historical figures who led seventeenth-century rebellions. In Yeats's poems the central conflict takes place in the hero's psyche; Mangan and (especially) Davis describe external conflicts between the forces of Irish good and British evil. Their heroes are one-dimensional figures presented as having fought the good fight and as meriting unadulterated reverence. Oisin and King Goll are multifaceted: they appear more as failed questers than as tragically sacrificed patriots.

Indeed, "King Goll" depicts a man who becomes dissatisfied despite his success in unifying Ireland politically, driving away its foreign enemies, and bringing it prosperity. This happens when, at the climax of yet another violent triumph, he enters a "whirling and a wandering fire" that grows in his "most secret spirit" and inspires a strange vision of the cosmos and of the "battle-breaking men" around him. This epiphany enriches his perceptions, changing him from a shouting warrior who tramples in bloody mire to a gentle intimate of the natural world. But, by arousing desires for otherworldly experiences that he can imagine but never consummate, it also exiles him from human society and ultimately drives him mad. His "inhuman misery" is temporarily "quenched" after he finds a tympan, an ancient Irish stringed instrument that emblematically suggests Irish music and poetry. By the time we hear him speak, however, the tympan's wires have broken, and he seems fated to wander endlessly. The tympan's broken condition recalls the death of European poetic traditions confronted by the Happy Shepherd. It also evokes the precipitous decline of the Irish language and of native Gaelic culture that occurred in the early nineteenth century as a result of repressive British policies and the desolation wrought by famine. In so doing, it hints at Yeats's dissatisfaction with the English-language poetry written in Ireland in the wake of that decline, perhaps reflecting his sense that such one-sidedly partisan poems as Davis's and Mangan's cannot provide the complex forms of inspiration needed by King Goll and his modern counterparts.

"King Goll" demonstrates Yeats's commitments not only through what it expresses on its own but also by virtue of its pivotal place in "Crossways." As the first of the collection's poems to take up Irish subject matter, it establishes a precedent followed by all succeeding poems. This allows the collection to dramatize Yeats as a poet who begins by deriving inspiration from such non-Irish sources as English pastoral lyrics and the literature of classical India but then quickly and permanently turns his thoughts toward home. Unlike "King Goll" and "The Wanderings of Oisin," however, the Irish poems from the second half of "Crossways" are not based on material from the written texts that preserve Ireland's heroic legends. They take their inspiration, rather, from the oral traditions of Irish folklore, from the songs and stories of the country people. The wit and beauty of these songs and stories made them ideal sources for a poet who wanted to portray Ireland favorably, and for someone who spoke only English they were more accessible than the poorly translated or untranslated texts of ancient Irish literature. Many readers – especially Irish immigrants in England or America – felt a strong appetite for nostalgic renderings of fairy tales and other peasant lore, an appetite Yeats fed not only with poems and essays but also with two anthologies of folk materials he assembled from the work of other Irish writers, *Fairy and Folk Tales of the Irish Peasantry* (1888) and *Irish Fairy Tales* (1892). Compiling these books made him something of a folklore authority, and he also gathered stories directly from the country people around Sligo. Although his own writing catered to popular expectations up to a point, he took folk beliefs far more seriously than most. His essays describe encounters with people who claim to believe in or even to have met the fairies; they also leave the door open on the question of his own belief. In one essay intended for fellow occultists, he carefully considered whether the fairies might be Irish emissaries from the ghostly netherworlds posited by Theosophy. Usually, though, he proceeded more tentatively, implying both beliefs and doubts. Probably the best example of his approach is "The Stolen Child," the most famous fairy poem from the 1889 volume to find a place in "Crossways."

This poem, based on the belief that fairies sometimes steal human children, is one of Yeats's best loved lyrics. Among the earliest to refer to such actual Sligo places as Sleuth Wood, Rosses Point, and Glen-Car Lough, it has been reprinted with glossy scenic photographs in many a picture book devoted to the "Yeats Country," inspiring countless literary tourists to make the Sligo pilgrimage. On the plain page, far away from Sligo, the poem may seem a bit too sweetly magical, a bit too quaint or twee. Yet like such apparent nursery-rhyme verse as William Blake's *Songs of Innocence* or Christina Rossetti's "Goblin Market," it offers more than first meets the eye. It gives off, first of all, at least the whiff of cultural politics: one can easily imagine Irish readers in Dublin, London, or Boston interpreting its refrain as an invitation to abandon their Anglicized, modernized selves and "come away" to the seemingly more authentic form of Irishness associated with western peasant traditions. There are also repeated indications that the fairies tempt the child with something genuinely dangerous, indications largely absent from such tamely conventional earlier treatments of the subject as William Allingham's "The Fairies." The final stanza, in particular, signals that when the child leaves the world of mortal weeping he also exiles himself – like the Happy Shepherd, Oisin, and King Goll – from the peacefully comfortable human world represented by the lowing calves, singing kettle, and bobbing mice. Even the fact that the fairies' new companion is a child proves troubling. Does the poem (like Wordsworth's "Intimations of Immortality") suggest in true Romantic fashion that innocent children are the best philosophers? Or does it imply that only a child unable to "understand" the world could be so immature as to yield to the fairies' temptations? Although Yeats closes the poem by revealing that the child goes with his tempters, he leaves such larger questions open.

Maud Gonne, gender, and *The Countess Cathleen*

The Wanderings of Oisin and Other Poems elicited a large number of reviews in Ireland and Britain, and a few more in America. One hostile Irish notice accused Yeats of substituting "obscurity" for "strenuous thought and sound judgment."[5] Others were more enthusiastic, suggesting that, while the book might include a few perplexing references or rough lines, it constituted a promising first effort. Oscar Wilde's unsigned response praised Yeats for "largeness of vision" and prophesied a "fine future."[6] William Morris, meeting him in the street, told him that "You write my sort of poetry" (A 135).

The volume's most influential reader, however, was neither a reviewer nor a famous fellow poet but rather a young, rich, beautiful nationalist agitator by the name of Maud Gonne, who called on the Yeatses in London shortly after the new book's appearance in January 1889. Dazzled by her beauty and her charismatic commitment to the Irish cause, Yeats promptly fell in love. Gonne spent a good deal of time with him – when she was in London – and rapidly came to treat him as a close friend and ally who shared her hopes and dreams. But neither spoke of love or marriage. Despite his book's success, Yeats remained a shy young man with little money who lived at home with his parents and siblings. Gonne's private life presented even greater obstacles. Mostly, she lived in Paris, where, unbeknownst to Yeats, she had embarked on a long-term love affair with the radical French journalist Lucien Millevoye, with whom she conceived a child several months after meeting the poet. Yeats knew nothing of this until much later, and remained unsure how to interpret her friendship. Eventually, in 1891, things came to a head. In July they met in Dublin, where Yeats took heart from Gonne's uncharacteristically gentle manner. Soon afterwards she wrote to describe a dream in which they had been brother and sister in a past life in Arabia and sold into slavery together. That this dream cast him as a brother rather than a lover did not discourage him. They saw each other again in August and yet again in October, and by the second of these two occasions Gonne was reeling from the recent death of her infant son, Georges. Turning to Yeats for comfort, she left Millevoye unmentioned but confided her sorrow about Georges, who she said had been adopted. Either in August or October, he proposed marriage. She refused, telling him she could never marry. But she also asked for his continued friendship and in any case did not rebuff him so strongly as to make him lose all hope. He continued to pursue her affections intermittently for the better part of the next twenty-five years, repeating his proposal on several occasions (with the same result), and writing dozens of compelling love poems pleading for her favor or meditating on her refusal to grant it.

This famously unrequited love will require frequent attention as we move forward with the poet's life and work. For now, it is most important to consider the reasons for – and consequences of – Yeats's initial attraction to Gonne. Her physical charms were part of the appeal, of course, but she inspired far more than sexual desire. Because she shared many of his un-orthodox religious interests, he quickly began to regard her as the embodiment of his spiritual beliefs. He was also attracted to her politics, though at times their violence troubled him. A fiery advocate of physical-force nationalism, Gonne made speeches, organized protests, and, generally speaking, did everything she could to hasten the overthrow of British rule. This combination of qualities encouraged Yeats to see her as an heroic symbol of an idealized Ireland. To a surprising extent, his responses to her also reflected the reevaluation of conventional Victorian gender roles that was beginning to occur in connection with the nascent women's suffrage movement. Gonne was aggressive and outspoken rather than submissive and quiet; her young admirer was more passive and dreamy than tough and hard-headed. At this stage, conventional gender stereotypes were especially entrenched in Ireland, reinforced by conservative religious institutions and (as some scholars recently have argued) by the colonial status quo: feeling their manhood to be threatened by British power, Irish men often developed hyper-masculine attitudes and expected Irish women to be correspondingly hyper-feminine. Yeats, however, had been conditioned in atypical ways by his sympathies for his mother and by his eccentric father, who, though domineering, was also uncommonly affectionate and who had exposed him from an early age to the emotive traditions of Romantic art. Hence he did not initially react with exaggerated masculine bravado to the threat of British imperialism. Instead he wrote works that explore and challenge gender norms, sometimes opposing heroic, "masculine" women to dreamy, "feminine" men and regarding both with a mixture of fascination and anxiety.

On reflection one can see that untraditional attitudes about gender began to emerge in Yeats's works even before his fateful first meeting with Gonne. His earliest poems not only depict otherworldly heroes grown discontented with the supposedly masculine realm of dusty deeds but also feature women sometimes portrayed as uncommonly powerful: Niamh, for example, leads Oisin, and not the other way around. Yeats's tendency to make friends with assertive and creative women also predated his acquaintance with Gonne. The best early example of this tendency is his close friendship with the young Irish writer Katharine Tynan, to whom he complained as early as 1887 that the women found in most contemporary poems by men were "essentially men's heroines with no seperate [sic] life of their own."[7] The challenge of understanding Gonne, however, forced some of the contradictions in his attitudes out into the open. Not surprisingly, he had grown up absorbing both conventional and unconventional notions. If from one angle Niamh appears uncommonly powerful, from another she resembles the sexist stereotype of the *femme fatale*. And if Yeats could make friends and fall in love with atypically strong women, he could also look to them for maternal nurturing. In his first and only published novel, *John Sherman*, completed in 1888 though not publicly issued until 1891, the eponymous hero vacillates between the successful London life he will lead if he marries the vivacious Margaret Leland and the quieter existence offered by his rural Irish home and the more traditionally feminine Mary Carton. Ultimately he takes the latter course. In contrast to John Sherman, Yeats began to wonder, after meeting Gonne, if he might not have it both ways. In her he clearly saw a rule-breaking, passionate woman. But he also thought he detected gentler, more spiritual attributes, and it became his fervent desire to illuminate these hidden depths with his love and art and thus to soften Gonne's strident surface. Yeats's wish to mend the contradictions he perceived in Gonne resembled his wish to resolve his own painful inner conflicts: his celebrations of figures like Oisin or King Goll or John Sherman – figures who abandon active lives for spiritual reveries – are invariably complicated by a latently envious preoccupation with outwardly powerful men. On some level he intuited that forging himself into unity would be easier if he had a soulmate whose conflicts mirrored his own.

Nowhere does all of this surface more interestingly than in *The Countess Cathleen*, the title work of his second major book, *The Countess Kathleen and Various Legends and Lyrics* (1892).[8] Written for Gonne in hopes that she might act its leading role, this play became Yeats's first truly memorable dramatic work. Its plot, derived from a story collected for one of his folklore anthologies, features an Irish countess who saves the famine-starved peasants of her district from selling their souls to the devil by first bartering her possessions and then finally her own soul (which God then intervenes to redeem). This scenario took on special meaning as Yeats became aware of Gonne's campaigns on behalf of the hungry and dispossessed in Ireland's rural west, campaigns that roused his admiration but also made him worry that his new love's all-consuming concern for the Irish poor would destroy her own health and soul (not to mention her capacity for devotion to him). The resulting play offers her – and Ireland – both tribute and instruction. To Ireland, it presents an anti-materialist, nationalist fable celebrating the native spiritual traditions that Yeats portrays as the nation's best defense against demons appearing in the guise of mercenary foreigners. At the same time, by stressing Cathleen's dual allegiance to her Christian servant, Oona, and the pagan poet, Aleel, it imagines Irish spirituality as including both orthodox and unorthodox elements, an implication that provoked controversy when it reached the stage in 1899. To Gonne, it offers the flattery of its unstated comparison between her own selfless efforts and those of the noble Cathleen. But it also invites her to emulate a model whose power derives from the sanctity of her soul rather than the ability to make angry speeches or lead violent protests. It provides her with a script that she is indirectly urged to perform both on the stage and off it, betraying Yeats's wish to cast her in a more traditional feminine role.

Indeed, most current readers attracted to the play's tacit advocacy of religious toleration will also be dismayed by its preoccupation with the virginal innocence and aristocratic status that elevate the value of its heroine's soul. Yet there is more to the play – and even to its treatment of gender – than at first may be apparent. Yeats created many of its intricacies during extensive post-publication revisions, some of which occurred many years later. In myriad ways, these changes gradually made Cathleen into a stronger figure.

In the original version, for example, she begins the play already resident in her native barony. In later versions, she arrives as a stranger, a returning exile who has long been wandering in an active search for her true place in the world. Later versions also present her as more decisive in her response to the demons: she spends less time praying and more time giving orders. Yeats made even more important changes to the role of Aleel, called Kevin in 1892. Kevin does not appear until near the end, and is all but ignored by Cathleen when he begs her to keep her soul and seek "the love of some great chief, / And children gathering round your knees" (VPl 148). Later versions, by contrast, depict Aleel traveling with Cathleen from the start. His heightened profile helps to create the revised play's balanced opposition between the pagan, poetic instincts he embodies and the orthodox Christian practicality of his verbal sparring-partner, Oona. Less obviously though perhaps more importantly, his unconventional masculinity acts as a foil to Cathleen's equally unconventional femininity. Despite having the courage to brave the weapons of Shemus and Teigue in Scene II, and to summon and grapple with the angels who announce Cathleen's redemption at the end, Aleel's principal powers are artistic and spiritual: he urges Cathleen toward a peaceful, contemplative life and does not attempt to rescue her by force. His refusal to use force distinguishes him from the unfavorably characterized Shemus, who strikes his wife Mary in a shocking display of masculine violence early in the play. Like Joyce's Leopold Bloom, Aleel contests the rigid parameters of Irish masculinity by behaving to some extent as a "womanly man," thus allowing Cathleen to move a little way toward becoming a manly woman.[9]

Aleel's behavior thus supports the premise that Yeats desired Gonne's softer side to complete, rather than cancel out, her harder, heroic qualities. And while such a desire may seem sexist by 21st-century standards, the poet was still miles ahead of those Victorian men who desired nothing more than a traditional "Angel in the House." He also deserves credit for subjecting himself to the same mix of implicit praise and blame he directed at Gonne and others. By emphasizing Aleel's artistic and spiritual potency and by having Cathleen suggest that she might have loved him in different circumstances, *The Countess Cathleen* indirectly asserts Yeats's masculinity. But the play's far stronger emphasis on Cathleen's rejection of Aleel also draws attention to the limitations of the poet's powers, unflinchingly registering their failure to inspire Gonne to alter herself for him. The play thus suggests that Yeats's need to become more heroic remains every bit as pressing as Gonne's need to become gentler and more soulful.

"The Rose"

Given this implication, it comes as no surprise to learn that while Yeats was writing *The Countess Cathleen* he was also throwing himself into the affairs of Irish cultural politics and embracing new aesthetic and spiritual commitments that entailed more aggressive stances. His *Autobiographies* exaggerate the extent to which he remained a passive dreamer until Gonne inspired him to become a man of the world. But certainly she did spur an increase in his real-world involvements, as did something else to which he later attributed mythic significance: the downfall of Charles Stewart Parnell, leader of the Irish Party. Parnell's adulterous liaison with Katharine O'Shea became publicly known in late 1889 when her husband filed for divorce; by the end of 1890 the ensuing scandal had split the Irish Party and destroyed its long campaign to legislate Home Rule. Yeats sympathized with Parnell, but also saw his failure as a sign that the time had come to turn Ireland's attention away from politics and toward more fundamental cultural and spiritual concerns. This belief – together with his need to impress Gonne and complete himself – soon prompted him to take a leading part in founding Irish literary societies in London and in Dublin. If founding literary societies does not seem a likely way for a would-be hero to save his country and win favor from his beloved, we must remember that Yeats was not organizing polite get-togethers for dainty aesthetes. The Parnell controversy had wrecked Ireland's best chance for greater autonomy in more than a generation, and a significant weight of real-world importance attached to anything that promised to gather the nation's most capable sons and daughters for the purpose of discussing its literary, cultural, spiritual, and (inevitably) political affairs. Yeats strove to convince the new organizations to share his core convictions. Steeling himself to overcome his timidity, he battled his way through innumerable public debates and committee meetings. In the end he succeeded in establishing himself as someone to be reckoned with in Irish literary matters. He failed, however, to persuade the new societies to endorse his heterodox cultural and spiritual visions and eventually made a bitter retreat after losing a protracted struggle for control of a book series called the New Irish Library. His plunge into public work also failed to alter Gonne's reluctance to see him as more than a friend. In fact, she sided with his opponents during the New Irish Library fight, a choice that temporarily estranged them.

Yeats's drive to balance his predilection for reverie with a greater capacity for action also led him to make several less worldly plunges at this time. One took him deep into William Blake, whose "Prophetic Books" and other works he co-edited with Edwin Ellis in a three-volume collection published in 1893. Like Yeats, Blake could not accept a universe in which human beings lived as isolated, broken individuals amid a welter of purely material objects. Instead of seeking to flee this universe, however, Blake worked to redeem it through bold imaginative action. He repeatedly declared that all forms of matter and consciousness derive from a single "universal Poetic Genius" and that humanity's experience of material creation is the legacy of a fall from grace that caused men and women to perceive the primal oneness erroneously as divided.[10] For Blake, individual percipients could reconnect themselves with this oneness only when the imagination cleansed their perceptions. Thus, to seek redemption by evading physical reality – and, in particular, to pursue the Puritanical transcendence of physicality advocated by much Christian orthodoxy – would be to commit the fundamental error known as "negation." True progress could not occur until such oppositions as matter *vs.* spirit and reason *vs.* imagination became what he termed "contraries": equal partners in never-ending processes of creative conflict. It would be years before Yeats fully absorbed the Blakean premise that "Without Contraries is no progression."[11] But his predecessor's basic beliefs began to influence him straight away.

Blake inspired Yeats in part because his works make confident artistic use of ideas the young poet had long encountered in his occult studies. The view that creation manifests a continual war of opposites emanating from a single universal soul was a tenet of Theosophy. It also accorded with the doctrines of another occult group known as the Order of the Golden Dawn, which he joined in 1890. Although these two groups had much in common, the Theosophical Society expelled Yeats soon after he entered the Golden Dawn. The Theosophists could not tolerate his interest in active magical experimentation, preferring students content to listen to Madame Blavatsky's teachings. In the Golden Dawn, by contrast, the pursuit of magical power presented no difficulties. Indeed, its major point of difference with Theosophy was that it stressed the western magical lore of the Cabala and Rosicrucianism rather than eastern mysticism. While mystics typically seek to discipline the self through meditation and thus gradually to merge it with the cosmic oneness, magicians attempt to reach that oneness – and control its energies – by means of rituals, spells, and symbols. All of these appealed to Yeats, and he eagerly began to ascend the elaborate hierarchy of arcane studies and secret initiation ceremonies prescribed by the Golden Dawn and its flamboyant leader, MacGregor Mathers. As an artist, he took a special interest in symbols. Eventually he came to believe that symbols could instill poems with powers like those of magical incantations, powers that brought both poet and reader into contact with the universal spirit. Symbols allowed individual souls to communicate with that spirit along supernatural paths that bypassed the conscious levels of the psyche. Unlike rationally defined allegorical emblems, they called up mysterious implications that could not be pinned down; they inspired dreams and reveries, but also called up forces potent enough to transform self and world.

Like all initiates in the Golden Dawn, Yeats offered special devotions to the central symbol of the Rose. This emblem quickly began to surface in his lyrics and eventually provided the title of "The Rose" section of his collected *Poems*, which he created in 1895 by revising some of the shorter works from *The Countess Kathleen and Various Legends and Lyrics*. The Rose suggested many things to Yeats, and, for someone straining to integrate so many competing impulses, this was part of its attraction. The first poem in "The Rose" – "To the Rose upon the Rood of Time" – introduces its presiding symbol as an emissary from the divine otherworld that permits mortal beings a vision of "Eternal beauty" by sacrificing itself (like Christ) upon the rood or cross of time. Subsequent Rose poems, however, supplement this basic implication by using the traditional connotative links between roses, romance, and beautiful women to create hymns to Eternal Beauty that also seem to function as paeans to Maud Gonne or, more generally, to the heroic-but-nurturing feminine ideal her young admirer wished her to fulfill. This is especially apparent in "The Rose of the World," where we learn that, though the Rose once embodied itself in the legendary forms of ancient Greece's Helen and ancient Ireland's Deirdre (for whom, respectively, "Troy passed away" and "Usna's children died"), it now resides in "this lonely face" (by implication, the face of Gonne). Other poems elaborate this implication by reflecting the split Yeats habitually perceived between Gonne's softer and harder sides. "The Rose of Peace" describes a sad comforter, who, like the Virgin Mary, intercedes in "gentle ways" between God and his fallen creation, while "The Rose of Battle" presents a proud comrade of spiritual warriors. Whether or not the Rose also participates in more worldly forms of conflict is an interesting question. In 1892 Yeats assured readers that he did not intend to follow the example of earlier Irish poets who had deployed the Rose as a "favourite symbol . . . not merely in love poems, but in addresses to Ireland, as . . . in Mangan's 'Dark Rosaleen'" (VP 798–99). Yet, in dismissing this possibility, he drew attention to it, and he can hardly have expected readers not to notice that his leading symbol shared many characteristics with the beautiful real-life nationalist often publicly associated with him. Many poems in "The Rose," furthermore, make perfectly explicit connections between the volume's central icon and the author's desire to "Sing of old Eire" (P 31).

It thus seems safe to conclude that, whatever else it may evoke, the Rose summons an eternal power associated with beauty, love, and femininity, a power that the poet implores to infuse itself in Ireland, in his beloved, and in himself so that all three can be joined in rapturous completion. In more practical terms, writing about the Rose allows Yeats to be spiritual poet, a love poet, and a (culturally nationalist) political poet at once; it remakes him as someone with a coherent identity and noble purpose who inhabits and acts powerfully upon a complex but harmonious cosmos. Or at least that's what he hopes it will do. As useful as it is to understand the theories that underlie his poems, we must never forget that Yeats's best writing usually focuses less on offering achieved solutions to life's problems than on dramatizing imaginative struggles to resolve human dilemmas that ultimately remain unresolvable. Such dramas are apparent throughout "The Rose." For example: although the speaker of "To the Rose upon the Rood of Time" begins by confidently petitioning the Rose, he falters when he considers that full absorption in the ultimate oneness may cut him off from "common things" and "mortal hopes." He wants to find Eternal Beauty not over but "under the boughs of love and hate," not beyond but "In all poor foolish things that live a day," and therefore, on second thoughts, he asks the Rose to preserve some distance, to leave "A little space for the rose-breath to fill[.]" Some critics have faulted the poem for hesitating in the face of conflict instead of engaging it squarely in the manner of Yeats's later work. And it is true that here he does not yet display a fully developed capacity for treating oppositions as Blakean contraries. Nonetheless, the poem's refusal to gloss over age-old spiritual contradictions distinguishes it from those myriads of mystically minded poems that are only too eager to imply that everything has been neatly sorted out.

Similar uncertainties appear again at the end of "The Rose," where the speaker of "To Ireland in the Coming Times" assures future generations that he is no less an Irish patriot for singing of "elemental creatures" who "hurry from unmeasured mind" to quicken "Ireland's heart." At once bold and defensive, this assertion implicitly recognizes that conventionally Christian Irish readers will be unlikely to embrace Yeats's occult convictions. The speaker's bravado may even suggest that he requires further convincing. It is as if he believes that his identity and his world will come into congruence if he only incants his poetic spell forcefully enough, but in the end he possesses no more surety than the Happy Shepherd before him that words alone can conjure certain good. This is not to say, however, that his failure to mask his anxieties ruins the poem: the cracks in the speaker's mask are the very things that bring him alive, that imprint him with Yeats's signature ability to blend imaginative power with moving displays of human frailty.

Together, "To Ireland in the Coming Times" and "To the Rose upon the Rood of Time" build a frame of italicized, declamatory poems around "The Rose" as a whole, encouraging readers to perceive it as a unit and to notice how its intervening poems keep faith with its central emblem. References in the opening lyric link this emblem both to "Fergus and the Druid" and "Cuchulain's Fight with the Sea," while several succeeding, previously mentioned poems (such as "The Rose of the World") reinvoke the symbol explicitly. Still, the Rose makes no obvious appearance in a number of the collection's middle poems, including one quick to take a place among the poet's best-loved works: "The Lake Isle of Innisfree." While this poem's popularity no doubt has much to do with its apparent lack of forbidding symbols, on examination one finds that it creates the same delicate layering of implication characteristic of the poems in which the Rose symbol is invoked, and that, read in the context of "The Rose" as a whole, it reflects the same occult cosmology. Most clearly, it hymns an ode to nature in the time-honored Romantic fashion of such city-weary writers as Thoreau (who partly inspired its vision of a cabined retreat among bean-rows and bee-hives). Yet because the landscape it calls to mind is distinctively Irish – Innisfree is a real islet, in Lough Gill near Sligo – it also softly sustains a culturally nationalist political challenge to prevailing British stereotypes about Ireland's primitive hinterlands, descriptively endowing an exemplar of the Irish west with much the same spirit of noble, soul-restoring innocence that Wordsworth so memorably located in the English Lake District. The second stanza, in particular, suggests that Innisfree promises both spiritual and natural fulfillments: its island confines create a middle space not unlike that in which the Rose-breath was urged to blow, a space in which abstractions like peace adopt physical forms and motions, and time passes in an ethereal flow that permits midnight to glimmer and noon to glow darkly. Readers who consider the poem's relationship to the rest of "The Rose" will have no trouble sensing a connection between "the deep heart's core" and the universal spirit.

Yet for all its evocative magic, "Innisfree" enacts a doubtful human drama much like those observed in "To the Rose upon the Rood of Time" and "To Ireland in the Coming Times." Its speaker expresses himself with a quiet resolve that bespeaks greater confidence than many of the bold assertions heard in nearby poems. Though he resolves for Innisfree, however, he stands on "pavements grey," and despite his power to make an imaginative pilgrimage within the "now" of the poem itself, his real-world plans seem little more than fantasies. If the poem exceeds its fellows in "The Rose," it is by virtue of the arresting directness of its balanced manner, which counterweights other-worldly aspirations and high-toned poetic music with effects that create the impression of a real person talking passionately but also naturally. Its rhythms, for instance, sometimes depart from their basically iambic pattern to swing into songlike anapestic movements (e.g., "from the veils of the morning" or "While I stand on the roadway"). Just as often, however, they force two or more strong beats together, slowing the poem and restraining its lyricism (as in the phrases "go now," "build there," "lake water," or "deep heart's core"). The poem's sound effects are similarly muted: in addition to alliteration and assonance (e.g., "*l*ake water *l*apping" or "*I* will ar*i*se"), it showcases the subtle music that occurs when vowels requiring facial tension give way to loose, smooth sounds ("bee-loud glade" or "deep heart's core"). And yet it never chimes with the highly perceptible sonority of such poems as "To the Rose upon the Rood of Time," where the stars "In dancing *s*ilver-*s*andalled on the *s*ea / *S*ing in their high and lonely melody." Its diction and syntax strike an even more noticeable contrast with most of the surrounding poems. It may glimmer with beautiful, even otherworldly images, but it builds them primarily with the vocabulary and phrasing patterns of ordinary (rather than stiltedly poetic) utterance. Instead of words like "thine," "whereof," "Lest," and "chaunt," it relies on "cabin," "lake water," and "road-way." Yeats probably had all of these traits in mind when he subsequently described it as the first of his lyrics to have any "of [his] own music" in it (A 139). For him (and others), "Innisfree" became a milestone in his slow but hugely influential effort to slough off the elevated language characteristic of nineteenth-century verse and thereby develop the power to evoke not only the poetic heavens but also what he later called "The fury and the mire of human veins" (P 248).

The Secret Rose and The Wind Among the Reeds

Like *The Wanderings of Oisin and Other Poems*, *The Countess Kathleen and Various Legends and Lyrics* elicited criticism from a few reviewers (usually for its obscure references or supposed stylistic *faux pas*) and praise from a few more, who managed to be charmed rather than baffled by what the poet's friend Lionel Johnson called its "Celtic notes of style and imagination."[12] Yeats's reputation climbed even higher after the publication of *Poems* (1895), an amalgam of his first two collections that for decades remained his best-selling book. It was also bolstered by his play, *The Land of Heart's Desire*

(1894), and by a series of prose sketches collected as *The Celtic Twilight* (1893). *The Land of Heart's Desire* appeared with Bernard Shaw's *Arms and the Man* at London's Avenue Theatre in 1894, becoming Yeats's first play to reach the stage and marking the first step in his lifelong quest to win a place for poetic drama in a theatrical world dominated by other modes. *The Celtic Twilight* blended descriptions of its author's visionary experiences with reports of his encounters with Irish country folk and retellings of their ghost and fairy stories. Eventually its title became associated with the vogue for "Celtic" writing that developed (especially in London) as the nineties progressed, a trend established not only by Yeats but also by the growing number of writers who began following in his wake. Fellow contributors to the Celtic Twilight trend included, among others, his boyhood friend George Russell (otherwise known as "AE"), the Scotsman William Sharp (who published under the name of his female alter ego, Fiona Macleod), the Welshman Ernest Rhys, and the thoroughly English Lionel Johnson, whose participation was made possible by his discovery of Irish roots. Yeats's essays and reviews make clear that he connected the Celtic Twilight not with the setting sun of a fading tradition but rather with the dawning of a new era of spiritually impassioned art that would soon eclipse the emphasis on external realities he saw as characteristic of late-nineteenth-century British culture. Although his belief in the coming of new artistic movements proved prescient, these did not develop along the lines he originally anticipated and largely failed to involve the mostly minor figures who surrounded him in the nineties.

While *The Celtic Twilight, The Land of Heart's Desire,* and *Poems* (1895) offer accomplished and influential writing, Yeats's early manner did not reach the summit of its achievements until *The Secret Rose* (1897) and *The Wind Among the Reeds* (1899). The first represents the apex of his career as a writer of short fiction; the second is one of the most fascinating collections of poetry he ever assembled, a work of uncanny power that rivals the poetry of his latest, greatest phase. What makes these two books stand out? Both bring richly polished surfaces into urgent juxtaposition with sexually troubled depths, thus creating examples of what the poet would later call "terrible beauty" (P 180). *The Wind Among the Reeds* in particular inspires pity and fear, admiration and revulsion: the passing of a century has done little to diminish its capacity for making the hairs on the back of one's neck stand on end. To arrive at a more considered appreciation, we must first turn back to Yeats's life and times in the middle and later nineties.

At the time of his thirtieth birthday in June 1895, Yeats was an acclaimed young writer known both for his published works and for his vigorous public efforts to reenergize Irish cultural nationalism and spark a Celtic Renaissance.

But he was also a thirty-year-old virgin who lived at home with his family, tormented by emotional, sexual, and financial frustrations. His relations with Gonne had been cool after her decision not to support him in the bitter feud over the New Irish Library in 1893. Since then he had shyly admired several other women, but seriously pursued none, unable to give up his deep-seated fascination with Gonne. At home, the strain produced by poverty, by his father's depressed brooding on his own artistic and personal failings, and by his mother's ever-worsening condition all but outweighed the intellectual and emotional sustenance derived from living amid a brilliant circle of family and friends. Occasionally his meager income permitted a trip to Sligo to write, to Dublin to politick, or to Paris to attempt to warm things up with Gonne, but mostly he plodded on at 3 Blenheim Road, the house in the London suburb of Bedford Park where the Yeatses had lived since 1888, having returned from Dublin in 1887. Beginning in 1890 he frequently sought escape from his private life and from Irish cultural politics in the company of a group of young London writers known as the Rhymers Club, which met in an upstairs room of the Cheshire Cheese inn. Regulars included Lionel Johnson, Arthur Symons, Ernest Dowson, and others; Oscar Wilde also looked in at times. These writers are often linked, sometimes too simplistically, with the aesthetically refined and morally decadent atmosphere of the English *fin-de-siècle*. Although they did not endorse any single artistic program, their urbane and apolitical conversation reinforced Yeats's commitment to high standards of poetic craft and to the idea of poetry as a high and lonely calling; in this way they contributed to the exquisitely finished luster of *The Wind Among the Reeds*. As the decade reached its midpoint, the social and artistic stimulation gained through the Rhymers also began to open up new artistic and real-life outlets for his long-repressed sexual and emotional energies.

By this stage the heyday of the Rhymers Club had come and gone. Several of its members, however, were renewing their ties through association with the newly established *Savoy* magazine, edited by Yeats's close friend, the poet, critic, and former Rhymer Arthur Symons. Founded in 1895 amid the uproar created by Wilde's trial and conviction for sodomy, the *Savoy* was conceived partly as a protest against the rigid sexual morality of late-Victorian Britain. Alluding in its title to the hotel made notorious by the revelations of Wilde's trial, the *Savoy* was published by the pornographer Leonard Smithers and featured artwork by Aubrey Beardsley, infamous for his provocative illustrations to Wilde's *Salomé* (1894) and for his tamer but still titillating designs for the *Yellow Book*, the periodical which up to this point had been the chief voice of English aestheticism. Yeats, who supported Wilde throughout his ordeal, eagerly aligned himself with the *Savoy* project, eventually contributing three of the stories and nine of the poems associated with *The Secret Rose* and *The Wind Among the Reeds*. One must be careful not to exaggerate the decadence endorsed by the *Savoy* or by Yeats: the former's contents were suggestive rather than pornographic and the latter continued to subordinate carnal to spiritual passions. He also suffered sexual anxieties every bit as intense as his desires. Still, there is no question that sexual impulses now began to affect his life and work more powerfully than ever before.

These impulses found a catalyst when Yeats met Lionel Johnson's attractive young cousin, Olivia Shakespear, at an April 1894 dinner for the *Yellow Book*. A writer herself, and unhappily married to a much older man, Shakespear was intrigued by Yeats, and initiated a flirtation. He responded with interest, but also with anguished hesitation. Not until February 1896, following nearly two years of increasing intimacy and awkward negotiations about whether Shakespear would leave her husband (and thus risk losing custody of her young daughter), did they agree to commence a secret sexual affair. (By this time Yeats had secured his own rooms in a working-class side street not far from the British Museum.) Though Shakespear was a woman of delicate sensibilities and certainly no sexual virago, Yeats bears primary responsibility for the slow pace of their affair. He also bears responsibility for its brevity. By the spring of 1897, it had collapsed under the strain of his continuing obsession with Gonne, who had begun to seek renewed closeness with him – though not sex or marriage – at roughly the same time that his liaison with Shakespear was first heating up. Though both his hesitancy in consummating this liaison and his decision to break it off can be explained by his fixation with Gonne, difficult questions remain about the true nature of his feelings, about his attitudes toward sex, and about how these things interacted with his other preoccupations and manifested themselves in his writings.

In considering these questions, we should keep in mind that the thirty-year-old Yeats lived at a time when the tide of new and more liberal attitudes about sex and gender that would later sweep over the twentieth century had only begun to gather. He was also possessed by a kind and degree of idealism that many find difficult to conceive, passionately aspiring to spiritual and artistic transcendence of the fractured imperfections of physical existence. Though familiar with writers like Blake, Rossetti, and Morris, who had done much to subvert the hierarchies traditionally posited between spirit and flesh or art and nature, he would only gradually accept the premise that such opposing terms could or should interact on an equal footing (or as what Blake had called contraries). In other words, he approached love with the same impractically Romantic, high-minded devotion he brought to his pursuit of a spiritually and politically reborn Ireland. A Freudian might trace this to his relationship with his mother, whose instinctive reserve and disappointed life prevented her from showing much affection to her children, possibly with the result of causing her eldest son's Oedipal hunger for unattainably complete forms of feminine nurturing to become so strong that it interfered with his ability to satisfy himself with the real thing.

Whatever the causes, the effect seems to have been a profound and partly unconscious fear of sex and female sexuality that induced Yeats to constrain his desires and ultimately to prefer the sexually distant Gonne to the attainable Shakespear. It also inspired him to write weirdly compelling stories and poems in which sexual desires and fears strain against elaborate textures of poetic artifice and otherworldly hope. In the most terrible and beautiful of these works, the resulting tensions open on prospects of death and apocalypse. Sometimes these are hopefully imagined as releases from – or consummations of – unfulfilled longings. At other times they are dreaded as the fearsome consequences of yielding to sexual or spiritual (or even political) passions. Because sexual intercourse may involve a loss of self through bodily and emotional union with another person, it has long been associated with a kind of psychic death (in some eras, forms of the words "death" and "die" have been used to make slangy sexual references). In a similar way, mystical union with divinity has often been imagined as involving a necessary death of self entailed in the joining of one's individual existence with the cosmic unity (and occurring whether one actually dies physically or not). Yeats encountered still another precedent for associating desire with death in Ireland's centuries-old proclivity for celebrating such nationalist martyrs as Wolfe Tone or Robert Emmet as men who heroically gave their lives for the love of a nation pictured as a lover or a mother. All of these traditions surface in the patterns of thought and instinct that emerge in *The Secret Rose* and *The Wind Among the Reeds*, patterns suggesting that the achievement of desire – whether for a woman, a mystical Rose, or an Irish nation – always requires some form of sacrificial death. In the most gripping of these stories and poems, the protagonists or poetic speakers both anticipate and dread such death, longing to consummate their desires but fearing the concomitant loss of self. Instead of finding the comforting middle space sought in "To the Rose upon the Rood of Time," they occupy a hellish no man's land where they are tortured by conflicting impulses.

Such dilemmas quickly come to the fore in the 1897 edition of *The Secret Rose*. The collection's initial story, "The Binding of the Hair," originally appeared in the *Savoy* in 1896. It concerns an ancient Irish bard named Aodh (pronounced "ay" rhyming with "day") who serves a young queen married to a king too old and sleepy to protect her from outside attackers. Aodh defends her, but perishes in the process; afterwards, she searches the battlefield and discovers his severed head, hanging by its hair from a bush. At this point, a strange miracle occurs: the head sings her a version of the poem ultimately known in *The Wind Among the Reeds* as "He gives his Beloved certain Rhymes" and then is battered by "a troop of crows" that smite its "ecstatic lips with the points of their wings" until it falls from the bush and rolls over to her feet (SR 181). On one level this violent, uncanny plot registers Yeats's fear of the metaphorical death of self demanded by sexual and emotional commitment to Olivia Shakespear (who, like the queen, was married to a lethargic older man). But because the queen is an Irish sovereign described by Aodh as "the Rose of [his] Desire," she calls to mind the equally demanding centers of Yeats's spiritual and political yearnings (SR 179). The severed head's song clearly implies that art may constitute a sacrificial tribute, a "sorrowful loveliness" laid at a beloved's feet. Indeed, this and similar songs have prompted some to suggest that in the 1890s Yeats wrote poetry partly as a substitute for sexual experience and other forms of painful sacrifice, as a way of offering himself to the feminine ideals he adored without actually undergoing any of the transforming sexual, emotional, spiritual, or political "deaths" he both desired and feared. Apparently, despite years of struggling to reconcile poetic reverie with active participation in the real world, part of him still wanted to take comforting refuge in dreams.

Though he later became dissatisfied with "The Binding of the Hair" and excluded it from succeeding versions of *The Secret Rose*, most of the other stories associated with the collection take up similar themes. Carefully arranged to chronicle Ireland's devotion to the Rose from pre-Christian times to the present, the 1897 book centers on a linked suite of narratives subsequently remade as *Stories of Red Hanrahan* (1905) and ends with its longest and most elaborate piece, "Rosa Alchemica" (in due course republished with two related stories, "The Tables of the Law" and "The Adoration of the Magi"). Like "The Binding of the Hair," "Rosa Alchemica" first appeared in the *Savoy* in 1896. Its slowly flowing rhythms and gradual accretion of phantasmal imagery create an aura reminiscent of Edgar Allan Poe. Set in the nineties, it begins in the old Dublin house of its first-person narrator, whose recent book, *Rosa Alchemica*, has attempted to tame the doctrines of the medieval alchemists by treating them as metaphors for artistic processes; whereas they had believed in "an universal transmutation of all things into some divine and imperishable substance," his book has offered but "a fanciful reverie over the transmutation of life into art" (SR 126). With similar ideas in mind, he has decorated his rooms according to the exquisite tastes of a *fin-de-siècle* aesthete, surrounding himself with beautiful images of "all gods because [he believes] in none" (SR 127). As one who wishes only to "[hold himself] apart, individual, indissoluble, a mirror of polished steel," he embodies the conviction that art provides safe substitutes for the self-sacrifices real commitments require (SR 127–28). Sometimes, however, intimations of "a divine world wherein [he has] no part" disturb his self-possession with a "thirst for destruction," a longing to be consumed by spiritual fires that will merge him with the cosmos (SR 128–29). These intimations quickly fan into flame with the unexpected arrival of Michael Robartes, a fellow student of occult lore whom he has not seen in many years (and whom readers will meet again in many succeeding works).

Unlike the narrator, Robartes has not forsaken the spiritual quest; for him, furthermore, art continues to offer real access to the divine rather than a mere alternative. When Robartes burns incense – a detail which may reflect Yeats's own experiments with hashish – the narrator receives a preliminary vision of "that Death which is Beauty herself" and agrees to accompany his guest to an isolated locale in the west of Ireland, where "the Temple of the Alchemical Rose" has recently been founded (SR 136, 138). On his arrival he reads a sacred book professing that magicians and artists can convert their dreams into realities by summoning immortal "moods" from the spirit realm: when they imagine beauty or ugliness they create forms that attract good or evil powers; once summoned, these powers gradually reshape the minds and even the bodies of human beings and through them cause "great events" (SR 143). Later he enters what appears to be a vast hall decorated with roses and other symbols; here he joins a visionary initiation ritual, a passionate dance led by "Eros himself" but with ordered rhythms derived from "the wheel of Eternity" (SR 147, 144). Pairing mortal adepts with immortal spirits and evoking a harmony of erotic and spiritual love, this dance seems to open a path back to the primal oneness. Before this transformation can fully absorb him, however, he draws back in horror at the perception that his superhuman dance partner is "drinking up [his] soul as an ox drinks up a wayside pool" (SR 147–48). Though aware that his fellow adepts regard the inhabitants of "the great deep" as "one and yet a multitude" (and thus not fully dispossessed of individuality), his terror that his soul will be changed beyond recognition prevents him from making the final leap of faith (SR 128). Waking after a long period of unconsciousness, he finds himself in a drab room surrounded by immobile figures, including Robartes. Suddenly he realizes that an angry crowd of country folk – outraged by what they regard as an outbreak of devilry – has gathered outside the Temple to destroy it and all inside. He alone escapes their wrath, making his way back to Dublin, where he tries to numb his anxieties through submission to Catholic orthodoxy.

This ending suggests that the narrator has made a crucial (if understandable) error: in avoiding what seemed a sacrifice of his individuality he has cut himself off from the ecstatic consummations sought by Robartes and his followers. And yet the story's first-person point of view prevents readers from knowing anything certain about Robartes's spiritual fate. What should we make of this ambiguity? One could reasonably argue that by focusing on the narrator's failures and leaving open the question of what happens to Robartes's soul, Yeats avoids the pretense of having solved life's eternal mysteries and instead creates a powerful dramatization of the dilemmas they entail. This reading allows one to conclude that, although the story's occult doctrines may strike some readers as bizarre, it tenders a recognizable depiction of the craving to preserve the self while simultaneously wedding it to some heavenly or earthly "other." This reading also allows one to praise Yeats for the self-critical way he maintains his distance from Robartes's alchemical wisdom and uses the narrator's fears to expose his own. Alternatively, "Rosa Alchemica" might function less as a skeptical interrogation of its author's most deeply felt occult convictions than as an assertion of these convictions that avoids an actual commitment. As such, it offers an all-too-characteristic demonstration of Yeats's pathological hesitancy to sacrifice himself to anything other than art itself. Such readings may not be mutually exclusive, and readers must decide for themselves how to navigate the story's complexities. The inference that persons perceived as beautiful or ugly have been made so by good or evil spirits demands especially careful scrutiny. An early manifestation of the aesthetics that eventually led the poet to embrace eugenics, this inference moralizes a beauty that is terrible indeed.

Things become no less weirdly fascinating – or problematic – in *The Wind Among the Reeds*, where Yeats takes full advantage of the evocative patterning of rhythm and imagery permitted by the lyric genre to generate a series of climactic moments even more hair-raising than those encountered in *The Secret Rose*. For many readers, the most disturbing of these moments occurs in "He wishes his Beloved were Dead." Here, a lover's frustrated craving for absolute possession of his uncooperative beloved becomes so unendurable that he longs to see her "lying cold and dead." Feminists have rightly pointed out that such violent thoughts about the flesh-and-blood woman are a predictable consequence of the lover's perverse demand that she conform to his idealized image of a motherly nurturer who dispenses "tender words." In Yeats's defense, however, we should note that the poem's speaker confesses his yearnings to the beloved herself: by admitting his need for forgiveness he indicates that to some extent both he and his creator have acknowledged the worrying nature of their desires. More to the point, the poem is not titled "*I* wish *my* Beloved were Dead." This opens the possibility that Yeats does not personally sanction what "He" wishes any more than Robert Browning personally endorses the murderous misogyny dramatized in "My Last Duchess." Yeats put even more distance between himself and his speaker in the volume's original version, where the poem was called "Aedh wishes his Beloved were Dead."[13] In 1899, Aedh appeared along with Hanrahan and Michael Robartes as one of three recurring personae specified in the titles of most of the poems that now identify their speakers as "The Lover" or "He" or "The Poet."

As suggested by its original version's references to Aedh, Hanrahan, and Michael Robartes, *The Wind Among the Reeds* has much in common with *The Secret Rose*. Like that book, it mostly focuses not on male protagonists who perversely long to see their beloveds dead, but rather on speakers caught between the yearning to consummate their desires and the fear that doing so will entail a death-like self-sacrifice. It begins with one of its most gripping poems, "The Hosting of the Sidhe," a bold demonstration of its author's late-nineties perception that his earlier depictions of Irish fairies had associated them too much with prettiness. As he explained to one correspondent, the Gaelic term *sidhe* (pronounced "shee") better reflects the fact that the "Irish peasant never thinks of the fairies as pretty [but rather] as terrible, or beautiful."[14] And indeed, the poem's sexy, dangerous, horse-riding host of male and female spirits is a far cry from the prancing troop that tempts "The Stolen Child." Their pale cheeks, unbound hair, heaving breasts, and parted lips recall the iconography of Pre-Raphaelite painting and poetry, of traditions associated with John Keats, D. G. Rossetti, William Morris, and (more recently) the *Savoy* magazine. Indeed, one might fairly say that the poem's (and the volume's) original artistic triumph centers on its success in bringing to Irish myth the same intoxicating combination of spiritual and erotic passions familiar from those traditions. Given the political insinuations of some of the collection's ensuing uses of Irish myth, its description of the fairy host may also imply a massing of ancient forces hostile to the modern, materialistic world of Britain and its empire. But despite these potentially attractive connotations, it is clear that one has to die to join the Sidhe: riding over the grave of an Irish goddess, described in Yeats's 1899 notes as one who beckons men to their deaths, they urge the speaker to "Empty [his] heart of its mortal dream."

Reluctant to yield to such urges, the speaker of the volume's second poem begs "The Everlasting Voices" who call in the wind to "be still." Though this poem seems paradoxically to ask the Voices both to be quiet and to continue always, it functions at least partly as an antithesis to "The Hosting of the Sidhe," turning from its predecessor in a way characteristic of the collection's subsequent movements, which gradually unfold additional implications having to do with Olivia Shakespear and Maud Gonne, politics and aesthetics. Tracing allusions to Shakespear and Gonne has long been a favorite pastime of expert readers. Such considerations can be enlightening, as they are with "The Lover mourns for the Loss of Love," where Yeats appears to be complaining to Gonne that Shakespear "has gone weeping away" after finding Gonne's image in his heart. A reductive approach to such allusions, however, has the unfortunate effect of flattening the rich symbolic layering of the collection's love poems; thus it may be best to imagine them as having speakers torn between the competing attractions of two rival women, one an idealized, unattainable beloved inspired by (but not equivalent to) Gonne, and the other an actual woman correspondingly based on Shakespear. A poem like "The Song of Wandering Aengus," for example, probably gains more through comparison with Keats's "La Belle Dame sans Merci," Shelley's *Alastor*, or similar poems in the Irish *aisling* tradition – works in which visions of otherworldly women inspire mortal men to begin an unending pursuit of perfection – than it does by considering its connection to Yeats's real-life feeling for Gonne. Biography matters somewhat more, however, in the case of "He bids his Beloved be at Peace," usually interpreted as relating to Olivia Shakespear (and originally spoken by Michael Robartes). In this poem, the mounted Sidhe of the collection's beginning have been replaced by ghostly, riderless horses, elemental forces that plunge at the speaker from all directions and that are described in terms – sighs, roses, penetrating hooves – linking them to spiritual and sexual "Desire." More like the narrator from "Rosa Alchemica" than that story's version of Michael Robartes, its speaker regards these bestial heralds of transformation as "Horses of Disaster" and turns from them in horror to the comforts of a real woman. While these involve physical contact, they seem to stop short of sexual consummation; apparently reflecting Yeats's own sexual anxieties, the poem's speaker wishes to be drowned in a "deep twilight of rest" where he can hide from tormenting impulses.

Political inferences also contribute to the collection's shifting currents. Its politics, however, do not lead toward real-world revolutions any more than its erotic energies move toward real sexual experiences. Typically, it advocates mystical substitutes for political change or looks ahead to a distant future reconfigured by apocalyptic violence. "Into the Twilight," for example, urges Irish readers to respond to "the nets of wrong and right" by remembering that their "mother Eire is always young" and will sustain them if they trade their everyday loves and hopes for the "mystical brotherhood" emanating from her shining dews and twilights grey. "He mourns for the Change that has come upon Him and his Beloved, and longs for the End of the World" and "The Valley of the Black Pig" augment such stances by recalling prophecies from Irish folklore about the coming of a mythical boar expected to defeat the nation's foreign enemies in an epoch-changing battle. "The Valley of the Black Pig" explicitly connects this battle with freedom for those who "labour by the cromlech on the shore" in weary service to "the world's empires." Both poems target the British empire and its materialist cosmos with the same impulse to destroy that appears in "He wishes his Beloved were Dead." It is hard to read them without remembering Freud's theory of the death drive, that profoundly destructive instinct thought to develop in response to an unconscious wish to reexperience an infantile symbiotic link with one's mother. Students of Irish writing may also recall the nightmarish "Circe" episode of Joyce's *Ulysses*, where – with a desperate cry of "*Nothung!*" – Stephen Dedalus tries to annihilate all that separates him from his dead mother by shattering the chandelier of Bella Cohen's whorehouse with his ashplant.[15]

Before we conclude, however, that Yeats's early efforts to hammer his thoughts into unity culminate only in disasters, we must reconsider the question increasingly pondered in the latter stages of *The Wind Among the Reeds*. Namely, how and to what extent can art allay or redirect the destructive urges that originate with frustrated desires? To some extent all of the poems in the collection strive to answer this question by restraining their turbulent depths with polished stylistic surfaces. But the second half of the collection takes up such matters more explicitly, for example in "A Poet to his Beloved," "He gives his Beloved certain Rhymes," and "The Cap and Bells," the last of these a striking allegory about a jester-artist who cannot conquer the affections of his young queen until he offers her the emblems of his talent, his cap and bells. Though this sacrifice enables his soul and heart to sing together and thus to win the young queen's love, making it requires his death. This plot clearly echoes that of "The Binding of the Hair," which is also recalled in this phase of the collection by "He gives his Beloved certain Rhymes," the lyric originally sung at that story's climax. We have already noted that such works suggest that Yeats in the late nineties had begun to see his art as a sacrifice offered to the much-adored feminine powers he associated with

Shakespear, Gonne, Ireland, and the Rose: a passionate tribute that could substitute for real sexual, emotional, political, or spiritual fulfillments. We have also observed that, although his poems frequently assert that he offers these artistic sacrifices only because his beloved will accept no others, certain features of both his poems and his biography suggest instead that he opts for art because he hesitates to make more substantial commitments. But would we really admire Yeats more if he had pursued Shakespear or Gonne – or an independent Irish nation – in some traditionally manly, forceful manner? Poems such as "He tells of the Perfect Beauty" and "He wishes for the Cloths of Heaven" suggest that his speakers know full well that their poems may not constitute adequate responses to "a woman's gaze" or to "the unlabouring brood of the skies" but instead may offer only pale substitutes produced by one too "poor" in spirit for something greater. No doubt there is something melodramatically self-pitying in such admissions. But there is also something self-critical that ought to make us respect the poet's request to "Tread softly" on his dreams. Nor is the aesthetics posited in *The Wind Among the Reeds* necessarily identical to the one encountered at the end of *The Secret Rose*. "Rosa Alchemica" tentatively asserts the dangerous doctrine that beautiful and ugly persons are made so by good and evil essences summoned by symbol-wielding poets and magicians. "The Fiddler of Dooney," by contrast, steers closer to the more modest and familiar claim that art makes us "merry" and thereby "good" ("Save by an evil chance"). Though obviously subject to challenge – not least by the pronounced lack of merriness in the preceding poems – this claim gives the artist an admirable purpose, one that lends worth to the death the fiddler must die before leading his brothers and people through the gates of heaven and beyond.

The fading of the Rose

Though their seemingly inscrutable Celticisms exasperated some reviewers, *The Secret Rose* and *The Wind Among the Reeds* received considerable public acclaim, especially in England. The latter won the *Academy*'s Poetry Award for 1899 and elicited a discerning notice from Arthur Symons, who praised its "extraordinarily intense inner life," and found in it an "atmosphere in which the illusion of love, and the cruelty of pain, and the gross ecstasy of hope, become changed into beauty."[16] Yeats's triumph was tempered, however, by the lasting effects of an evil chance that befell him in December 1898, when his new book was in press. This involved Maud Gonne, and hastened the close of the first phase of his life and work. Having put to rest their 1893 quarrel over the New Irish Library, Yeats and Gonne had rekindled their friendship in late 1895 and since drawn ever closer. At first their renewed amity sprang mainly from shared spiritual experiences, but by early 1897 – a point in time that also witnessed the end of the poet's liaison with Olivia Shakespear – it was becoming reentangled with Irish nationalism. Once again (and with an intensity that partly belies the fear of real-world commitments repeatedly suggested by his works) he threw himself into politics, ascending to the Presidency both of the 1898 Centennial Association of Great Britain and France and of the Wolfe Tone Memorial Association. Ostensibly devoted to celebrating the centennial of the United Irishmen's failed 1798 rising against the British, these two organizations provided cover for a range of nationalist activities; Yeats hoped to use them to heal the wounds that had festered since Parnell's fall. Gonne was much involved in these plans and also in other more overtly revolutionary schemes. When Dublin Unionists prepared to celebrate the sixtieth anniversary of Queen Victoria's reign in the summer of 1897, she helped to lead nationalist protests, one of which devolved into a violent riot that Yeats physically restrained her from joining. Although this infuriated her – and although both her attempts at fomenting insurrection and his at building new coalitions came in the end to nothing – their mutual attraction to nationalist activism strongly recharged their connection. By contrast, Gonne's relationship with her French lover, Lucien Millevoye, had by late 1898 deteriorated badly; on December 7, in her Dublin hotel, she told Yeats of a dream in which an Irish god had joined her to him, and, bestowing the first kiss she had ever given him, "begged [him] to see her no more."[17]

When he ignored this request and came again the next day, she at last revealed her long affair with Millevoye, with whom she had not only conceived the short-lived Georges in 1889 but also a daughter, Iseult, born in 1894. This revelation shook Yeats to the core. He had spent the better part of the last ten years celebrating her as the incarnation of his ideal of a powerful (but also virginal and nurturing) feminine force connected with the essence of Ireland and the Eternal Rose. Now he was forced to see her as a sexual being caught up in physical passions prompted more by the worldly attractions of Millevoye's politics than by any spiritually meaningful notion of love. Ten gut-wrenching days later he proposed marriage and she refused, agreeing instead to commence an unofficial "spiritual marriage" founded on the sharing of dreams, visions, and out-of-body experiences. While many commentators have assumed that both this proposal and its rejection can be taken at face value, some recent critics have suggested that Gonne actually wanted to marry Yeats, and turned him down only because she perceived his offer to be a chivalrous gesture masking deep reluctance. Either way, the effect on his work was profound. Though roses would long continue to appear in his verse, never again would he write about the Rose with a capital "R"; that tradition reaches its apogee in *The Wind Among the Reeds*, and especially in the poem titled "The Secret Rose," a superb expression of desperate apocalyptic hope and desire. From now on his idea of woman – and of the spiritual and political principles associated with her – would be represented not by the soft enfoldings of an eternal and "inviolate" Rose, but rather by the cold silver lights of a changing moon.

Chapter 2

Middle Yeats

The Irish National Theatre   *36*
Early plays: *Cathleen ni Houlihan, On Baile's Strand,* and
   The King's Threshold   *41*
Drama's influence on Yeats's verse style: *In the Seven Woods*   *46*
Revisions, masks, and *The Green Helmet and Other Poems*   *51*
Responsibilities   *58*
Ireland's "Troubles"   *63*

Romantic Ireland's dead and gone, / It's with O'Leary in the
grave.   "September 1913"

According to W. H. Auden, the minor poet may spend a lifetime writing
similar poems, but the major poet "continues [to mature] until he dies so
that, if confronted by two poems of his of equal merit but written at different
times, the reader can immediately say which was written first."[1] Few poets
measure up to Auden's standard more fully than Yeats, who never stopped
searching for new ways to unify his fragmented experience. One turning point
came at the end of the nineties, when instead of seeking to repeat his recent
triumphs as a story writer and lyric poet, he set himself the fresh task of
founding an Irish national theatre. The frustrations arising from this endeavor
and from his failures with Gonne affected his work in ways that established
important precedents for younger modernist writers. This chapter traces his
evolution through his middle phase's culmination in *Responsibilities and
Other Poems* (1916).

The Irish National Theatre

Yeats reacted to Gonne's confession of her affair with Millevoye by writing no
lyric poems for nearly a year and a half. He took some solace, however, in his
"spiritual marriage." By 1901 and 1902 he was beginning to idealize a revised
feminine archetype in such plays and poems as *On Baile's Strand* and "The

Old Age of Queen Maeve," which celebrate sexually assertive heroines rather than otherworldly virgins.[2] Then, in February 1903, Gonne suddenly ended the spiritual marriage by actually wedding the nationalist revolutionary Major John MacBride. Even before this bombshell, a new attitude of "masculine" anger and skepticism had begun to permeate Yeats's work. Afterwards, this attitude reshaped his views about women, politics, poetry, and the nature of human selfhood. To understand why this began even before Gonne's marriage, one must look to the poet's theatrical commitments. These changed him in three principal ways: by allying him with new friends and collaborators; by involving him in disputes that put him at odds with much of his public; and by compelling him to master a genre traditionally focused on tragic conflict rather than on the evocation of ethereal moods.

Drama attracted Yeats from the start: it appealed to the same fascination with ritual performance that drew him to such occult groups as the Golden Dawn. He also believed that his vision of Ireland's destiny might be publicized more effectively on the stage than in books appealing to small audiences of poetry readers. The opportunity to act on these ambitions first emerged in the summer of 1896, when he escorted Arthur Symons on a tour of the Irish west that included a stay at Tillyra Castle, the County Galway home of Symons's wealthy and artistic friend Edward Martyn. Martyn subsequently assumed a crucial role in founding the new theatre: when the first performances occurred in Dublin in 1899 he supplied the financial backing as well as one of the two plays offered (the other being *The Countess Cathleen*). He also, in 1896, introduced his guests to a neighbor whose part in the project and in Yeats's life soon upstaged his own. This was Lady Augusta Gregory, an aristocratic 44-year-old widow with literary inclinations whose husband had been an Anglo-Irish landowner and former British governor of colonial Ceylon. Impressed by Yeats, Lady Gregory sought him out frequently in London during the following winter, and in July 1897 he returned to her Galway estate – Coole Park – for the first of many extended summer visits. Yeats, Martyn, and Lady Gregory spent much of this second Galway summer planning the venture they initially christened the Irish Literary Theatre. Lady Gregory saw the project as a chance to do important work for her country while fulfilling her own ambitions. In Yeats she saw a talented young man who desperately needed her help. During and after his first lengthy stay at Coole, she tactfully began to provide the solicitous maternal care he seldom received from Gonne (or from his actual mother, who died in 1900). She listened to his troubles, loaned him money, sent him food, bought him a comfortable armchair, and made sure he consulted the dentist. She also became a co-worker. Initially, her contribution consisted of helping him gather folklore, but later she surprised them both by writing a series of successful plays and other works, by co-writing several plays he is often supposed to have written on his own, and by bringing strong leadership to the theatre movement.

Lady Gregory also made a deep impact on Yeats's politics. Like him, she possessed an intense desire to work for her country's good, and despite her "Ascendancy" origins, she gradually exchanged the Unionism of her husband and family for an increasingly fervent Irish nationalism. She did not, however, renounce her identity as a Protestant aristocrat or her faith in traditional justifications of class privilege. Like her forebears, she believed that inherited wealth and position freed the gentry from the worries of those caught in the struggle to survive, thereby allowing them to cultivate social and artistic refinement. These views appealed to Yeats. Though he had grown up despising the complacent respectability of the Unionist Ireland inhabited by his ancestors (who had been merchants and professionals rather than aristocrats), he was not immune to the anxieties of middle- and upper-class Irish Protestants in the aftermath of the Land War, when the decline of their own fortunes occurred in tandem with the growth of an aspiring Catholic middle class. Yeats's early work had celebrated the blend of pagan and Christian belief he observed among Ireland's mostly Catholic country folk and had excoriated middle-class values wherever it found them. But it had also indulged nostalgia for the nobility embodied in such protagonists as the Countess Cathleen. As he absorbed Lady Gregory's generosity, witnessed her devotion to the national theatre, and admired the refinements of Coole, he increasingly embraced the belief that a landed class acted an essential role in any satisfying social order and that, in modern Ireland, this role had been played mainly by well-born Protestants such as his friend and patron. This belief found its way into many of the plays and poems written during his middle and later years. At their best these works exemplify his impressive capacity for critical interrogation of his own convictions. Many in his own day and later have nevertheless objected strongly to their emphasis on noble bloodlines and their romanticized depictions of a class usually remembered more for exploiting Ireland than for displaying disinterested magnanimity.

Yeats's fascination with the Protestant Ascendancy's supposedly large-minded temper developed in response both to Lady Gregory and to the hostile reception given the Irish Literary Theatre by many Dublin nationalists. Many of these nationalists – including Maud Gonne – did not share the poet's goal of using the theatre to explore complex ideas about the nation's culture. Embittered by centuries of negative stereotypes, they expected a national theatre to represent Irishness and Irish nationalism in a wholly favorable light. Most had roots in Dublin's up-and-coming Catholic middle class: their concerns had less to do with Britain's spiritual and aesthetic failings than with their daily experience of an oppressive socio-economic order. The belief that the Catholic Church constituted one of the few legitimate authorities in their lives had also reinforced their orthodox religious faith. Although the nationalism evinced in Yeats's writing and in his leadership of such organizations as the Wolfe Tone Memorial Association had distanced him from Dublin's Unionist elite, his Anglo-Irish background and unusual religious convictions aroused intense suspicion. He in turn began to perceive the blend of Catholic and nationalist beliefs held by his middle-class Dublin critics as the mechanical group-think of a caste that opposed Britain's political authority but embraced its bourgeois values. He sometimes allowed his mounting obsession with the virtues of aristocratic Protestants and the deficiencies of middle-class Catholics to obscure his lasting attraction to the folk beliefs of the rural, Catholic west. Gonne's marriage to the Catholic MacBride exacerbated these tendencies. As Yeats saw it, by marrying MacBride and committing to his faith, Gonne had betrayed her spiritual husband, turned her back on unfettered spiritual exploration, rejected her upper-class Protestant heritage, and given credence to the demoralizing assumption that only Catholics could be truly Irish.

The earliest attacks on Yeats's theatrical activities occurred during the lead-up to the May 1899 production of *The Countess Cathleen*. Though the play's emphasis on Ireland's pagan traditions and its depiction of starving peasants rejecting their Catholic faith had caused few objections in the seven years since its publication, its prominent place in the new movement attracted heightened scrutiny. When misgivings about its orthodoxy seized the scrupulously Catholic Martyn two months before its scheduled debut, he threatened to withdraw his own play, *The Heather Field*, as well as his financial support. No sooner had Martyn's qualms been soothed than the irascible patriot Frank Hugh O'Donnell opened a campaign of opposition, expressing outrage not only with the play's supposedly blasphemous theology but also with its failure to conform to the nationalist custom of idealizing Irish peasants as paragons of unspoiled virtue. Though this led to heated exchanges in the Dublin papers, to condemnation for the play from Cardinal Michael Logue, and to a raucous mixture of heckling and applause during performances, the most tangible effect of O'Donnell's antics was to launch the Irish Literary Theatre amid a frenzy of headline-grabbing publicity.

Still, the controversy exposed cracks between Yeats, his audience, and his theatrical colleagues, and these soon widened appreciably, both in response to his own plays and even more in reaction to the work of a brilliant newcomer who entered the scene in 1903, John Millington Synge. Though by origin a Protestant Dubliner, Synge knew Irish and had spent several observant summers soaking up native speech patterns and stories in Ireland's remotest western reaches. He now produced a series of superb Irish-English dialect plays treating the darker realities of Irish country life. The first of these, *In the Shadow of the Glen*, centers on an unfulfilled rural wife who abandons both her husband and her lover to seek freedom with an impoverished vagabond. The howls of indignation from nationalists scandalized by this perceived insult to the purity of Irish Catholic womanhood were deafening, and this time came from a greater number of more formidable opponents: from influential journalists and politicians, from the newly married Gonne, and from several of the theatre's own contributors. Gonne had previously been a key participant in the movement, but now withdrew in protest, accompanied by the poet and playwright Douglas Hyde, and the actors Maire Quinn and Dudley Digges.

Yeats wasn't caught off guard. Since the uproar over *The Countess Cathleen*, Dublin's nationalist papers had attacked him with ever greater vehemence. He had responded by writing essays professing literature's transcendence of partisan propaganda, and by maneuvering to make the theatre movement less dependent on uncompromising patriots. By 1903, Martyn had abandoned the movement, but Lady Gregory remained steadfast, and Yeats was supplementing her support with important new alliances. One of these began in 1902 when the Irish Literary Theatre merged with a company of talented Irish amateur actors headed by Frank and Willie Fay to become the Irish National Theatre Society. Previously, the movement had relied on English professional companies, and association with the Fays allowed it to end this expensive and politically inflammatory practice; it also established a partnership between Yeats and the best available Irish actors, most of whom agreed that plays could serve Ireland without following a narrow party line. Meanwhile, he had also cultivated Annie Horniman, a theatrically minded English heiress and member of the Golden Dawn. When he appeared before the curtain on the night of the first performance of *In the Shadow of the Glen*, she was so inspired by his defense of Synge's artistic freedom that she offered to fund a permanent home for his theatre, which up to this point had shifted between different venues. By December 1904 a renovated hall in Abbey Street – ever after known as the Abbey Theatre – stood ready for use. Soon afterward, the Irish National Theatre Society reorganized again as the National Theatre Society, a professional company controlled by Yeats, Synge, and Lady Gregory. Years of struggle had given Yeats a confident public persona and a platform from which to speak. But his audience mostly continued to reject his vision of its spiritual fate.

Early plays: *Cathleen ni Houlihan, On Baile's Strand,* and *The King's Threshold*

As these storms gathered and broke, Yeats began writing new plays that gradually manifested important shifts in attitude and technique. He became increasingly fascinated with – and skilled at dramatizing – manly tragic heroes. This trend evolved partly in response to his bruising public battles and his vexed relationship with Gonne, but also reflected his growing aware- ness that plays must dramatize conflict to hold an audience's attention. His development as a playwright unfolded slowly, however, and, especially at first, involved much collaboration. One of his most noteworthy new efforts, the prose-drama *Cathleen ni Houlihan*, required extensive contributions from Lady Gregory before it appeared in April 1902. Set in a western cottage at the time and place of the French invasion that supported the United Irishmen's failed 1798 uprising, it adapts the conventions of the *aisling*, an Irish literary genre in which a vision of the nation personified as a woman (and sometimes called Cathleen ni Houlihan) inspires a male hero to dedicate himself to her cause. In this case a young man about to be married meets a poor old woman (originally played with "weird power" by Maud Gonne).[3] Complaining that strangers have stolen her fields, the old woman intones a series of thrilling songs glorifying those who die in her service. Her young listener responds by forsaking his worldly concerns to join the doomed rebellion, thus enabling bystanders to glimpse the old woman transformed into a "young girl" with "the walk of a queen" (line 300).

In our own day, memories of the violence related to the Irish "Troubles" of 1916–23 and to the more recent conflict in Northern Ireland have caused many to regard the imperiled femininity and violent masculinity encoded in the *aisling* tradition as profoundly problematic. In 1902, however, these motifs fell on receptive ears, earning Yeats the biggest popular success of his life. This came at some cost to his principles: while the play's focus on the terrible beauty entailed in sacrificial death strikes a typically Yeatsian note, the patriotic allegory that made it popular erodes the divide between litera- ture and propaganda his essays had begun to stress. This uncharacteristic straightforwardness owes much to Lady Gregory, whom textual evidence identifies as author of most of the play's actual words. In 1902, Yeats remained too much the aesthete to generate convincing peasant dialogue in prose. Lady Gregory, by contrast, had already developed a knack for such writing, and would soon go on to compose a succession of one-act dramas that, like *Cathleen ni Houlihan*, make relatively clear-cut thematic statements. Though Yeats acknowledged her help in an edition of his dramas issued in 1903, the decision to list him as the play's sole author has until recently prevented the extent of her contribution from being realized. This decision took advantage of the publicity value of his more famous name. But it also reflected the era's bias against female authorship, and thus gives us another reason to think twice about the play's depiction of feminine dependence on masculine agency.

More plays quickly followed, including *The Pot of Broth*, a peasant comedy co-written with Lady Gregory and initially performed in October 1902. Next came *The Hour-Glass*, a one-act prose morality play about a scholarly atheist who relearns faith from a fool after confronting the angel of death; it reached the stage in March 1903. The same year saw the arrival of *The King's Threshold* and *On Baile's Strand*, the first new verse dramas Yeats had written since the onset of the theatre movement, and, apart from *Cathleen ni Houlihan*, the most significant plays he composed during its early years. *The King's Threshold* materialized in the immediate aftermath of Maud Gonne's marriage and debuted on the same night as Synge's *In the Shadow of the Glen*. *On Baile's Strand*, by contrast, first emerged much earlier: though unpublished until August 1903 and unperformed until December 1904, its earliest drafts date from the summer of 1901. Its conception thus took place at a time when Yeats had begun to adjust to Gonne as a sexual being and to be influenced by his rough-and-tumble interactions with Dublin audiences, but had not yet been embittered by his beloved's marriage to MacBride or the nationalist reaction to Synge. Though it reflects an increased commitment to manliness – prompting its author to claim, "My work has got far more masculine. It has more salt in it" – it suggests that masculinity's most heroic form depends on productive opposition from an assertive femininity.[4] It therefore dramatizes conflicts more complex than those encountered in *Cathleen ni Houlihan*.

On Baile's Strand directs its audience's sympathies firmly toward its hero, the mythic Irish champion, Cuchulain (pronounced "Kuh-HOO-lin" by Yeats). At the same time, however, it explores its hero's frailties, and pits him against credible opponents, most especially the High King Conchubar ("KAWN-a-hoor"). It characterizes Cuchulain, and distinguishes him from Conchubar, by suggesting that he blends qualities symbolized by the sun and moon. Though Yeats had long deployed the sun and moon as emblems, after the decline of his commitment to the Rose they began to stand out more sharply in his work. The Cabalistic lore of the Golden Dawn had taught him to associate the sun with an elemental masculine principle connected with discipline and pattern; the moon evoked an opposing feminine force linked to passion and infinitude. Sexual, political, aesthetic, or spiritual harmony required these two cosmic forces to enter into sustaining conflict, in the manner of Blakean contraries. Cuchulain epitomizes such conflict: he is ancient Ireland's mightiest warrior, but also a pleasure-seeking nonconformist who hunts and dances with "wild companions" and remains close to the spirit world (line 176). Begotten by the sun-god upon a mortal, he has

> never . . . known love but as a kiss
> In the mid-battle, and a difficult truce
> Of oil and water, candles and dark night,
> Hillside and hollow, the hot-footed sun
> And the cold, sliding, slippery-footed moon –
> A brief forgiveness between opposites
> That have been hatreds for three times the age
> Of this long-'stablished ground.   (lines 299–306)

Conchubar, by contrast, embodies such solar qualities as kingliness and rationality: he wants to build a well-regulated society with himself and his heirs on top. He needs the backing of Cuchulain's sword, but is threatened by the hero's turbulence, which he attempts to negate by convincing Cuchulain to swear an oath of fealty.[5] After Cuchulain reluctantly agrees, Conchubar stages a ceremony to "blow the witches out," ritually banishing the feminine forces that have heretofore enlivened Cuchulain's masculinity (line 355). Immediately after this ceremony, Cuchulain confronts a strange young warrior, who, unbeknownst to him, is his only son, the offspring of a tempestuous encounter with a Scottish queen who has trained her son for revenge. Intuiting something familiar, Cuchulain cajoles his challenger into friendship, thus dismaying Conchubar, who demands that the foreign invader be repelled. Eventually, Cuchulain concludes that his attraction to the young man has been the work of "witchcraft," and agrees to fight and kill him (line 566). Later, after learning his victim's identity, he turns his wrath on Conchubar, who magically deflects him into a doomed assault on the sea, which is said at the end to have "mastered him." *On Baile's Strand* thus gives realm-defending violence a very different treatment than it receives in *Cathleen ni Houlihan*, suggesting that it may be deeply misguided if unleashed for the sake of materialists and xenophobes. The negation of Cuchulain's lunar qualities initiated by his oath and reflected in his son's death and his mastery by the waves bolsters an oppressive political order. The play offers neither a nationalist allegory nor an uncritical defense of the hero's own rights and powers. Nor does it assume that government by a man of noble blood necessarily fosters justice and beauty. Rather, it laments for the enlivening mixture of passionate masculinity and strong femininity associated with Ireland's heroic era, encouraging audiences to ponder the place of such qualities in the modern world.

The King's Threshold is more problematic. Written soon after Gonne's marriage, at a time when Synge's arrival was inflaming Yeats's relationship with nationalist Dublin, it tells the story of a poet deprived of honor by an ancient Irish king whose materialistic courtiers have convinced him to see poetry as trivial; in addition to decrying such Philistines, it critiques women who refuse to subordinate their bodies' reproductive powers to poetry's spiritual guidance. In all of the play's texts, its aggrieved poet-hero, Seanchan (pronounced "SHA-na-han"), goes on hunger strike to shame King Guaire's court into restoring his rights. In early versions, Guaire ("GWAI-ra") capitulates when it becomes clear that Seanchan's death will provoke popular unrest. Many years later, in the midst of the Irish War of Independence and following the hunger-strike death of the imprisoned nationalist politician Terence MacSwiney, Yeats altered the play's ending so that Guaire refuses to yield and Seanchan perishes. In this revised version, nothing less than an accomplished sacrifice and imminent turmoil can properly reorder society.

Why does restoring Seanchan's rights justify the threat – or fulfillment – of a sacrifice calculated to inspire violent change? Both early and late versions of the play answer by reasserting the disturbing aesthetics more tentatively put forward in "Rosa Alchemica": namely, that poets mediate between the super-natural and the natural by using images of beauty or ugliness to summon good or evil spirits who in turn take control of the reproductive powers of women and thereby shape the minds and bodies of individuals and races. Good poets hang "Images of the life that was in Eden / About the child-bed of the world, that it, / Looking upon those images, might bear / Triumphant children" (lines 129–32). When, by contrast, the arts decay, "The world that lack[s] them [becomes] like a woman / That, looking on the cloven lips of a hare, / Brings forth a hare-lipped child" (lines 137–39). This explains why the King and his court must be the "world's model" by fostering poetry (line 163). Seanchan takes this very literally. When angered by princesses who tempt him with food, he tells one of them that she has been "contaminated" as a result of the fact that, just before her birth, her mother welcomed a leper into the town (line 613). Later, he asks a group of cripples, "What bad poet did your mothers listen to / That you were born so crooked?" (lines 649–50). Finally, he suggests to his beloved that the artistic deficiencies of Guaire's court have delayed the coming of

> that great race
> That would be haughty, mirthful, and white-bodied,
> With a high head, and open hand, and [that],
> Laughing, . . . would take the mastery of the world.   (lines 690–93)

These troubling lines posit a supernatural basis for the racial taxonomies elsewhere associated with slavery and imperialism and the Nazis' horrific attempts to impose "white-bodied" masters on the world.

We must keep in mind, of course, that Yeats lived in a world that had not yet experienced the Nazi Holocaust, a world in which the superiority of some races to others was widely assumed, and where anxiety about the perceived degeneration of Nordic and Anglo-Saxon "races" had begun to stimulate widespread support for the eugenics movement in Britain and the United States (as well as in Germany).[6] We must also keep in mind that his imaginative experiments did not always carry him to such outrageous lengths. His important essay on Edmund Spenser, dated October 1902, sharply qualifies conclusions similar to Seanchan's. It centers on the question of how the man responsible for the beautiful poetry of *The Faerie Queene* (1590–96) could also produce *A View of the Present State of Ireland* (written in 1596; published posthumously in 1633). In *A View*, Spenser suggests that, because the Irish appear barbaric, they deserve brutal subjugation. Yeats critiques this position not by renouncing the premise that beauty and ugliness derive from good and evil but rather by arguing that Spenser misperceived the Irish when he saw them as barbaric. To recognize that someone as imaginative as Spenser may make such an error is tantamount to admitting that anyone may be similarly deceived, and thus to conceding that real-world decisions should not be based on moral judgments deriving from aesthetic perceptions. Yeats may have suffered from the class and racial prejudices typical of his time, but we go too far if we accuse him of being a fascist. His skeptical accounts of King Guaire and Spenser demonstrate that he does not advocate a totalitarian state power acting in accordance with aesthetic judgments. The power he prays for is a spiritual one, a supernatural wind emanating from the universal spirit. It is this power he calls on to reshape human minds and bodies. Artists summon divinity by creating beauty, and according to Yeats they do so best when an enlightened aristocracy fosters them.

Drama's influence on Yeats's verse style:
In the Seven Woods

The bold protagonists of *The King's Threshold* and *On Baile's Strand* reflect the extent to which Yeats's post-1899 troubles with theater audiences and Maud Gonne disenchanted him with the (usually) less assertive heroes of his earlier work. Both plays also manifest formal innovations necessitated by the dramatization of such figures as Cuchulain. Yeats's best works had always dramatized conflict, but in the 1890s they had done so most effectively in brief lyrics featuring dream-burdened speakers and elaborate but static symbols. "The Secret Rose," for instance, accumulates layer after layer of symbolic description before climaxing in its speaker's desperate plea to the unresponsive Rose. Such agonized lyrical epiphanies typically fall flat in the theatre: plays must sustain themselves for longer periods than lyric poems and can easily bewilder audiences if they use language too richly textured to be understood on first hearing. Such language may also sound odd when spoken by forceful heroes. Coming to terms with these issues, Yeats developed new theories of poetic drama and its performance that quickly began to affect both his plays and lyrics. He hated the "realistic" theatrical traditions established by such playwrights as Henrik Ibsen and Bernard Shaw: these put too much stress on the merely material world. Instead, he sought to synthesize drama's customary emphasis on action and conflict with modes of visual and verbal minimalism intended to produce visionary theatrical experiences.

Although the minimalist movement did not come into vogue until after Yeats's death, its slogan of "less is more" aptly describes his evolving philosophy of drama and performance. Influenced by such continental playwrights as Maurice Maeterlinck, by the Fay brothers' acting methods, and eventually by the English actor, producer, and set designer Gordon Craig, Yeats came to believe that poetic drama must maximize its expressiveness by minimalizing all but a few highly salient features. Like a lens concentrating light to a point of burning intensity, it must focus the audience's attention; only thus could it create and sustain intense, transforming moments similar to those evoked in his lyrics. As a poet, he wanted the strongest emphasis to fall on the spoken word (though he later developed an equally strong interest in dance). This meant that simple costumes and patterned backdrops must replace the eye-catching garb and ornate sets used in most contemporary productions. It also meant that instead of improvising movements, actors must adopt stylized poses and move only to enact essential gestures:

> We must simplify acting, especially in poetical drama, and in prose
> drama that is remote from real life like my *Hour-Glass*. We must get rid
> of everything that is restless, everything that draws the attention away
> from the sound of the voice, or from the few moments of intense
> expression, whether that expression is through the voice or through the
> hands.[7]

At first, Yeats enjoyed more success in explaining these principles than in bringing them to the stage. The Fay brothers proved kindred spirits, but other actors resisted, and he had difficulty in finding like-minded set and costume designers. The debut production of *The King's Threshold*, for example, adopted garishly baroque costumes designed by his wealthy bene-factor, Annie Horniman. Not until 1916 and his experiments with forms derived from Japanese Noh drama did he truly realize his proto-minimalist vision of dramatic performance.[8] In the meantime, he applied minimalist principles to poetic language itself. Instead of building up layers of symbol-ism, he cut back on poetic artifice, introducing, as his *Autobiographies* explain, "such numbness and dullness . . . that all might seem, as it were, remembered with indifference, except some one vivid image" (A 321). Such vivid images as remained derived less from dim netherworlds and more from the realm of the physical eye and of ordinary speech. Diction, syntax, rhythm, and sound became simpler, more direct and vigorous: still elo-quently beautiful, but more like a passionate hero speaking and less like an ethereal fairy singing or a magician chanting a spell.

Some of these qualities inhere in the passage from *On Baile's Strand* quoted earlier, which opts for words familiar from ordinary speech, rhythms invi-gorated by enjambment, and imagery focused on one vivid picture of two hostile forces in turbulent symbiosis. They are even more apparent in the poetry of *In the Seven Woods* (1903). This collection's initial, title poem summons a very different imaginative universe than the one evoked in *The Wind Among the Reeds*. That volume begins by mustering the wraithlike Sidhe. Here, we start with a speaker who seems a version of the real-world poet and who uses everyday language to locate himself in an actual place and time, the Seven Woods of Lady Gregory's estate, in August 1902. He also alludes to two real events that had recently demonstrated Ireland's continuing subservience to Britain: the coronation of King Edward VII ("new common-ness / Upon the throne"), and the excavation by crackpot English archeolo-gists of the ancient seat of Irish kingship at Tara. Though the speaker's rueful tone undercuts his claim to have "put away / The unavailing outcries and the old bitterness, / That empty the heart," he avoids the effusive lyricism typical of early Yeats. Instead he offers a series of numb, dull images – pigeons, bees, flowers – that hint at emotional and political distress. Only at the end do such images defer to symbols. At this point, the speaker avers that "Quiet" – personified as a woman and seeming to embody the feminine principle – still "Wanders laughing" at Coole. Within Lady Gregory's cultivated demesne, she enjoys the masculine protection of the constellation Sagittarius, that "Great Archer" who, the speaker hopes, will one day unloose apocalyptic forces and remake the fallen cosmos.

In its 1903 version, *In the Seven Woods* followed up the apocalyptic prophecy of its introductory poem with two long narratives subsequently removed from the collection, "The Old Age of Queen Maeve" and "Baile and Aillinn."[9] These combine accounts of ancient Irish legends with first-person interjections by modern-day narrators who contrast Ireland's legendary glories with its spiritless, fallen present; this technique later prompted T. S. Eliot to remark that Yeats had "adumbrated" the mythic-modern parallelism of Joyce's *Ulysses*.[10] "Queen Maeve" is the more interesting of the two. Depicting its heroine as beautiful and fierce, "great-bodied and great-limbed, / Fashioned to be the mother of strong children," it joins *On Baile's Strand* in celebrating an image of female valor less virginal and removed from the world than those idealized in "The Rose" or *The Wind Among the Reeds* (lines 25–26). For the narrators of both "Queen Maeve" and "Baile and Aillinn," however, such images of bygone greatness remain painfully distant from modern Ireland. This may explain why the volume's next several poems turn away from the nation's heroic age to face its present actualities. In such first-person, real-world lyrics as "The Arrow," "The Folly of being Comforted," and "Adam's Curse," the realities of modern, middle-class life prompt ever greater dejection. Finally, the intensity of this dejection breaks open a new set of visions best exemplified by "Red Hanrahan's Song about Ireland" and "The Happy Townland." Here, both the inaccessible glories of Ireland's past and the disillusioning realities of its present give way to the hope that it will be revitalized through communal sharing of its surviving folk traditions. These concluding lyrics mostly feature plural speakers and folk-based forms and hence evoke collective, ritualized experience. "The Happy Townland," for example, uses an approximation of ballad stanza to herald a populist paradise where beer-drinking, bagpipe-playing peasants mix with dancing queens and fighting warriors, where the archangel Michael blows his trumpet for supper instead of judgment, and where miracles actually occur "On wet roads where men walk." *In the Seven Woods* thus satisfies the apocalyptic expectations of its first poem by moving away from the impossibly idealized Romanticism of its heroic poems – and through the disillusioning realities encountered at its mid-point – to conclude with a synthesis of the miraculous and the earthly.

Despite the volume's harmonious conclusion, most current critics prefer its disheartened personal lyrics, which now appear as turning points in modern poetry's rejection of the idealism and elevated language of late-nineteenth-century verse. Eliot's influential summation of Yeats's career, for example, praises both "The Folly of being Comforted" and "Adam's Curse" for their "particularity," arguing that "in beginning to speak as a particular man [Yeats] is beginning to speak for man."[11] One need not share Eliot's disparagement of Yeats's earlier work to see that the lifelike dialogue and clear-eyed description of "The Folly" mark a significant new departure. "Adam's Curse" represents an even more remarkable achievement. It uses all of the lyric genre's formal resources to bring its speaker's high-minded passions into forceful contact with ordinary realities. Its despairing vision of beauty and truth thus becomes more palpable, more distinctly outlined, than the ethereal moods that haunted Yeats in the nineties.

Like "In the Seven Woods" and "The Folly of being Comforted," "Adam's Curse" establishes a real-world setting and cast of characters: a poet who seems a version of Yeats himself addresses a beloved more like a real woman than an emblem. Recalling an earlier conversation shared with her "close friend," he remembers grumbling that, despite poetry's apparent artless-ness, poets must work harder than servants scrubbing floors or paupers breaking stones and still end up dismissed as idlers by "the noisy set / Of bankers, schoolmasters, and clergymen / The martyrs call the world." This had prompted the beloved's friend to tease him with the remark that women, too, "must labour to be beautiful." He had then admitted that, since Adam's fall, even true love requires skilled effort. This was bad enough in the old days, when poets wrote "beautiful old books" full of precedents for lovers to follow. But now, in the capitalist, empirical era of "bankers, schoolmasters, and clergymen," poetry attracts few followers, and love itself has consequently degenerated into "an idle trade." This admission leads to a memorable example of Yeats's new talent for isolating single vivid images, in this case a vision of the dying daylight and the waning moon that symbolizes the near extinction of the vital mixture of masculine and feminine energies associated with the conjunction of the sun and moon. The poet's memory of this vision prompts him to tell his beloved something left unstated in their earlier conversation: that, her beauty notwithstanding, his attempt to love her "in the old high way of love" has failed, leaving both of them "As weary-hearted as that hollow moon." The beloved herself remains silent in both of the poem's time frames, and the fact that we cannot know how or whether she responds to the poet's anguished confession greatly augments its effect. More than anything she could possibly say, her wordlessness dramatizes their relationship's excruciating paradox: she is close enough to be intimately addressed, but immune to the power of his words, even when they come straight from the heart, undisguised by veils of myth.

"Adam's Curse" disavows faith in poetic words through both the matter and manner of its language. Virtually all of its words and phrases derive from everyday speech, and some are more mundane than any previously encountered in Yeats (e.g., "maybe," "all kinds of weather," and "the noisy set / Of bankers, schoolmasters, and clergymen"). Its "sweet sounds" are mostly muted, and occasionally offset by the mild ticks and thuds created when a word ending with a phonetic stop precedes another word beginning with a similar sound (as in "That beautiful" and "not talk"). Speechlike rhythms roughen its iambic pentameter meter, and its sentences often strengthen the impression of spontaneous, colloquial speech by extending themselves over several lines, sometimes by means of enjambment. The poem's rhymes also merit careful attention. Yeats possessed an extraordinary knack for using rhyming sounds to call attention to rhyming words and thereby enhance their significance. By the time he wrote "Adam's Curse," he had learned to tone down the music of his rhymes by making some of them imperfect. The result is a rhyming *tour de force* that reinforces the poem's major conflicts with such resonant pairings as "school / beautiful," "fine thing / laboring," "enough / love," and "poetry / maybe." The dissonant chord of sound and connotation characterizing the last of these masterfully encapsulates the poem's deflated mood.

Even so, few readers will conclude that Yeats gives up entirely on poetry, beauty, and love. Though colloquial language, muted sounds, irregular rhythms, and dissonant rhymes check the poem's artfulness, that artfulness preserves considerable latent strength. This is especially evident at the end, where the dying sun and hollow moon imply a measure of hope both through their trembling blue-green beauty and by virtue of being heavenly bodies that wane only to wax again. Even the beloved's silence is not absolutely daunting: she confirms neither a commitment nor a disavowal. Like many of Yeats's most admired works, "Adam's Curse" dramatizes painfully unresolved conflicts.

Revisions, masks, and *The Green Helmet and Other Poems*

Between Maud Gonne's marriage and the debut of such works as *On Baile's Strand*, *The King's Threshold*, and *In the Seven Woods*, 1903 was an important year for Yeats. He capped it by embarking on his first North American lecture tour. The Protestant background and occult convictions that alienated him from Dublin nationalists mattered little to the admiring thousands he encountered half a world away: to academic audiences in university towns he appeared a charismatic literary trendsetter, while hero-hungry Irish-Americans in big cities hailed him as a native son made good. He recrossed the Atlantic in March 1904 with a fur coat, a slight middle-aged paunch, and more money than he had ever possessed, a welcome reprieve from years of relying on his writing's meager earnings and the generosity of better-off friends. The side of him that envied successful men of the world was brimming with confidence, eager to pursue plans for the Abbey Theatre. But the dreamy, fragile side had worn as hollow as the moon in "Adam's Curse," exhausted by the effort to make sense of his rejection by Maud Gonne and by nationalist Dublin. Many of his friends from the eighties and nineties had now either died or grown distant, and disputes within the Golden Dawn had estranged him from another important source of spiritual and emotional support.

Thus divided, Yeats began a four-year period of artistic and personal struggle during which the demands of managing the Abbey sapped his creative energies and often forced him to trade his comfortable London rooms or the tranquility of Coole for a dreary life of cheap Dublin lodgings and petty backstage quarrels. With the exception of a few important prose essays and the play *Deirdre* (first performed in November 1906), most of what he wrote between 1904 and 1908 took the form of revisions to existing works. In such compilations as *Poems, 1899–1905* (1906) and the monumental eight-volume *Collected Works in Verse and Prose* (1908), he subjected his oeuvre to the most sweeping changes it had experienced since *Poems* (1895). *In the Seven Woods* underwent particularly significant transformations as the poet inserted the handful of brief, dispirited love poems that trickled from his pen in the aftermath of Gonne's marriage. Such lyrics as "Old Memory," "Never give all the Heart," and "O do not Love Too Long" speak to and about women in tones more embittered than any he had used before. The speaker of the first informs his beloved that her lofty, world-transforming "strength" owes its existence to his own imagination and then patronizingly chides her for having strayed beyond his guidance; the other two adopt attitudes of ironic knowingness to lament the deceptions of "passionate women" capable of changing "in a minute." A volume of poems that had once begun in a world of heroic love and ended with a vision of paradise became much more thoroughly skeptical.

Yeats devoted himself to revision not merely because he was too consumed with theatre business to generate fresh compositions or too angry with Gonne to leave his earlier praise of her unqualified. The onset of middle age spurred him to assess his progress as an artist, to discover and reinforce the patterns underlying half-a-lifetime's labors. This process eventually inspired new creation by prompting the exciting realization that the defining characteristics of his recent work took root in a new understanding of the human self and of the imagination's role in harmonizing it with others and the cosmos. One of his clearest acknowledgments of this realization – and of revision's part in fostering it – came in a prefatory quatrain to his 1908 *Collected Works*:

> The friends that have it I do wrong
> When ever I remake a song,
> Should know what issue is at stake:
> It is myself that I remake.

These lines suggest that the poet now regards his identity as something deliberately constructed in his works, an artifact he can alter and perhaps redeem by remaking these works. In the nineties Yeats had conceived of the self as more passive and unchanging, an entity that escaped the choice between solipsistic entrapment in individual, material existence and sacrificial surrender to some human or spiritual "other" only when protected by an idealized feminine intermediary such as the Rose. Revising his oeuvre allowed him to see that his post-nineties development had been a function of his desire to reimagine the self in more active and "masculine" terms, as something that sought union with other beings by standing up to them rather than by submitting or pleading for mercy. It was this desire, he now saw, that had occasioned his turn from the private reveries of lyric poetry to the public arena of the theatre, that had inspired his interest in such sexually and spiritually forceful protagonists as Queen Maeve and Cuchulain, and that had roused him to exchange wavering rhythms, elevated diction, and elaborately layered symbolism for a more impassioned, speechlike manner.

Yeats explored these realizations not only in the quatrain quoted above but also in such critical writings as *Discoveries* (1907), where he recanted his early preoccupation with "impersonal beauty" and concluded that "we should ascend out of common interests, the thoughts of the newspapers, of the market-place, of men of science . . . only so far as we can carry the normal, passionate, reasoning self, the personality as a whole."[12] He pushed even further in a journal begun in 1908, a text from which he later extracted the sections of his *Autobiographies* known as "Estrangement" and "The Death of Synge." Here, he suggested that ascending out of common interests without leaving the ordinary self behind required the creation of a mask: a deliberately imagined second self wrought from everything the ordinary self lacked and therefore able to complete that ordinary self by confronting it in the manner of a Blakean contrary. At first he focused mainly on such a mask's role in making someone a more compelling lover or public figure, but eventually, in his occult treatise *Per Amica Silentia Lunae* (1918), he revealed that as a mask completed a person's individual identity it also summoned from the universal mind that person's own special guiding spirit, a "Daemon" who enabled ascent toward the cosmic oneness. *Per Amica Silentia Lunae* also suggested that nations could fashion collective masks – and call up "more general" Daemons – if their cultures deliberately fostered the virtues not instinctive to their peoples, a premise that accorded well with the poet's evolving view of the Ascendancy's role in Ireland (LE 29). In some respects, then, Yeats's doctrine of the mask resembled his earlier theory of the symbol, though with important differences. The symbols in his early work had been intended to induce states of passive reverie that opened up the poet and his readers to powerful forces flooding in from without. The masks created in his middle and later works, by contrast, do not attempt to quiet the self or expose it to transformations controlled entirely by outside forces. Instead, they represent Yeats's efforts to rouse himself and others to acts of imaginative self-unification, acts empowering individuals and even entire nations to engage their lovers or guardian spirits in mutually strengthening opposition.

Yeats's doctrine of the mask also established him as an influential proponent of the new conceptions of selfhood adopted by modernist writers. Since the late eighteenth century, the Romantic traditions associated with such figures as Jean-Jacques Rousseau and William Wordsworth had suggested that our truest, most natural selves lie deep within us, buried by modern civilization, and must be rediscovered and expressed if we are to find real happiness. Such thinking had often been applied not only to individuals but also to nations (and would-be nations) like Britain and Ireland, where many people longed to preserve or resurrect the older, seemingly more genuine national identities obscured by industrialism, capitalism, and imperialism.

When Yeats concluded that it wasn't enough to express the natural self of a person or a nation, he anticipated ideas soon explored by Ezra Pound, James Joyce, T. S. Eliot, and others. Though these writers rejected many aspects of their predecessor's thought, all agreed that human fulfillment required the natural self to undergo deliberate re-creation. Adopting the Latin word for masks as its title, Pound's *Personae* (1926) fashions models for the present by breathing new life into artistic and political heroes from medieval Europe and ancient China. Joyce's *A Portrait of the Artist as a Young Man* (1916) suggests that, while art originates in the artist's urge to express his personality, the proper shaping of artistic materials ultimately obliges this personality to "[refine] itself out of existence."[13] As for Eliot, his contention in "Tradition and the Individual Talent" (1919) that the individual writer finds "complete meaning" through confrontation with the "ideal order" formed by literary tradition parallels Yeats's conviction that the natural self achieves wholeness through struggle with a created mask and with a Daemon emanating from the ideal order of the universal mind.[14] In fairness, it should be acknowledged that earlier writers equally anticipated Yeats, whose use of the mask metaphor owes much to Oscar Wilde (not to mention Friedrich Nietzsche, whom he began reading in 1902).[15] Even so, Yeats's commitment to carefully crafted personal and national identities deserves recognition as an important contribution to one of modernism's definitive features.

Some elements of Yeats's mask theory surface as early as the disillusioned lyrics added to *In the Seven Woods* after Maud Gonne's marriage: both "Never give all the Heart" and "O do not Love Too Long" suggest that only a carefully refashioned self can win a passionate lover. It took a fresh set of energizing experiences, however, to produce a steady current of new creative accomplishments. The first of these experiences occurred in January 1907, when the Abbey debut of Synge's masterpiece, *The Playboy of the Western World*, sparked a furor far more riotous than those incited by *The Countess Cathleen* or *In the Shadow of the Glen*. *The Playboy* tells the story of a strange young rural renegade who makes himself attractive to women by claiming to have killed his father. Infuriated Dublin nationalists decried it in print and packed the theater with boisterous crowds who drowned out the actors by booing, singing, and blasting on toy trumpets. When the reticent Synge refused to defend himself, Yeats leapt into the breach: he called in the police, appeared on stage to hurl defiance at the protesters, and, at a forum held after the play's week-long run, angrily defended Ireland's need for uncensored public expression. This episode greatly hardened the confrontational stance he had begun to take toward his audience. It also inspired *The Green Helmet*, his most interesting new verse play since *On Baile's Strand*. First performed in March 1908 in a prose version known as *The Golden Helmet*, *The Green Helmet* satirizes Synge's detractors by dramatizing a farcical incident from Cuchulain's early life. This time the hero must deal with an Ireland made defenseless by the self-interested quarreling of an absurdly intolerant mob. When the country's internal divisions expose it to the sacrificial demands of a monstrous supernatural Red Man, Cuchulain demonstrates his own disinterested nobility by offering to die for his people. In response, the Red Man proclaims himself Ireland's "Rector" and crowns Cuchulain as its champion (line 275). By claiming a clerical title usually associated with Protestantism, the Red Man underlines the play's daring departure from the nationalist tradition of personifying Ireland as feminine and Catholic: here, the nation's presiding spirit is masculine and quasi-Protestant, and its hero is a chivalrous blueblood who sets a selfless example instead of leading the rabble to arms. Though no mention is made of masks, Cuchulain plainly epitomizes the aristocratic virtues Yeats believed were necessary to complete the disordered energies of his country's masses.

Meanwhile, Maud Gonne's marriage had long since fallen apart. Early in 1905 she shocked the poet by revealing that her hard-drinking husband had sexually abused both her seventeen-year-old half-sister, Eileen, and her eleven-year-old daughter, Iseult. Yeats supported her gallantly during the long ordeal that followed, which involved bitter political skirmishes with MacBride's nationalist allies as well as a legal battle to obtain a separation. By the summer of 1908, these scandalous matters had been largely settled, but Gonne was faltering privately. Repeating a familiar pattern, she turned to her old friend for comfort, inviting him to visit her in Paris. Here, old passions soon rekindled, and the two former soulmates resumed their spiritual union. Most biographers believe that at some point during the next few months they also conducted a brief sexual affair that ended when Gonne insisted on reverting to a non-sexual relationship. The poet presumably took solace in the fact that, since April, he had been conducting a secret sexual liaison with a 33-year-old Dublin actress and exercise teacher called Mabel Dickinson. This continued until 1913, when an erroneous (and possibly dishonest) claim of pregnancy convinced him to end it. His feelings for Dickinson, about which we know little, probably did not go beyond affection and physical attraction. Still, when Yeats's ideas about the mask encountered the stimulants associated with the *Playboy* controversy, his rapprochement with Gonne, and the Dickinson dalliance, he experienced a burst of lyric creativity more prolific than any since the days of his affair with Olivia Shakespear. The resulting poems combined with

The Green Helmet to form *The Green Helmet and Other Poems* (1910), his first volume of new verse in more than seven years.

This collection begins with a series of love lyrics inspired by the spiritual marriage's revival and then shifts to less intimate matters. Most of its poems took shape on the pages of the same journal in which Yeats first employed the mask metaphor, and most explore the philosophy that backs up this metaphor, at least to some degree. This is clearest in "The Mask," where a lover refuses to reveal his natural self to his beloved on the grounds that "It was the mask engaged your mind, / And after set your heart to beat." Though the more obviously autobiographical poems leading up to "The Mask" also consider the premise that a fulfilled and compelling self must be deliberately reconstructed, they do so in more skeptical terms. "His Dream" starts things off by restoring the eerie, suicidal aura of the poet's late-nineties work: its speaker dreams himself the oarsman of a gaudily decorated ship carrying a shrouded figure who entrances him and others into an "ecstatic" state resembling the deathlike transformation embraced by Michael Robartes and his disciples in "Rosa Alchemica." Recapitulating the course of Yeats's subsequent development, the following poems turn from praises for "the sweet name of Death" to the quest for fulfillments that avoid self-obliterating sacrifices (P 89). But instead of simply outlining the hope that a carefully imagined mask may prepare the self for satisfying encounters with other beings, they focus on the difficulties entailed in realizing such ambitions.

Both "Words" and "The Fascination of What's Difficult," for example, suggest that Yeats's imaginative endeavors have impoverished rather than enhanced his life. "Words" begins with the poet seeking consolation in the thought that his failures to enlighten his "blind bitter land" and his equally uncomprehending "darling" have at least had the effect of spurring him to song. Though this thought tallies with the idea that great achievement results from imagining masks that remedy the insufficiencies of ordinary existence, Yeats never limited his ambitions to the mere writing of fine poems. From the beginning, his devotion to poetic words assumed that they would bring him added control over spiritual and material realities. In "Words," he ends by conceding that he did not "come into [his] strength" as soon as "words obey [ed] [his] call" and by expressing regret that he has not "thrown poor words away / And been content to live." "The Fascination of What's Difficult" reveals yet more directly and bitterly that, instead of leading him toward completion, the poet's artistic struggles have "dried the sap out of [his] veins, and rent / Spontaneous joy and natural content / Out of [his] heart."

Though the poems that follow "The Mask" exude greater assurance than the anguished personal lyrics preceding it, they imply more self-doubt than at first may be apparent. Most apply Yeats's conception of the mask to Irish politics, professing the virtues of aristocracy more overtly than any of his previous works. Written after a court decision lowered tenants' rents at Coole, "Upon a House shaken by the Land Agitation" angrily contends that an Ireland deprived of such estates will lack access to the cultural masks "Wrought" by "written speech" out of "high laughter, loveliness, and ease." "These are the Clouds" advances similar notions, while "At Galway Races" praises the "one mind" created when the plebian crowd "closes in behind" aristocratic "men / That ride upon horses." These poems do not, however, suggest that the political corollaries of Yeats's mask doctrine will enable some final triumph: his new thinking may allow him to diagnose Ireland's problems more forcefully, but it does not permit him to effect real change in the present. All of these poems assume that clouds are gathering "about the fallen sun" of aristocratic Ireland's "majesty" and that any glorious rebirth will have to wait for "some new moon" (P 96–97).

These topical poems become still more complex if read in relation to the *Green Helmet* volume's final two lyrics, "All Things can tempt Me" and "Brown Penny." Though we may be initially inclined to read the angry political poems of the collection's second half as evidence that an instinctively dreamy poet has at last completed himself with an active, worldly mask, Yeats's journal reveals that, by this stage, years of theatrical and political controversy had made him so prone to bitter outbursts that he now considered his mask to be a posture of proud, imperturbable sweetness. The journal describes "petulant combativeness" as his "worst fault," and records his resolve to "set up a secondary or interior personality" that "must be always gracious and simple."[16] Such qualities are presumably what the speaker of "All Things can tempt Me" has in mind when he says that he "would be now, could [he] but have [his] wish, / Colder and dumber and deafer than a fish." In other words, all of the poems in which Yeats denounces his "fool-driven land" for failing to adopt the cultural masks offered by aristocratic Ireland are simultaneously dramatizations of his own failure to embrace the sweet silent serenity he sees as his self's necessary complement (P 97). The poet's closest approach to this mask of sweetness comes in the final poem, where a wishfully thrown "Brown Penny" tells him to "go and love." Yeats has once again created compelling poetry by dramatizing turbulent emotions and thoughts (and not by dressing up his convictions in the fine clothes of eloquent words).

Responsibilities

Yeats continued to dramatize his emotions and thoughts in the half dozen years following publication of *The Green Helmet and Other Poems*. As the Abbey became more established he shifted attention to his own creative efforts. He took added encouragement from a strong rise in his income that made him comfortably well off for the first time. His relationship with Gonne kept on an even keel, and he also repaired his friendship with Olivia Shakespear, whose circle of acquaintance now included the young American poet Ezra Pound. By the summer of 1914, he had released another volume of poetry – *Responsibilities* – and was making good progress with the first installment of his memoirs, *Reveries over Childhood and Youth*. The publication of *Reveries* in 1916 coincided with the release of *Responsibilities and Other Poems*, which combined the lyrics of the 1914 volume with those from *The Green Helmet and Other Poems*. These two books brought the work of his middle years to a high point every bit as remarkable as the late-nineties zenith reached by *The Secret Rose* and *The Wind Among the Reeds*.

Compared to *Responsibilities and Other Poems*, none of Yeats's recent poetic collections had attracted very much notice. Both *In the Seven Woods* and *The Green Helmet and Other Poems* had appeared during a time of preoccupation with the poet's theatrical work. Both had also been hand-printed in expensive, limited editions by his sister Lolly, who ran a press dedicated to furnishing Ireland with books untainted by soulless mass production. Though *Responsibilities* likewise debuted as one of Lolly's deluxe editions, the expanded 1916 version appeared in more accessible form under the auspices of Macmillan & Co., a major firm which had recently become Yeats's principal British publisher. Even in 1914, *Responsibilities* attracted a scattering of crucial reviews, including one by Pound that heralded "a manifestly new note in [Yeats's] later work," a "gaunter," "harder" note that aligned the Irish poet with the emerging avant-garde the American saw himself as leading.[17] Pound and Yeats had first become acquainted in 1909; their friendship reached its most intense phase during the winters of 1913–14, early 1915, and early 1916, when Yeats rented a cottage in southern England and invited Pound to accompany him as his secretary. Here, they wrote and studied together, and the younger poet pressed the older to continue the stylistic reforms he had begun almost ten years before. Though Pound's influence has sometimes been exaggerated, his private and public judgments affected both the substance and reception of Yeats's writing. Not everyone agreed that the "hard light" of *Responsibilities* shone more radiantly than the ethereal glows of the nineties.[18] But, by 1916, partly through

Pound's efforts, interest in Yeats as a lyric poet was approaching levels not reached since the appearance of *The Wind Among the Reeds.*

Though capable publishers, animated reviewers, and the interest stirred up by *Reveries* all helped put *Responsibilities* in the limelight, the collection's enduring reputation derives from its own poetic merits. Eliot made no mistake when he identified *In the Seven Woods* as the starting point for Yeats's metamorphosis as a twentieth-century poet, and such *Green Helmet* lyrics as "No Second Troy" and "The Fascination of What's Difficult" are no doubt as gaunt and hard as anything in *Responsibilities*. But *Responsibilities* forms a more ambitious body of work than either of its two immediate predecessors: it includes more (and generally longer) poems, and ranges through a greater variety of themes, from the legacies bequeathed by the poet's ancestral, artistic, and political "old fathers" to the spiritual quest for "uncontrollable mystery" (P 101 and 126). Unlike *The Wind Among the Reeds*, which accumulates uncanny power by constraining terrible depths with layers of polished beauty, *Responsibilities* unleashes an onslaught of proud assertions, savage accusations, mocking fables, and anguished revelations. Many of these counterpoint traditional poetic forms with emphatic, fist-pounding rhythms, slangy turns of phrase, and imagery that revels in indecorous descriptions of brawling beggars and urinating dogs. The collection pushes Yeats's post-nineties fascination with heroically masked versions of his own personality to a new level of intensity, bringing home the conflict between his commitment to the masks worn by those able to "Be secret and exult" and his urge to express "naked" pride, anger, and fear (P 109 and 127). The clash between the laughing mask and the angry self permeates *Responsibilities*.

Like "The Rose," *Responsibilities* frames itself with two italicized and, in this case, untitled poems. The first – according to Eliot, a "violent and terrible epistle" – instantly establishes the sinewy mode commended to Yeats by Pound.[19] Constructed as a single, intricate sentence, it builds the syntactic and emotional tensions released in its final quatrain by devoting its first eighteen lines to phrase after appositional phrase. It also relies on forceful, colloquial language and repeatedly invigorates its iambic meter with the insistent rhythms created when two or more trochaic words follow in jolting succession (as in the phrase, "Old country scholar, Robert Emmet's friend"). These stylistic energies summon neither an idealized feminine comforter nor a devouring whorl of wraiths. Instead, the poet calls on and praises the masculine attributes of his Anglo-Irish "old fathers," (and, by extension, of Anglo-Ireland generally). Proudly delineating a family tree filled with seafaring merchants, public-spirited scholars, and brave soldiers, he implies that, whatever their allegiances, his ancestors earned honored places in Ireland's history when, like William Pollexfen, that "silent and fierce old man," they transcended bourgeois aspirations to set examples of selfless courage. Despite the poet's haughty celebration of his forebears, he ends by begging their pardon that "for a barren passion's sake" he has "nothing but a book" to "prove" their blood and his. As someone who sacrificed ordinary pursuits to create works he hoped would change his country, he has lived up to his old fathers' boldness and public spirit. But, lacking a flesh-and-blood child, and as unsure as ever that words alone really are certain good, he cannot match the assurance that allowed his grandfather to wear a mask of wordless self-mastery. Here and elsewhere, his angry outcries bespeak as much self-doubt as arrogance.

Between these opening lines and their equally dejected closing counter-parts, *Responsibilities* moves from the legendary narrative recounted in "The Grey Rock" to a suite of bitter political poems, then to a series of Rabelaisian parables followed by a concluding miscellany.[20] The bitter political poems provide the most accessible point of entry. These begin with "To a Wealthy Man who promised a second Subscription to the Dublin Municipal Gallery if it were proved the People wanted Pictures," a work prompted by Yeats's irri-tation with the failure of Dublin's affluent classes to take responsibility for a priceless collection of French Impressionist paintings that Lady Gregory's nephew, Sir Hugh Lane, had donated to the city on the condition that a permanent gallery be built. The poem reflects Yeats's growing interest in the Italian Renaissance as an example of the cultural greatness fostered by aristocracy, contrasting the deference to public opinion of its unnamed "Wealthy Man" with the far-seeing generosity of the Italian princes praised by Baldassare Castiglione in *The Book of the Courtier* (1528). The next several poems open broader perspectives on Irish history by linking Dublin's penny-pinching response to Lane to the impotent rages that had boiled up against Parnell and Synge. "September 1913" is the most far-reaching and striking of these. Both its title and position in the volume suggest that the Lane controversy forms part of its backdrop, and its depiction of an Ireland deprived of passionate leaders by an obsession with sexual transgression calls Parnell clearly to mind. But the angry tones of its refrain decry something more significant than one or two isolated failures: they proclaim the death of the high-minded nationalist traditions the poet has wished to inherit from his political "old fathers," traditions that once allied Catholic activists like John O'Leary with such eighteenth-century Protestant patriots as Robert Emmet, Edward Fitzgerald, and Wolfe Tone.

"September 1913" stands out from its surroundings not only because its perspective is more sweeping. Even more than the collection's untitled opening salvo, it confronts readers with stunning directness. Yeats's nineties lyrics had relied on the theory that esoteric symbols draw readers quietly toward the universal spirit. But "September 1913" forces us to decide whether we will take sides with the poet or stand against him with the "you" he directly and contemptuously addresses. His compelling voice – gliding between free-spoken denunciations of Ireland's present and chanted laments for its past – is not easily resisted. Anyone who has ever tried to write metered poetry knows how hard it is to recreate the changing intonations of authentic speech amid the repeated patterns of conventional verse forms. In this respect, at least, "September 1913" triumphs. Most of its lines drum out a resounding four-beat rhythm that strengthens itself by stressing, and sometimes alliterating, the plosive initial sounds of words like "fumble" and "prayer." At the same time, the first six lines of each stanza unwind a single shifting sentence that counters this regular beat with the varying inflections created by enjambments, colloquial expressions, rhetorical questions, and bursts of dazzling eloquence. The result is a pulse-quickening blend of heroic song and angry speech that cannot be appreciated fully unless recited aloud.

After "September 1913," *Responsibilities* tempers its bitterness in two ensuing poems. "To a Friend whose Work has come to Nothing" advises Lady Gregory, who campaigned endlessly on Lane's behalf, to assume the proud, self-reliant posture of one able to "Be secret and exult." In publicly giving this advice, however, it makes clear that the poet himself lacks such a mask, which is "of all things known" the "most difficult." He comes closer to secret exultation in "Paudeen," where the recognition that he has "stumbled blind" in response to "obscure spite" suddenly fills him with the thought

> That on the lonely height where all are in God's eye,
> There cannot be, confusion of our sound forgot,
> A single soul that lacks a sweet crystalline cry.

Though his anger flares again in the next several poems, the premise that redeeming sweetness descends on those who adopt poses of self-mastered nonchalance resurfaces in the series of verse fables on beggars and hermits found at the volume's midpoint. "The Three Beggars" contrasts the "secret thought" of a laughing, generous king with the self-defeating quarrelsomeness of a trio of materialistic tramps: its moral seems to be that intense passions cannot lead one toward fulfillment if one lacks the grace to complete them with a mask. Its counterpart, "The Three Hermits," reemphasizes that this is less a matter of earnest piety or certain doctrinal knowledge than the capacity to sing "unnoticed like a bird," a capacity apparently also possessed by the giddy vagabond who intones "Running to Paradise." Perhaps the most delightful of these lyrics is "Beggar to Beggar cried." Here, we listen to a "frenzy-struck" beggar announce his intention to "make [his] soul" by assuaging "the devil in [his] shoes" with "a comfortable wife and house." This wittily implies that middle-class desires originate when beggars madly decide to "put off the world" of their beggary. Unlike the brawling rogues mocked in "The Three Beggars," the frenzied anti-hero of "Beggar to Beggar cried" elicits sympathy as well as disgust, especially when he imagines himself confined within his garden, hearing "The wind-blown clamour of the barnacle-geese." Paltry as they are, his desires resemble those of the poet who begins *Responsibilities* by expressing regret for his failure to father children. The sense that Yeats includes himself among those he mocks adds greatly to the poem's appeal.

"The Hour before Dawn" concludes the set of beggar and hermit poems by underscoring the difficulty of discovering paradise. It describes a stalemate between two opposing figures: one violently committed to the realm of "comfortable thing[s]" and the other nihilistically awaiting the hour when "flesh and bone may disappear, / And souls as if they were but sighs, / And there be nothing but God left." A similar sense of frustrated deadlock pervades the remaining poems. Like Blake's "The Lamb" and "The Tyger," "A Song from 'The Player Queen'" and "The Realists" move between states of innocence and experience without establishing how or whether the two may come together, and the same might be said of "To a Child dancing in the Wind" and "Two Years Later." "Friends" offers a moving tribute to Olivia Shakespear, Lady Gregory, and Maud Gonne, concluding with the revelation that, when the poet overcomes his bitterness toward Gonne, "sweetness" shakes him "from head to foot." Any suggestion that such sweetness has now lifted him into a permanent state of ecstasy is quickly put to rest in "The Cold Heaven." Here, a sudden vision of the burning, icy firmament grips him with the fear that, after death, bitter memories "of love crossed long ago" will oblige his ghost to be "sent / Out naked on the roads . . . and stricken / By the injustice of the skies for punishment." "The Magi" offsets this vision by imagining kingly spirits "in the blue depth of the sky" who scan the earth for "uncontrollable mystery." But even "The Magi" has its downhearted counterpart in "The Dolls," which Yeats described as illustrating the observation that "all thought among us is frozen into 'something other than human life'" (VP 820). Instead of using his "mind's eye" to see and summon higher powers, the dollmaker manufactures diminutive imitations of merely material realities. He thereby dooms his household to an existence devoid of mystery, an existence that makes even a human baby seem but an "accident."

As long as materiality constrains him, a man who fathers a child is no better off than a poet whose barren passions leave him "nothing but a book" (P 101). Though hopeful moments of masked serenity occur in such poems as "Paudeen" and "Friends," *Responsibilities* seldom permits such states of grace to do more than flicker on the verge of perception.

What, then, should be said of the collection's final two poems? "A Coat" proudly recounts Yeats's decision to exchange the mythological "embroideries" of his early work for the directly autobiographical poetry of "walking naked." The untitled final poem employs similarly haughty tones to claim that he has forgiven "even that wrong of wrongs, / Those undreamt accidents that have made [him] / . . . / Notorious, till all [his] priceless things / Are but a post the passing dogs defile." Despite these triumphant notes, the collection's earlier emphasis on the sweetness that flows from the ability to "Be secret and exult" raises the possibility that such declarations of victory manifest subtle failures. *Responsibilities* succeeds artistically by enacting Yeats's mostly unsuccessful struggle to sing "unnoticed like a bird" in the face of Romantic Ireland's death (P 109 and 114).

Ireland's "Troubles"

Like *Responsibilities*, *Reveries over Childhood and Youth* derives artistic power from moving evocations of failure and stalemate. Its famous concluding passage, for example, reveals that remembering his early life leaves Yeats "sorrowful and disturbed."

> It is not that I have accomplished too few of my plans, for I am not ambitious; but when I think of all the books I have read, and of the wise words I have heard spoken, and of the anxiety I have given to parents and grandparents, and of the hopes that I have had, all life weighed in the scales of my own life seems to me a preparation for something that never happens.   (A 108)

These words had scarcely been printed, however, when something did indeed happen, something that made the poet question whether Romantic Ireland was really as dead and gone as he had come to think. In 1914, the British Parliament had at last approved Home Rule, but the outbreak of World War I had suspended its implementation. Frustrated by this situation – and determined to take advantage of Britain's preoccupation with the fighting in France – roughly 1,800 nationalist revolutionaries launched an armed uprising in Dublin on Easter Monday 1916, and proclaimed an Irish

Republic. After a week of heavy fighting with British troops that entailed the shelling of central Dublin and thousands of civilian casualties, the rebel leaders surrendered. Fifteen were quickly court-martialed and shot, and another was subsequently hanged. Though most Irish people, including Yeats, initially opposed the Rising, the execution of its leaders produced a ground swell of sympathy. In the general election held after the end of World War I in late 1918, the hard-line nationalist party known as Sinn Féin (pronounced "shin fain" and meaning "Ourselves") won 73 of the 105 parliamentary constituencies in Ireland. Instead of taking their seats in London, the Sinn Féin members set up an independent Irish parliament and ratified the Republic declared in 1916. Guerrilla attacks on the police by the obliquely affiliated Irish Republican Army soon followed, eventually causing the British to deploy such quasi-military forces as the so-called Black and Tans, named for their two-tone uniforms and notorious for revenging themselves on civilians in retaliation for IRA attacks. Widespread unrest continued through the first half of 1921. Finally, having lost public support both in Ireland and at home, the British government opened negotiations. These led to the establishment of the Irish Free State in 1922, but because this state did not obtain full independence from the British Crown and did not include the six counties of Northern Ireland (where Protestant Unionists formed a solid majority), a breakaway faction of the IRA resisted it in a bloody civil war lasting until May 1923, when Free State forces finally found themselves in control of a broken and embittered new nation.

These occurrences inspired many of Yeats's finest later works. They also set off a chain of events in his personal and spiritual lives that led him out of the impasse so memorably captured in *Responsibilities* and *Reveries over Childhood and Youth*. Among the Rising's executed leaders was Maud Gonne's estranged husband, John MacBride. Shortly after MacBride's death, Yeats visited Gonne in France and, for the final time, asked his soulmate to marry him. She declined, having once again become more interested in radical nationalism than in the role of a poet's wife. This time, however, something deep inside him refused to accept rejection, something wrenched to the point of agony by decades of unfulfilled searching for an emotional and spiritual partner. Almost immediately, he found himself struggling with a surge of strong feelings for Gonne's daughter, Iseult, now twenty-one and strikingly beautiful. Iseult had long since learned to treat her mother's famous suitor with a mixture of filial and flirtatious affection. After wrestling with his emotions for more than a year, Yeats returned to France in August 1917 and proposed marriage to Iseult. She refused. He returned to London in a state of intense agitation, determined, come what may, to escape companionless solitude. By the end of October he had married Georgie Hyde Lees, a 24-year-old Englishwoman he knew through Olivia Shakespear's social circle and the Golden Dawn.

Yeats had first met George, as he called her, in 1911, and may have considered marriage with her as early as 1915. Still, his sudden lurch from one woman to another suggests something akin to desperation. To some extent this may have been the ordinary desperation of a 52-year-old man desirous of finding a young wife. But it can only be fully appreciated by remembering how intensely Yeats had always dreaded solipsistic isolation. In time, his marriage brought him love, children, and domestic comfort. Initially, however, it prompted anxious regret: the fear that by marrying someone he did not yet deeply love he had betrayed both himself and her. To relieve his evident misery on their honeymoon, George, who shared his occult interests, attempted automatic writing, entering an apparent trance during which spirits took control of her pen. This attempt excited her husband enormously, and he asked her to repeat it. For the next several years, they conducted such experiments on an almost nightly basis, receiving messages from a wide range of supernatural "communicators" who introduced themselves with names such as "Apple" and "Fish." At first these spirits (seemingly) moved George's pen, usually in response to Yeats's questions; later she often spoke out of a trance-like sleep. Gradually, what began as a series of reassurances about the poet's personal life evolved into a complex system of belief based on immutable cycles of individual reincarnation and historical development. This system inspired the two versions of Yeats's *A Vision* (1925 and 1937). Together with Ireland's "Troubles," it set the stage for the astounding phenomenon subsequently known as "late Yeats."

Chapter 3

Late Yeats

Lunar visions: *The Wild Swans at Coole* 66
Four Plays for Dancers and *Michael Robartes and the Dancer* 70
The Tower 78
The Winding Stair and Other Poems 92
Blueshirts, eugenics, "lust and rage": Yeats's final works 101
Death 113

> All changed, changed utterly: / A terrible beauty is born.   "Easter, 1916"

Yeats's late poems and plays rejuvenate the impassioned spirit of his nineties work without disregarding the fiercer, more skeptical disposition that directed his subsequent development. Their rejuvenated spirit derives from the terrible beauty of the Easter Rising and its aftermath, from the emotional and occult energies set free by the poet's marriage, and from the international recognition reflected in such honors as the Nobel Prize for Literature. But while such occurrences partly restored Yeats's early hopes, he always had to settle for something short of his initial desires. He found love and marriage, but not with Maud Gonne. He became a Senator in an independent Irish state, but that state was born in appalling violence, and in his view did not properly accommodate the Anglo-Irish. He achieved spiritual illumination, but that illumination postponed individual redemption until after death and cultural redemption for some future era. Yeats succeeded more and more in constructing his own self, his own art, his own house, family, and religion. But he failed to revive a unified Irish tradition in which he could root these individual triumphs. This chapter explores his life and work between the tumults of 1916–17 and his death in 1939.

Lunar visions: *The Wild Swans at Coole*

The first version of *The Wild Swans at Coole*, published by Lolly Yeats's handpress in 1917, reads more like a continuation of Yeats's middle period than the start of something new. Though less angry in tone than *Responsibilities*, it evokes a similar aura of disheartened stalemate; all of its contents predate the poet's marriage and none addresses the Rising. "The Fisherman" is typical: in scorn of Dublin knavery, it seeks the same elusive exultation that remains maddeningly out of reach for most of the earlier volume. "Upon a Dying Lady" also recalls images and concerns from the poet's preceding collection, using dolls to symbolize an art too worldly to deal with death. Completed in 1913, it probably would have been included in *Responsibilities* had not tact required postponement until the lady in question had died. (This was Mabel Beardsley, sister of the illustrator, Aubrey.) Even "Ego Dominus Tuus" stems from long-established lines of thought. More explicitly than any previous lyric, this poem sums up Yeats's thinking about masks and daemons, those opposing images and spirits that rouse keen imaginations to turbulent but fulfilling contact with all that their natures lack. For a naturally "lecherous" man like Dante, setting one's "chisel to the hardest stone" entails pursuing an "exalted lady." For "poor, ailing" Keats, it leads to "Luxuriant song."

Of all the volume's poems, "The Wild Swans at Coole" has proven most popular. Suggestive imagery, graceful music, and an easily understandable premise make it one of the most eloquent and accessible lyrics in the poet's canon. Its basic situation could not be more straightforward. A middle-aged man observes a flock of swans first seen years before; contrasting their unwearied energies to his own diminished spirits, he wonders what will happen when the vitality they symbolize leaves him behind for good. Each stanza blends melancholia with mysterious expectancy. The expectancy arises partly from such vividly elemental images as "brimming water among the stones." It also derives from the speaker's resonant voice, which coaxes the diction and syntax of mildly elevated speech into harmony with gentle rhythms, lilting undulations of longer and shorter lines, and the music of assonance and rhyme. (The first stanza's pairing of "stones" and "swans" is one of the most oft-admired off-rhymes in the language.) Can anyone capable of such imaginative seeing and speaking really possess a heart that will grow old? The poem's concluding reference to an eventual awakening suggests that the end of ordinary life may bring the start of something else.

The 1917 collection follows its title poem with a series of similar lyrics written during the lead-up to Yeats's desperate bid for Iseult Gonne's affections. Such poems as "Men improve with the Years" and "Lines written in Dejection" present him as "worn out with dreams," an aging man abandoned by "heroic mother moon" who now must "endure the timid sun." But they also register strong countercurrents of persistent desire for "burning youth" and the "angry tears" of "wild witches" (P 136 and 145–46). Instead of resolving these tensions, the original volume progresses to a group of mostly earlier poems praising Iseult's mother; these run from "Memory" to "Presences." For signs of the new energies that reshaped Yeats's work after 1916–17, readers must turn to the revised edition of *The Wild Swans at Coole* published by Macmillan in 1919. This version adds several lyrics apparently inspired by Iseult, including "The Living Beauty," "A Song," "To a Young Beauty," and "To a Young Girl." Even greater differences result from the insertion of two sets of more substantial poems, one inspired by the death of Lady Gregory's son Robert, shot down in 1918 while serving in the Royal Flying Corps, and the other by the revelations of George's automatic writing.

In the 1917 book, Yeats's only reaction to World War I had been the brief demurral offered in "On being asked for a War Poem." Though no believer in the rebel dictum that "England's difficulty is Ireland's opportunity," his antipathy to Britain's empire left him largely indifferent to the fighting on the continent, especially after the Rising. Robert Gregory's death presented a dilemma: the poet could not remain silent in response to the loss of his dearest friend's only son, but mixed feelings about that son and his cause made honest commemoration awkward. The most imposing of the three elegies he produced, "In Memory of Major Robert Gregory," includes some stirring panegyrics. And yet, readers aware of Yeats's real estimation of his subject's moderate talents may balk at hearing Gregory described as "Our Sidney and our perfect man." The poem's most convincing moments occur in its early stanzas, which dramatize the recently married poet telling his new wife about the dead friends of his youth (as usual, he analyzes his comrades in relation to their masks). "An Irish Airman foresees his Death" memorializes Gregory indirectly, putting Yeats's own ambivalence about the war into the mouth of a pilot not specifically identified. It celebrates this airman's courage, but also raises questions about the nature of a sacrifice made for "A lonely impulse of delight." Is the airman pursuing the mask of secret exultation that prepares the self for satisfying contact with something beyond its bounds? Or is he numbed by suicidal desire for obliterating absorption into the cosmic oneness?

Surprising speculation about such questions provides the main point of interest in the 1919 volume's third Gregory poem, "Shepherd and Goatherd," an elegiac dialogue spoken by two idealized rustics. The Goatherd's concluding passage represents one of Yeats's earliest efforts to describe the curious features of the afterlife he explored during George's trances, features that eventually inspired such important poems and plays as "Byzantium" and *Purgatory.* The Goatherd tells the Shepherd that, after death, the soul returns to innocence by dreaming through its worldly experiences in reverse order, growing "younger every second" as it "unpacks the loaded pern" – or, in more familiar language, unwinds the wound-up spool – "Of all 'twas pain or joy to learn." Though the poem itself provides little to clarify this burst of peculiar lore, the volume ends with a succession of extraordinary new lyrics that offer extensive explanation of the doctrines that later informed *A Vision*. The most revealing of these is "The Phases of the Moon."

This poem stems from the central revelation of George's otherworldly communicators: that each human life corresponds to a stage in a cycle of twenty-eight incarnations analogous to the phases of the moon. The full moon of Phase 15 symbolizes a superhuman condition of pure subjectivity during which a being's body and soul become one completely beautiful and self-sufficient form; the unseen moon of Phase 1 stands for a similarly superhuman state of utter objectivity during which a being's essential stuff is beaten up into the primal dough in preparation for a new cycle. Between these extremes the being progresses through a series of material incarnations, deriving its changing selves and masks from changing proportions of object-ive and subjective influences (what Yeats had previously designated the solar and lunar principles). From Phase 2 to Phase 8 ("the first crescent to the half") the being moves toward Phase 15 but remains close enough to Phase 1 that its nature – and masking "dream" – stay mainly objective: "the dream / But summons to adventure, and the man / Is always happy like a bird or a beast." Later, as the being pursues the mask of "whatever whim's most difficult / Among whims not impossible," its subjective powers grow so strong that even "His body moulded from within his body / Grows comelier." Eventually, such physically potent specimens as Achilles and Hector meta-morphose into more mentally powerful figures (e.g., Athena and Nietzsche) as the soul begins "To die into the labyrinth of itself." After Phase 15, the process reverses: the being withdraws from its solitude and into the world, pursuing the mask of "whatever task's most difficult / Among tasks not impossible" as it sinks back on the "deformity" associated with Phase 1. Between the physical deformity of Phase 26 and the mental deformity of Phase 28, emblematized by the Hunchback and the Fool, the potential Saint incarnated in Phase 27 may "escape" the cycle for good by renouncing both subjective selfhood and the objective world, thus opening the way to per-manent harmony with the cosmic oneness. For those not ready to be saints, the wheel continues to spin.

These doctrines are not as bizarre as they at first may seem. Reincarnation features not only in the Theosophical and Cabalistic teachings familiar to Yeats and George but also in such major religious traditions as Hinduism and

Buddhism (not to mention the classical wisdom of Pythagoras and Plato). Since the time of Descartes, moreover, most Western philosophers (and many Western poets) have shared Yeats's preoccupation with the relationship between the mind's subjectivity and the objective, exterior world. In sum, the poet's convictions are rooted in well-established traditions. By imagining a cosmos in which beings move between union with other spirits (at Phase 1) and absolute individuality (at Phase 15) until they are ready to escape into ultimate harmony, he balanced his longing for cosmic oneness against his fear of losing his selfhood. He also correlated differing states of the soul with differing degrees of physical beauty without yielding to the notion that persons perceived as ugly are made so by evil spirits. Still, there is no avoiding the fact that many find his views outlandish and unappealing. The most sympathetic usually take the same approach to his religion that some take to his politics, focusing their admiration on the power with which he dramatizes his unusually intense perceptions. "The Phases of the Moon" provides a good opportunity for indulging such admiration. Framed as a dialogue between Michael Robartes and Owen Aherne – those subjective and objective alter egos familiar from the early stories and poems – it recreates the eerie atmosphere that typifies those earlier works.[1] Moreover, by projecting Yeats's beliefs onto fictive characters who mock their creator's ignorance, it depicts the poet as a struggling off-stage presence caught in an arduous, uncompleted quest. "The Saint and the Hunchback," "Two Songs of a Fool," "Another Song of a Fool," and "The Double Vision of Michael Robartes" make similar use of personae. The last of these begins by invoking the violent melding of spirits experienced at Phase 1 and then shifts to a vision of a perfectly individuated spirit dancing at Phase 15 between a Sphinx and a Buddha, symbols of knowledge and love. This poem closes the 1919 version of *The Wild Swans at Coole* with Robartes's elated announcement that years of futile dreaming have been "rewarded" "at last." Only a few of Yeats's subsequent works focus so completely on the forbidding occultism that flowed through his wife's pen. But readers who neglect the rudiments of this lore will have difficulty appreciating the cosmic assumptions that underlie his later writing.[2]

Four Plays for Dancers and *Michael Robartes and the Dancer*

Between 1918 and 1922 the Yeatses lived mainly in Oxford, the poet's London rooms having proved unsuited to married life. They also devoted some of their time (and more of their money) to refurbishing Thoor Ballylee, an ancient, four-storied stone tower near Coole that Yeats had acquired in 1917 for use as a summer residence. The intensifying round of guerrilla ambushes and government reprisals connected with the War of Independence limited their time in Ireland, especially after the birth of their daughter Anne in 1919 (followed by a son, Michael, in 1921). To some extent, their obsession with George's automatic writing distanced them from everyone else. But eventually, as the situation in Ireland worsened, their thoughts – and Yeats's writing – turned back to the world at large. Having concentrated first on the twenty-eight phases of the soul's incarnation and then on its experiences after death, George's spiritual guides gradually shifted to historical matters, mapping out cycles of European history governed by larger oscillations of the same subjective and objective impulses that directed individual fates. This shift had a pronounced effect on the two crucial books Yeats published in 1921. Both *Four Plays for Dancers* and *Michael Robartes and the Dancer* demonstrate how thoroughly his work had been transformed by his marriage and by the onset of Ireland's "Troubles."

Four Plays for Dancers makes these influences apparent in three of its four plays: *The Only Jealousy of Emer*, *The Dreaming of the Bones*, and *Calvary*. The first resumes Cuchulain's story in the aftermath of *On Baile's Strand*, placing him at the center of a love triangle comprised of a supernatural temptress, an earthly mistress, and a long-neglected wife who saves him from the temptress by sacrificing her claims to his love. It makes elaborate use of material generated during Yeats's sessions with George, and is sometimes read as his distraught attempt to sort out his tangled feelings for Maud Gonne (represented by the temptress), Iseult Gonne (represented by the mistress), and George (represented by Cuchulain's devoted wife). *The Dreaming of the Bones* is more straightforward. It depicts a bitter encounter between a fugitive participant in the Easter Rising and the ghosts of two royal Irish lovers who cannot purify themselves of their earthly experiences until one of their countrymen forgives their centuries-old betrayal of Ireland to the English. *Calvary* takes up matters even more controversial, and remained unperformed in Yeats's lifetime. It advances the theory – also considered in such poems as "The Second Coming" – that the Christian incarnation embodied the objective principle only. According to the Yeatses' emerging system, Christ's sacrificial effort to absorb humanity into the oneness of God's love offers no redemption for subjective persons whose phases make them hunger for perfected individual existence.

In contrast to these plays, *At the Hawk's Well* came to light before either the Easter Rising or the poet's marriage. It portrays the turning point of

Cuchulain's early life: having journeyed to a sacred well about to fill with the waters of immortality, he succumbs to the distracting charms of the same hawklike spirit who tempts him in *The Only Jealousy of Emer*.[3] As the first of the *Four Plays for Dancers* to be written, *At the Hawk's Well* pioneered a new dramatic mode followed by the volume's other plays and by several of Yeats's later dramas. Its famous first performance enhanced his standing as a trend-setting experimental playwright. He wrote it during his final winter with Pound, who had recently introduced him to translations of Japanese Noh drama. The aristocratic and religious associations of this ancient form strongly appealed to a dramatist long out of patience with the middle-class audiences who filled the Dublin and London theaters. Inspired by the Noh, he invented his own new mode, one that at last allowed him to realize the proto-minimalist theatrical principles he had been advocating since the early years of the national theatre movement. Because the "dance plays" based on this mode required no elevated stage, no realistic scenery, and no special lighting, they could be inexpensively produced for forty or fifty poetry lovers in relatively small and ordinary rooms. *At the Hawk's Well* debuted in April 1916 in the London residence of Lady Cunard, an aristocratic patron of literary modernism. Those in attendance – an avant-garde elite that included both Pound and Eliot – took their seats in front of a "bare space before a wall against which [stood] a patterned screen" (Pl 297). Neither rising curtain nor altered lighting announced the Three Musicians who sang the opening lines while ceremoniously unfolding and refolding a cloth emblazoned with the image of a hawk.

The legendary performance that followed featured starkly evocative poetry sung or spoken by actors whose faces were either masked or made up to resemble masks and whose words and rhythmic movements took emphasis from music played with a drum, a gong, and a zither. The climax came when the silent and previously motionless Guardian of the Well – played by the Japanese dancer Michio Ito – suddenly threw off a black cloak to reveal the glittering costume of a hawk and begin the mesmerizing dance that fires Cuchulain's passions even as it leads him from his quest. As Yeats explained in his essay "Certain Noble Plays of Japan" (1916), these innovations were intended to create the separation from ordinary life needed to give an artwork extraordinary power while simultaneously reducing the physical and perceptual distance between that artwork and its audience. By putting a small group of receptive spectators into intimate proximity with ritually emphasized verbal and visual images, he hoped to "enable [them] to pass for a few moments into a deep of the mind that had hitherto been too subtle for [their] habitation."[4] Put another way, *At the Hawk's Well* presents its audience with a mask designed to stir up the passions Yeats regarded as missing from the modern world. It gives its audience an experience analogous to Cuchulain's encounter with the hawklike mask or daemon who, in tempting him to a painful fate, rouses his intrinsic selfhood to its most heroic expression. By confining its first performances to the homes of English aristocrats, the poet's new mode entailed a temporary retreat from his dream of using a national theatre to revitalize Irish culture. Even so, *Four Plays for Dancers* represents a breakthrough: for the first time, Yeats's drama attains the same spine-tingling intensity that electrifies his most powerful lyrics.

The other major Yeatsian book of 1921 – *Michael Robartes and the Dancer* – embodies an equally remarkable achievement. It centers on a set of political poems that, along with *The Dreaming of the Bones*, comprise the poet's most explicit literary responses to the Easter Rising. He wrote the foremost of these, "Easter, 1916," in the rebellion's immediate aftermath, but not wishing to be inflammatory, withheld it from publication until October 1920, when it appeared in a British periodical. By this stage, Ireland had already been convulsed by violent exchanges between the Irish Republican Army and ill-disciplined British forces who often targeted civilians in retaliation for guerrilla attacks. One of the British atrocities took the life of a young mother near Coole, shot outside her house while holding a baby in her arms. Soon afterward, in February 1921, Yeats awed students at Oxford University with an impassioned oration mixing furious denunciations of Britain's policy with appeals to its better nature. A comparable balance distinguishes the political lyrics at the heart of his new volume. Two of these – "Sixteen Dead Men" and "The Rose Tree" – throw off as much angry nationalist heat as any rebel song. But the other Rising poems reaffirm Yeats's gift for acknowledging the complexities of Ireland's dilemmas.

"Easter, 1916" opens by recalling Dublin before the Rising as a spiritless, disunited city that found its fitting emblem in the mottled garb of a fool. There, the routines of modern commerce "among grey / Eighteenth-century houses" had so camouflaged the "vivid faces" of the Rising's future leaders that the poet remembers greeting them with "polite meaningless words" even while thinking "Of a mocking tale or a gibe / To please a companion / Around the fire at the club." Now, after the Rising, everything has changed: it no longer matters that the poet's old friend Constance Markievicz has traded her youthful beauty for shrill-voiced activism, that Patrick Pearse and Thomas MacDonagh might have mastered poetry's "wingèd horse," or even that John MacBride "had done most bitter wrong / To some who are near my heart." In sacrificing themselves, all of the Rising's leaders have resigned their parts in the "casual comedy" of the nation's former life. Yet their transformation has produced both beauty and terror, a mystery the poet contemplates by means of the third stanza's symbolic landscape. In contrast to the more static, two-dimensional descriptions characteristic of Yeats's earlier verse, this stanza creates a fluid virtual space that draws us deep into its interior. Using the intersection of the "living stream" and the crossing road to evoke a two-dimensional plane, it lifts our vision up and down the third dimension occupied by the horse and rider, the birds, and the shadowing cloud, depicting all of these as moving. It thus not only invites us into a beautiful landscape but also brings home the contrast between the living, moving world and the unchanging stone that symbolizes the hearts of the fallen rebels. This stone gives the world a new center, a permanent locus of meaning and interconnection. But it is also dead. The creation of its unmoving oneness has required the sacrifice of many individual lives.

The concluding stanza dramatizes the poet's struggle to face the implications of this insight. No English-language poet surpasses Yeats when it comes to building up a stanza's power by shaping its grammar, imagery, and argument into a single unfaltering current. Here, however, he employs an unusually halting moment to express his anguished uncertainty. After daring to imply some blame for the fallen heroes, he quickly falls back on one of the polite, meaningless conventions elegies usually employ (in this case, the notion that death is merely sleep). But just when he seems on the verge of some predictably uplifting conclusion, a stutter of alliterated negatives brings the poem to a standstill: "No, no, not night but death; / Was it needless death after all?" This moment establishes the poet as an active thinker rather than a mere propagandist. For anyone who believes that artists have an obligation to model complex responses to complex events even when audiences clamor for simple reassurance, "Easter, 1916" surely must stand as one of Yeats's finest achievements. By its end, the Rising's organizers have been praised for leading their country toward a future in which the fragmented "motley" of the past yields to the greenness of communal Irishness, a condition that allows the isolated "I" who begins the poem to speak as part of a "We." But it reaches this point only after admitting that England's pre-war commitment to Irish Home Rule may yet prove the rebels to have been "Bewildered" by love for a cause that did not require their sacrifice.

The other major Rising poem in *Michael Robartes and the Dancer* is "On a Political Prisoner," a work inspired by Constance Markievicz, the rebel officer reproached for shrillness in "Easter, 1916." Constance and her sister Eva Gore-Booth hailed from a landed Anglo-Irish family based in County Sligo, and Yeats had known them since his youth. After the Rising, he came to regard both sisters as exemplars of an Anglo-Irish gentry that had increasingly neglected its duty to mask Ireland's peasant energies with upper-class refinements. (Lady Gregory continued to represent this trend's heroic exception.) The sisters' rejection of conventional gender roles added to their fascination. Eva campaigned for women's rights and also wrote poems and plays. Constance played such a key part in the rebellion that only her status as a woman saved her from the firing squad. "On a Political Prisoner" begins by picturing her in a prison cell. Like "Easter, 1916," it climaxes in a description of a three-dimensional scene centering on a symbol: a "rock-bred" bird "balanced on the air" at the moment of its first flight. The poem associates this bird with the harmony Markievicz realized between her individual and group identities when her "youth's lonely wildness" upheld the traditions of her class by riding to the hunt. Now that her male compatriots' hearts have been turned to stone, Yeats wonders if she can recover her innocence. Though his question remains unanswered, the intensity of his own perceptions suggests that his mind, at least, has not become an "abstract thing."

How might a feminist respond to this poem? At first, it may not seem especially problematic: nothing in its critique of Markievicz's activism explicitly blames her for violating gender norms, and the lyric that follows it, "The Leaders of the Crowd," applies similar criticisms to others whose sex remains unspecified. But if we look elsewhere in *Michael Robartes and the Dancer* and *The Wild Swans at Coole* we soon encounter a tendency to censure "opinionated" women (P 189). From the outset, Yeats had both desired and feared strong women. He spent years seeking the perfect synthesis of feminine heroism and maternal nurturing before finally conceding failure. Later, bruising theatre battles hardened his masculinity and strengthened his desire for women less uncontrollable than Gonne. Hence his affair with Mabel Dickinson, his pursuit of the demure Iseult, his marriage to George, and such poems as "On Woman," which praises God "for woman / That gives up all her mind" to man. Still, it would be reductive to conclude flatly that Yeats became a sexist. The real women in his life continued to be anything but shrinking violets: George Yeats may have been more willing than Gonne to play the part of a devoted wife but she was also an extraordinarily intelligent and resourceful woman who had a major impact on her husband's work. And even the most problematic examples of that work grant women greater sexual and spiritual power than the era generally allowed. The sexual innuendo increasingly found in the poet's later work reflects the temperament of a man who – unlike many men, then and now – could see a woman as a sexual being without condemning her as impure.

Yeats valued female sexuality in part because his occult studies had taught him to regard a beautiful woman's body as a manifestation of redeeming spiritual impulses. His cosmic system suggests that all individual fulfillments derive from the subjective, feminine force. His heroes only achieve greatness – only glimpse their masks – when, like Cuchulain confronting the Guardian of the Well, they discover potent female counterparts. To some extent, this thinking merely adapts the patriarchal tradition of endowing women with power in mythical higher realms while withholding it from them in the real world. But as he adapted this tradition, Yeats rejected parts of it. Nowhere do these matters come to the fore more clearly than in the poems about gender and sex that open and close *Michael Robartes and the Dancer.*

The volume's title poem enacts a dialogue between Michael Robartes and a woman whose occupation as a dancer constitutes a significant detail. Because dance makes art literally from the human body, Yeats saw dancers as emblems of the unity of body and soul associated with Phase 15. (Hence his preoccupation with "dance plays" and his use of dancer symbolism in "The Double Vision of Michael Robartes.") Here, Robartes contends that women fulfill their destinies when they reject ugly opinions and thus make their bodies into beautiful vessels for supernatural wisdom. In achieving "uncomposite blessedness," they "lead [men] to the like." This isn't quite the same as suggesting that women should be dumb and good-looking, but it comes uncomfortably close. Two things preserve the poem from an utterly devastating feminist critique. First, it affirms the human body in terms that avoid the usual implication that women's bodies are less pure than men's: the Renaissance paintings and sculptures praised by Robartes honor both male and female "sinew." Second, it dramatizes the dancer getting the better of Robartes at every stage of his argument. When he asserts an elaborate allegorical interpretation of a painted altar-piece, she deflates him in one line. By the end, her witty objections have so agitated him that he finds himself in the ironic position of supporting his criticisms of learning with citations from learned texts. The poem creates a real dialogue, in which the poet pits a representative of one part of his mind against a female antagonist who appears well up to the challenge.

"Solomon and the Witch" presents another verbal sparring match between male and female interlocutors. Solomon half jokingly tells Sheba that sexual intercourse can spark the end of the world if the lovers perfectly unite the "imagined image" they bring to the "bride-bed" with the "real image" they find there (thus blending the subjectivity of "Choice" with the objectivity of "Chance"). Sheba deftly replies that she's willing to give it a try. After two more poems centering on male-female relationships, *Michael Robartes and the Dancer* shifts to the Easter Rising poems previously discussed. But in the end it comes back to gender issues in its final major lyric, "A Prayer for my

Daughter." This poem, spoken by a version of Yeats himself rather than an alter ego, places less emphasis on female beauty than does "Michael Robartes and the Dancer." Citing Helen and Aphrodite as examples, it concedes that women who "Consider beauty a sufficient end" must inevitably sacrifice much. At the same time, however, it places more emphasis on the need for women to be Angels in the House, and allows no sharp-witted dancer to undercut its assertions. Here, readers irritated by Yeats's views must seek compensation in emphatic rhythms, evocative imagery, striking turns of phrase, and the emotional crescendo that culminates in the poet's confession that his mind, though "dried up of late," "knows that to be choked with hate / May well be of all evil chances chief."

The mood of millenarian anxiety that opens "A Prayer for My Daughter" carries over from "The Second Coming," the lyric that precedes it in *Michael Robartes and the Dancer* and that eventually displaced "The Lake Isle of Innisfree" as Yeats's single best-known work. This poem's immense popularity arises partly from the sheer thrill induced by its blasphemous vision of the stony Egyptian sphinx slouching towards Bethlehem to take the place of Christ, a vision that draws readers into its uncanny interior with three-dimensional imagery similar to that of "Easter, 1916" and "On a Political Prisoner." Here, a voice breathless with elated horror evokes a "pitiless" beast stretching its limbs at the focal point of a space inscribed by reeling desert birds and their shadows far below. The poem gains additional appeal from its finely calculated ambiguity, which encourages readers to interpret it in relation to their own experiences. Because falconry is the sport of kings, critics have often construed the opening image as another of Yeats's laments for the demise of aristocracy, but nothing confirms this. The significance of the "blood-dimmed tide" and "ceremony of innocence" also lies open to question. The poet's drafts allude to the execution of Marie Antoinette and the Russian Revolution, but finished versions specify only that "Things fall apart; the centre cannot hold; / Mere anarchy is loosed upon the world." Yeats wrote the poem in January 1919, a time when the destructive legacy of World War I was infusing most of Europe with apprehensions of radical change. "The Second Coming" encapsulates the era's mood of crisis.

Later readers have discovered farther-ranging applications for the poem's evocation of cultural collapse. In 1958, the Nigerian novelist Chinua Achebe titled his requiem for the breakdown of Igbo culture *Things Fall Apart*, and even now one can scarcely pick up a newspaper without coming upon a reference to a center that cannot hold, a politician who lacks all conviction, or a passionately intense fanatical movement. Yet for all its general appeal, "The Second Coming" manifests the particular conceptions of European history that developed from George's automatic writing. Like *Calvary*, it reflects the belief that Christ's birth "twenty centuries" ago precipitated an epoch of objectivity that reached its apogee in modernity's scientific materialism, an epoch soon to be overtaken by a renewal of the subjective impulses Christ's "rocking cradle" "vexed to nightmare." The poem's connection to this theory comes across most clearly in its reference to a "gyre," the gradually widening spiral shape that Yeats's later work uses to represent the ebb and flow of the subjective and objective principles. In *A Vision*, he draws an analogy between the cyclical fluctuations of these two principles and two interpenetrating gyres configured so that the narrowest point of one coincides with the widest point of the other. One gyre stands for subjectivity, the other for its opposite; as one expands the other contracts until finally an extreme is reached and the process reverses itself. The combined effects of World War I, the Russian Revolution, and the ongoing turmoil in Ireland suggested that Europe was beginning to witness the chaotic onset of just such a reversal. The resulting poem dramatizes an intensely conflicted state of mind, mingling excitement at the prospect of a new era with horror at the violence its coming will entail.

The Tower

In December 1921, negotiators for Sinn Féin – the guerrillas' political party – signed a treaty with the British. This proposed to conclude Ireland's War of Independence by dividing the island into two political entities, one composed of the twenty-six predominantly Catholic counties known until 1937 as the Irish Free State and the other of the six predominantly Protestant counties identified as Northern Ireland. Though the Free State gained more independence than Northern Ireland did, both remained subject to the British Crown. In January 1922, the parliament set up by Sinn Féin – the Dáil Eireann (pronounced "doyle air-an") – ratified this treaty, a decision indirectly endorsed by the Irish electorate in June. For a large section of the Irish Republican Army, however, the prospect of a divided Ireland subject to the British Crown remained unacceptable. Civil War broke out after the June elections between the part of the IRA that became the Free State Army and the part that rejected the treaty. Now, former guerrilla comrades ambushed, assassinated, arrested, and executed each other. In August, anti-Treaty "Irregulars" bent on sabotage blew up the ancient bridge adjacent to Thoor Ballylee, and many historic buildings with irreplaceable collections of documents and artworks suffered more serious damage. By May 1923, the

Irregulars had suspended operations, but the conflict never entirely ceased. Guerrillas professing allegiance to the anti-Treaty IRA continued to be sporadically active for decades, and were responsible for much of the violence that beset Northern Ireland between the later 1960s and the middle 1990s.

Despite the dangers of living in a city unsettled by intermittent explosions and frequent sniper fire, Yeats moved his family to Dublin and cast in his lot with the Irish Free State, which he regarded as a first step toward a fully independent, united Ireland. The beleaguered new state embraced his support and in December 1922 appointed him to a six-year term in its Senate, an upper house of sixty members designed to review government policy and legislation from the Dáil. Though subordinate to the Dáil, the Senate exerted considerable influence, and Yeats gave it careful attention, concentrating on cultural matters. He chaired committees charged with creating a new coinage and with encouraging study of the nation's ancient manuscripts. He inspected schools, and, when the subject was copyright law, offered the advice of a seasoned professional author. He also lobbied successfully for state funding for the Abbey, which he and Lady Gregory continued to oversee. His participation came with huge risks during the Civil War. Thirty-seven of his fellow Senators had their houses burned down, and all were potential assassination targets. On one occasion shots were fired into the Yeatses' Dublin home, striking a wall next to George as she held their daughter. Yeats's Senate career also put him at odds with Maud Gonne, who sided with the anti-Treaty forces and opposed the Free State's authoritarian policies, which entailed imprisoning its armed antagonists and summarily executing their leaders.

The poet supported such strong-arm tactics, seeing them as necessary for the establishment of public order. But after the crisis had passed, he began to have doubts about the order being established. The new state quickly developed a tendency to base legislation on Catholic moral doctrines and Catholic conceptions of Irishness. The first hints of Yeats's unease came in response to efforts to promote the Irish language by requiring its study in school and insisting that signs, railway tickets, and other public notices be printed in both Irish and English. In several Senate speeches and an essay on "Compulsory Gaelic," he made it clear that, while he wished to see the country speaking Irish, he did not support the language's imposition on those who refused to regard it as a feature of their heritage (at one point he implied that forcing a Protestant to learn Irish was like "compelling a Jew to eat bacon").[5] He reacted less gently when the Dáil and Senate enacted legislation making divorce all but unobtainable, even for Protestants and others whose religion (or lack thereof) posed no bar. In the press and in the

Senate, he denounced this step as an assault on the civil rights of the Free State's Protestant minority, a people whom he proudly – many would say, arrogantly – described as "one of the great stocks of Europe," the creators of "most of the modern literature of this country" and "the best of its political intelligence."[6] Plans to institute state censorship of materials judged sexually "indecent" by pious Catholics incensed him just as much, and he ardently defended the supposedly objectionable works of James Joyce and Sean O'Casey. In February 1926, the combination of sexual frankness and anti-nationalist political heresy in O'Casey's *The Plough and the Stars* touched off an uproar at the Abbey that brought back memories of the *Playboy* riots. Yeats responded by once again taking the stage to hurl defiance at the protesters. Much of his own writing from the mid-twenties onward challenges the official orthodoxies of the Irish Free State by making deliberately audacious assertions about sex, politics, and religion.

Meanwhile, the larger literary world was reevaluating his work. In 1923, he won the Nobel Prize for Literature, an accolade that reflected his growing reputation as a writer still relevant to the contemporary scene. Though the term "modernism" would not be widely used for many years to come, it had already become apparent that a new spirit of artistic experimentation was spreading through Europe and North America. In 1922, both Joyce's *Ulysses* and Eliot's *The Waste Land* had suddenly burst into view, and much of the most influential work of Pablo Picasso, Arnold Schoenberg, Gertrude Stein, and Virginia Woolf was already famous or soon would be. Yeats made his mark on modernism's *annus mirabilis* by publishing *Later Poems* (1922), which contained all of his nondramatic poetry from *The Wind Among the Reeds* through *Michael Robartes and the Dancer*. Previously, most readers had known him through *Poems* (1895), for decades his best-selling book, and for every reviewer who preferred the hard lights of his latest efforts, there had been another who pined for the Celtic Twilight's mists. Now, with all of his recent poetry gathered together, it became clear that much of Yeats's genius had to do with his ability to transform himself in response to changes in his life and in the larger culture. The concurrent publication of *The Trembling of the Veil* reinforced this perception by providing his own autobiographical account of his first phase as a writer. The resulting critical verdict was summed up by a reviewer who praised him for "keeping pace with the gradual change from the aestheticism of the Eighteen Nineties to the verse experimentation . . . of the last decade."[7]

Should Yeats be called a modernist? Not everyone agrees on this question's answer or even on the term's definition. Most generally, modernism refers to the experimental forms and attitudes that western artists evolved as the

political, social, and psychological certainties of nineteenth-century life collapsed under the pressure of such twentieth-century occurrences as World
War I and the dawn of Freudian theory. Exemplary modernist works include
the cubist paintings of Picasso, the allusive, collage-like poetry of Eliot, and
the "stream of consciousness" novels of Joyce and Woolf. Those who don't
see Yeats as a modernist point to his use of traditional forms, and argue that
his doubts about Europe's religious and artistic traditions were never as
profound as Eliot's. They also point out that Yeats did not regard himself
as part of Eliot's school, which he disparagingly associated with "impersonal
philosophical poetry" (LE 100). Proponents of Yeats's modernism contend
that his reformation of the elevated language of late nineteenth-century verse
contributed to Pound's celebrated insistence on "Direct treatment of the
'thing.'"[8] They also posit similarities between the rapid movements and
compressed allusions of Yeats's later verse and the sudden juxtapositions
and piled-up references employed by his modernist peers. Chapter 2 aligned
his theory of the masked self with the modernist reaction to Romanticism,
and his use of myth as a lens for understanding modernity adumbrated both
Joyce and Eliot. Who, moreover, can read "The Second Coming" without
conceding that its author remained in touch with the angst-ridden temper of
Europe after World War I?

Whether they term him a modernist or not, critics generally agree that
Yeats produced one of the modern era's definitive books of poetry in *The
Tower* (1928), which combines three limited-edition collections previously
printed by his sister.[9] To some extent, this volume's reputation derives from
its epical scope: it includes the poet's principal artistic responses to Ireland's
War of Independence and Civil War as well as such memorable forays into
ancient times as "Leda and the Swan" and "Sailing to Byzantium." *The Tower*
also features a new profundity of tone and attitude. Though it concludes with
"All Souls' Night," which heralds Yeats's new cosmic system and also serves as
epilogue to both versions of *A Vision*, many of the volume's poems suggest
that the advent of *A Vision* failed to make life much easier. The poet's new
convictions comforted him with the thought that the cosmos's cycles would
eventually bring redemption, but they did not offer clear-cut or appealing
answers to questions about how he should live the remainder of his life.
Should he prepare for the afterlife by renouncing his worldly attachments? Or
should he continue to feel and express the passions of his aching heart
whatever the spiritual risks? Yeats devotes much of *The Tower* to protesting
the cosmos revealed in *A Vision*, to raging against the way its cycles toss
human beings about, deceiving them, cheating their desires, demanding they
renounce what they love. He had written *Michael Robartes and the Dancer* at a

time when the unexpected heroics of the Easter Rising and the adventure of fresh occult discoveries were tempting him to indulge what "A Prayer for My Daughter" calls "excited reverie," a mood of elated expectation inspired by the prospect of violent change. By the time he finished *The Tower*, he had seen violent change close up; he had also grown older and reflected further on George's harshly fatalistic prophecies. The resulting volume deepens its excited reveries with influxes of tragic knowledge. One of its presiding figures is Oedipus: the man who understood his terrible fate only after he lacked the power to alter it.

"Sailing to Byzantium" opens the volume by dramatizing a speaker who has repudiated the "sensual music" of his home country to travel to the place and time identified in *A Vision* as the destination Yeats would most wish to visit "if [he] could be given a month of Antiquity and leave to spend it where [he] chose."[10] The poet's fascination with the early medieval city now known as Istanbul had begun during a trip to Italy in 1907, when he had seen Byzantine mosaics in Ravenna. By the time he wrote *A Vision*, he had come to regard sixth-century Byzantium as a city in which the waxing subjective gyre had fostered "Unity of Culture":

> I think that in early Byzantium . . . religious, aesthetic and practical life were one, that architect and artificers . . . spoke to the multitude and the few alike. The painter, the mosaic worker, the worker in gold and silver, the illuminator of sacred books, were . . . absorbed in their subject-matter and that the vision of a whole people. They could copy out of old Gospel books those pictures that seemed as sacred as the text, and yet weave all into a vast design, the work of many that seemed the work of one, that made building, picture, pattern, metal-work of rail and lamp, seem but a single image.[11]

This privileged realm – similar to the new subjective world Yeats hoped would slouch out of modernity's turbulence – has been forged into unity by spiritually inspired artists. The speaker of "Sailing to Byzantium" seeks it for the sake of his soul. For him, the soul can only learn to "clap its hands and sing" by studying artistic "Monuments of its own magnificence" in a city made "holy" by its golden mosaics. He regards these monuments in the same way Yeats had long regarded symbols and masks: as magical icons empowering him to call down otherworldly "sages" who will "Consume" his mortal attachments and gather him "Into the artifice of eternity."

Though the poem's speaker may initially come across as a man on the verge of transcending mortal desires, careful analysis suggests latent difficulties. When he links his rejection of "That . . . country" to his body's tattered state, he implies that, were he in his prime, he would gladly sing the song of sex and birth and death. In the first stanza he associates this song with a cohesive world where all things enact their natural destinies; he also bespeaks suppressed attraction to this world with the ear-pleasing sensuousness of his vigorous rhythms and alliterations. Further hints of persistent desire for the body surface in stanza two, where he describes the soul in bodily terms, as something having hands and wearing clothes. In stanza three, he asks the sages to unfasten him from his body only after requesting them to "Come from the holy fire" of their unearthly reality and "perne" part way into his. Thus it comes as little surprise to learn in stanza four that he has no wish to exist "out of nature" without a "bodily form" or without communication with the temporal sphere. Though he now pursues spiritual purgation, he intuits that, as a spirit, he will crave contact with mortals, with "a drowsy Emperor" and his court. His incipient understanding of this inversion recalls Yeats's longtime belief that material and spiritual beings hunger to consume each other, that they "die each other's life, live each other's death."[12] The speaker's yearning for "God's holy fire" is no doubt deeply in earnest, but he has already begun to apprehend the truth confronted in "The Wanderings of Oisin," namely, that translation to the spirit realm offers no sure cure for mortals "sick with desire."

Another way to apprehend the poem's basic tension is to contemplate the gulf separating its speaker from the real-life poet. By hammering his visions into golden poetry, Yeats could gather part of himself into the artifice of eternity. But his everyday, bodily self could no more sail to a sixth-century city than it could live in a wattled cabin on a tiny island in Lough Gill. The dilemmas faced by this daily self take center stage in "The Tower," where a speaker readily identifiable as a version of Yeats himself begins by asking his "troubled heart" how he should respond to "Decrepit age." He thus makes clear that he has not yet decided to renounce the world or to open his heart to consumption by purgatorial spirits. Though it "seems" that he must untie himself from the "battered kettle" of his body and study philosophers linked (in a note) with "transcendence," he makes a reluctant Platonist (VP 825–26). Unlike Plato's Socrates, so eager to detach soul from body that he willingly drank poison, Yeats considers restricting himself to "argument" and "abstract things" only as a last resort. This would require him to give up poetry, to tame an imagination never "more / Excited, passionate, fantastical." The poem's second major section quickly confirms that he has not yet "bid the Muse go pack." Here, we find him on his tower's roof, staring at his physical surroundings, sending imagination forth. As his eyes rove over the landscape, he summons images and memories of figures associated with his neighborhood, figures emblematic of mortal life rather than of God's holy fire. All have been led by the "brightness" of lunar impulses to commit acts of passionate foolishness. One incited her servant to clip "an insolent farmer's ears," another wandered into a deadly bog after being maddened by poetry and drink. Still another, the poet's own creation Hanrahan, neglected his real-world beloved after being lured into frenzied pursuit of a hare and pack of hounds conjured from a pack of cards.[13] Like Cuchulain in *At the Hawk's Well*, these figures have been roused to disastrous but strangely stirring exuberance by the cosmos's mysterious workings, and Yeats seems both repelled by and attracted to the "horrible splendour" of their destinies. He readily admits that, as a poet, he desires to see "the moon and sunlight seem / One inextricable beam" and thereby bring himself and others to mistake "the brightness of the moon / For the prosaic light of day."

Once he has summoned his hearers, he poses the question on his mind from the start: did all of these "old men and women . . . rage / As [he does] now against old age?" Their "impatient" eyes suggest an affirmative response, and he dismisses all but Hanrahan. As the archetype of an "Old lecher with a love on every wind," Hanrahan evokes the "mighty memories" and "deep considering mind" needed to answer a more intimate and painful question:

> Does the imagination dwell the most
> Upon a woman won or woman lost?
> If on the lost, admit you turned aside
> From a great labyrinth out of pride,
> Cowardice, some silly over-subtle thought
> Or anything called conscience once;
> And that if memory recur, the sun's
> Under eclipse and the day blotted out.

Critics sometimes read the "you" of this passage as referring to Yeats himself (as well as to Hanrahan), thus taking the "woman won" to be George and the "woman lost" to be Maud. On this level the stanza functions as a keenly self-critical admission that the poet's dread of "the labyrinth of another's being" – and not Gonne's supposed pitilessness – kept their love from blossoming. The stanza also summarizes everything previously suggested about the doom awaiting mortals governed by subjective inclinations: driven by "over-subtle thought," they turn from the actual to pursue elusive phantoms. Even in old age, their memories ensure that the moon eclipses the sun.

By the end of the poem's final section the poet has again resolved to compel his soul "to study / In a learned school." But he does this only after rejecting what he takes to be Plato's and Plotinus' belief in a reality transcending human subjectivity; for him, all spiritual and material realities proceed out of the "bitter soul" he elsewhere terms the "Spiritus Mundi" or universal spirit. His art, he now declares, has not madly distracted him from ordinary life or from the necessity of making his soul. Instead, it has given him a way of preparing his peace, of using "Poet's imaginings / And memories of love" to make "a superhuman / Mirror-resembling dream." And he has not constructed this dream only for himself. Like a bird slowly assembling a nest for its young, he has put together a legacy of "faith and pride" that – in apparent defiance of the Free State's emerging Catholic theocracy – he presents as the inheritance of an Anglo-Irish people bound "Neither to slaves that were spat on, / Nor to the tyrants that spat." Previously, Yeats's praises for the Anglo-Irish had been comparatively muted: there is little in such poems as "In the Seven Woods," "These are the Clouds," or "In Memory of Major Robert Gregory" to confirm them as tributes to a specifically Anglo-Irish gentry rather than to aristocracy in general. "The Tower," by contrast, overtly affirms allegiance to "The people of Burke and of Grattan."[14] Though this candor occurred in response to the poet's anger with the Free State's treatment of its Protestant minority, his claims about this minority's history have prompted justifiable skepticism from critics concerned to scrutinize Ireland's colonial experience of Anglo-Irish oppression. Still, his poem's magnificence is hard to deny. He perceives the world so intensely and speaks his perceptions so passionately that he seems to embody the same "horrible splendour" he observes in the figures gathered in Section II.

Whereas "The Tower" takes up the painful consequences of allowing the moon's brightness to inspire bold action, "Meditations in Time of Civil War" weighs the equally unsatisfying alternative of retreating into inaction and solipsism. The first of its seven parts – "Ancestral Houses" – begins by suggesting that "Surely" the sheltered estates of the rich encourage "Life [to overflow] without ambitious pains." Almost immediately, however, Yeats concedes that the "inherited glory of the rich" is "now" more like an "empty sea-shell" than a fountain filled by the "abounding glittering jet" of "life's own self-delight." The beauty preserved at great estates was paid for and created by "Bitter and violent men," conquerors who forged completing masks of "sweetness." Such completion cannot be handed down to later generations like a collection of rare objects: those who merely inherit their culture may find that its sweetness "take[s] [their] greatness with [their] violence." This supposition inevitably raises the possibility – given the sequence's general rubric – that the current Civil War is necessary to reinfuse Ireland with the turbulence that inspires fresh creation. Yeats's attitude toward this possibility remains untinged by the excitement that typifies his earlier prophetic poems. He can scarcely bring himself to imply it, and spends most of the last two stanzas affectionately describing the artifacts for which it augurs obsolescence and destruction.

In "My House," the second part of "Meditations," the poet turns from rich estates to describe his own "ancient tower" and its "acre of stony ground." These seem unlikely to domesticate anyone's bitterness: they are too rough and craggy, too permeated by the aura of "ragged elms" and "old thorns innumerable." Built by an Anglo-Norman "man-at-arms" to shelter a "dwindling score" of "castaways" from "long wars and sudden night alarms," the tower and its keep are also unlikely to foster overflowing cultural abundance. The Anglo-Irish poet who has now retreated to this place with his own family during a time of civil strife may succeed in escaping the violence, in cultivating "the symbolic rose," and in pursuing the "daemonic rage" that "Imagined everything." But anything created or discovered here promises to remain unshared with the "benighted" outside world that looks on uncomprehendingly. (A note informs readers that, before these poems were finished, anti-Treaty forces had blown up the tower's "ancient bridge," symbol of its connection to the outer world; VP 827.) Here, the poet's only remaining hope is that, by bringing his "bodily heirs" to a realm of his own creation, he can bequeath them "emblems of adversity" and thus exalt their minds.

"Meditations in Time of Civil War" moves further into Thoor Ballylee's private world in "My Table," where the poet sits at an old-fashioned trestled table, admiring a 500-year-old sword given him by a Japanese admirer. This delicately crafted weapon, covered with "A bit of an embroidered dress," reflects the same conjunction of violence and artistry taken up in the sequence's first two poems. It prompts the poet to draw an implicit contrast between the Japanese culture that forged it and the world assumed by "Ancestral Houses" and "My House." According to the poet, ancient Japanese artists did not simply refine the culture of a single generation or create their own private retreats. They passed the "marvellous accomplishment" of their art undiminished "From father unto son." This art did not domesticate its "rich inheritor[s]" because they kept their passions focused on "Soul's beauty." Only "an aching heart / Conceives a changeless work of art," and as long as a culture's heart aches for spiritual refinement, it will never produce "inferior art" or find its "wits" grown dull.

This admiring account of a spiritually purposed culture makes it difficult to take the poet's words at face value when, in "My Descendants," he dismisses his "dreams" for the future by resigning history to the cycles of the "Primum Mobile" and by declaring that, for him, private "love and friendship are enough." "The Road at My Door" puts these statements under additional pressure. In this poem, two representatives of the violent outer world – an "affable Irregular" fighting against the Free State and a "brown Lieutenant" in its army – intrude upon the tower's isolation, prompting the poet to offer the same sort of "polite meaningless words" he remembers exchanging with the Easter Rising's leaders in "Easter, 1916." Here, his self-conscious account of himself bespeaks surging awareness of the drawbacks of the attitudes expressed in "My Descendants." Perhaps the tower's cloister of private affection and contemplation provides nothing more than "the cold snows of a dream." Don't the bitter, violent men at his door require something more than trivial conversation from the chief poet of their divided nation? In response to some such question, Yeats finally nerves himself, in "The Stare's Nest by My Window," to confront his dilemma head on, without any intervening generalizations about ancestral houses, ancient Japan, or the Primum Mobile. In lines as powerful as any he ever wrote, he admits that, in the tower, he and his family "are closed in, and the key is turned / On our uncertainty," leaving the only "clear fact to be discerned" that "Last night they trundled down the road / That dead young soldier in his blood." Yet even as he admits his isolation and uncertainty he partly redeems himself from them. By the final stanza, he has not only faced up to the suffering that surrounds him but also begun to speak for a "We" that plainly refers to the Irish people as a whole (and not just to his family or the Anglo-Irish inheritors of the overlords who built the tower). The act of speaking to and for this whole – and thereby attempting to constitute it – represents Yeats's modest but moving effort to feed his own and Ireland's aching hearts something sweeter and more loving than the fantasies that have made them "brutal." Though he has no powerful man or unified tradition to support him, he lifts his voice in a prayer to Ireland to become like the "honey-bees" and "build in the empty house of the stare."

Any suggestion that he thereby achieves some final release from his predicament is quickly put to rest in his final meditation, "I see Phantoms of Hatred and of the Heart's Fullness and of the Coming Emptiness." Here, the ghostly procession flowing past the poet offers a reminder that, even if subjective fulfillment follows hatred and chaos, such fulfillment eventually will also pass away. Now that the poet has witnessed violent horrors and not just dreamed about them, the endless cycles of the cosmos no longer inspire excited reverie. He concludes the poem – and "Meditations" as a whole – by shutting himself back into the tower, dejectedly conceding that "The half-read wisdom of daemonic images / Suffice the ageing man as once the growing boy."

No sooner do we finish "Meditations in Time of Civil War" than *The Tower* confronts us with yet another important, multipart poem, "Nineteen Hundred and Nineteen." Instead of evoking the Civil War period of 1922–23, this poem treats the aftermath of World War I and the beginning of Ireland's War of Independence. Its first section compares the destruction of ancient Greek civilization with developments in the United Kingdom since the hopeful time of its pre-war commitment to Irish Home Rule.[15] Before the war, most British and Irish people believed that they lived in a world of fair-minded laws, ripening social justice, and great armies maintained for show. "Now," in 1919, "days are dragon-ridden," drunken British soldiers "Can leave the mother, murdered at her door, / To crawl in her own blood" (as they notoriously did not far from Thoor Ballylee), and "The night can sweat with terror as before / We pieced our thoughts into philosophy." Nowhere does Yeats seem more like a modernist than in this poem's initial section. Like Pound and Eliot, he presents the violence of the times as evidence of the shallowness of the rationalist, materialistic era that preceded World War I, probing this era's classical roots for clues about its fate. Like Eliot in particular, he lacks confidence in art's ability to tie itself to a reality higher than the one "That pitches common things about." But as the author of *A Vision*, he also has his own idiosyncratic reading of "the signs" of the times. This tells him not only that "no work can stand" but also that any lasting "triumph" would only "break upon [its maker's] ghostly solitude" (an insight not explained until Section III, which affirms that, in the afterlife, we must "cast off" our mortal experiences, and will find it more difficult to do so if great accomplishment cements us to life). Before the poet can take comfort in his conclusions, it dawns on him that the evanescence of mortal triumphs is precisely what makes us love them. The fact that great works vanish does not make it easier to cast off our attachment to them. Indeed, it makes it harder.

At this point the poem makes the first of the nimble associative leaps that tie its six sections together. Though not as disorienting as the abrupt juxtapositions encountered in Eliot and Pound, these leaps reflect a typically modernist sense of modernity's disorder, of the dexterity required to perceive connections between its shattered pieces. Section II compares the evanescent triumph of a famous modern dancer to the ebb and flow of the cosmos's cyclical patterns, taking no more comfort in these patterns than any other part of *The Tower*. Section III positions its explanation of how earthly triumph can "mar" the afterlife's solitude between two slightly different comparisons of "the solitary soul" to a swan. The first offers an image of the living swan in the process of lifting in flight; the second imagines the swan after it "has leaped into the desolate heaven." The poet strains to satisfy himself with the first, associating the second with a rage against mortal existence that implicates him in the era's violence. Section IV adds cohesion to the whole by reinvoking sentiments and imagery from Section I. Its condemnation of the cynical pleasure post-war culture has begun to take in confessing its own imperfections carries over into Section V, which recapitulates the entire poem in a torrent of ironic mockery that includes among its targets such mockers as the poet. Section VI concludes the poem by offering a final, startling apparition of violent specters "upon the roads." Like the vision that ends "Meditations in Time of Civil War," this apparition prompts little excitement. It imagines the Sidhe – long associated by Yeats with the Germanic goddesses known as "Herodias' daughters" – degenerating from "handsome riders" into sinister quintessences of lust and hatred, appropriate harbingers of the infamous fourteenth-century Kilkenny witch Lady Kyteler, and her fiendish incubus Robert Artisson. The physical violence that makes 1919 "dragon-ridden" evidently occurs in tandem with a breakdown in the spirit realm. If there is any redeeming purpose to this process it remains concealed "in the labyrinth of the wind."

The remainder of *The Tower* features such notable works as "Leda and the Swan," "Among School Children," and the eleven-part sequence "A Man Young and Old." "Leda and the Swan" appears also in *A Vision*, and depicts the annunciation of the subjective Greek epoch Yeats believed to have preceded the objective Christian era. Defying associations between sonnets and tender expressions of love, it pictures the mythical rape of the mortal Leda by the god Zeus in the guise of a swan. According to the poem, this rape led to Greek civilization's defining episode by engendering Helen of Troy and her sister, Clytemnestra. (Helen's elopement with Paris triggered the Trojan War, and at its conclusion Clytemnestra murdered King Agamemnon.) Yeats concludes by asking whether Leda understood how the god was acting through her. Though this question bespeaks pity for her, the poet's god-like perspective aligns him equally with Zeus. Feminists have often criticized the poem as an example of a larger cultural tendency to see rape as part of the natural order, objecting in particular to the acquiescence suggested by Leda's "loosening thighs." The poem may also be read as a deliberately audacious protest against the prudery that led the Irish Free State to prohibit divorce and to censor "indecent" publications. "Leda and the Swan" first appeared in Ireland in the short-lived journal *To-morrow*, which, like the nineties' *Savoy* magazine, was founded by writers intent on challenging the restrictive mores of their day.

"Among School Children" may also reflect Senator Yeats's concerns about the status of bodily experience in the Irish Free State. Its immediate inspiration

came from a 1926 visit to a model school in Waterford, paid as a member
of a government committee investigating Irish education. In the poem, the
sight of so many children prompts the poet to daydream about Maud
Gonne's youthful body, "Ledaean" because of its long association with the
body of Leda's daughter, Helen. Remembering an occasion when he and
Gonne seemed blended into a unity as perfect as that evoked in Plato's
Symposium, he wonders "if she stood so at that age," and finds his "heart . . .
driven wild" by the sensation that "She stands before me as a living child."
Her present form then "floats into the mind," so "Hollow of cheek" that it
resembles a ghostly image from a fifteenth-century Italian painting. He too is
now an "old scarecrow." By the end of the fourth stanza, references to Leda,
Plato, and the poet's own scarecrow of a body have created associative links
with many other poems in *The Tower.* Such associations prepare readers to
hear deep resonances in the four concluding stanzas.

These begin by acknowledging that, because the body withers, it cannot
offer "compensation" for the pangs of earthly life (pangs awaiting unborn
spirits whose desire for "Honey of generation" betrays them into taking
"shape" upon a mother's lap, and who later either accept or resist their
mortality depending on whether they remember their former spiritual condition). Plato, Aristotle, and Pythagoras reacted to the body's limitations
by positing transcendent ideals or trying to master the solid world or
listening for the music of the spheres. They ended as scarecrows all the same.
As for the sacred icons revered by nuns, though they may not wither like the
human body, by symbolizing heavenly glory they mock all earthly "enterprise" and thereby also "break" their worshippers' hearts. In this respect they
resemble the mosaics that summon spirits to consume the heart in "Sailing to
Byzantium" or the "changeless work[s] of art" described as keeping ancient
Japan's wits awake in "My Table." All of these "images" exemplify what Yeats
had once called masks: they are emblems of adversity that lure us into
fulfilling our destinies by simultaneously calling up the passions of our
mortal hearts and calling down the daemonic energies that act as those
passions' Blakean contraries. What pious Catholics presumably do not realize, however, is that such necessary "mockers of man's enterprise" are "self-
born" creations of what "The Tower" terms man's "bitter soul" (and what
Yeats elsewhere calls the universal spirit or "Spiritus Mundi"). Like the Greek
philosophers derided here and in "The Tower," Catholic Ireland sees matter
and spirit as negations of each other and therefore assumes that the former
must be transcended for the latter to blossom. Speaking to the "Presences"
called up by Catholic icons, Yeats proclaims that "Labour is blossoming or
dancing where / The body is not bruised to pleasure soul," and concludes by

asking "How can we know the dancer from the dance?" On one level this famous concluding passage functions as another of his hymns to the glories of Phase 15, that superhuman state where, for a time, body and soul – dancer and dance – come together in perfect fulfillment. As such, it counterweights the more despairing responses to the cosmos's fatalistic gyring encountered earlier in *The Tower*. But on another level, it also defies those elements in the Irish Free State – and perhaps in the poet's own psyche – that believed the body should be renounced.

"Among School Children" forges associative links with other poems in *The Tower* not only by recalling their allusions, imagery, and cosmic convictions, but also by sharing their form. Along with "Sailing to Byzantium" and parts of "Meditations in Time of Civil War" and "Nineteen Hundred and Nineteen," it employs *ottava rima*, an eight-line, iambic pentameter stanza rhyming *abababcc*. Other poems in the volume create octaves with different meters and rhyme schemes, and several more establish a ten-line stanza rhyming *abcabcdeed*.[16] Yeats's previous collections had featured a greater proportion of poems written in shorter tetrameter lines arranged as quatrains or sestets. In *The Tower*, his repeated use of lengthy and complex stanzas creates an aura of technical virtuosity that reinforces his imaginative authority, assuring us that, at the least, he possesses extraordinary powers of expression. The simplest way to appreciate this virtuosity is to read the poems out loud. Notice how often the ear finds pleasure in a balance of emphatic or alliterated consonants and musically assonant vowels, and how deftly the poet's rhymes match important words (as well as pleasing sounds). Notice too how consistently his intermittent off-rhymes, moderately irregular rhythms, and colloquial diction and phrasing allow him to create a tone of ceremonious intensity without losing the jagged energy of speech. To sustain this sort of poise in tetrameter lines arranged in quatrains or sestets is to be a very fine craftsman. But to extend it repeatedly and with apparent ease through the length of *ottava rima* and other similar structures is to rival such all-time masters of stanzaic verse as Spenser and Keats.

One's admiration becomes all the greater when one reaches "A Man Young and Old" and discovers that Yeats's mastery of elaborate stanzas has done nothing to diminish his gift for brief, evocative love songs. This sequence moves from four poems spoken by a young man to several more spoken by the same man grown old. Several seem to offer new assessments of the poet's obsession with Maud Gonne and all she represented. "First Love," "Human Dignity," and "The Mermaid" rue the devastating influence of a *femme fatale* who at once resembles a cruelly indifferent lover, a deceptive lunar daemon, and such "murderous" icons of physical-force nationalism as Cathleen ni

Houlihan (P 221). Like Cuchulain in *At the Hawk's Well*, the man dramatized in the sequence has encountered a female embodiment of subjective beauty and power who has stirred him into action. In his case, however, the exertions thereby induced appear less heroic than tragically misguided: "I have attempted many things / And not a thing is done" (P 221). As in "The Tower," subjective influences appear as maddening if not lethal for ordinary mortals, doomed to spend their old age caught between regrets for the earthly life they might otherwise have lived and undiminished desires to "sail up there / Amid the cloudy wrack" of the moon (P 226). The only escape would seem to be the stoical renunciation advised in "From 'Oedipus at Colonus,'" a translated excerpt from Sophocles' play that Yeats added to the sequence in 1933. As the rest of *The Tower* makes clear, however, articulating such advice is one thing and following it is another. Even if one enters the artifice of eternity, the cosmos's inexorable inversions ensure that "Honey of generation" will eventually draw one back to mortal life (P 216). Like Yeats's cosmos, *The Tower* gyres between such visions of temporary fulfillment as those granted in "Sailing to Byzantium," "Among School Children," and "All Souls' Night," and the nightmares that ride upon sleep in "The Tower," "Meditations in Time of Civil War," "Nineteen Hundred and Nineteen," and "A Man Young and Old."

The Winding Stair and Other Poems

The Tower inspired many admiring notices in Britain, Ireland, and America. Most reflected the increased preference for Yeats's later manner that had set in after *Later Poems*. Virginia Woolf spoke for many when she declared that "Mr. Yeats has never written more exactly and more passionately."[17] Some reviewers expressed reservations about the poet's political or religious beliefs, but nearly all praised his gift for dramatizing intricate motions of thought and feeling. By the time these praises reached his ears, he was badly in need of a lift. He had not enjoyed a major public triumph since winning the Nobel Prize in 1923. Since then, he had seen the first version of *A Vision* appear to tepid, uncomprehending reviews, and endured constant attack in Ireland from such pillars of zealous orthodoxy as the *Catholic Bulletin*. More recently, he had been shocked by the assassination in July 1927 – by remnants of the anti-Treaty IRA – of his friend Kevin O'Higgins, the Free State Minister for Justice and External Affairs. A few months later he had also been afflicted with a congested, bleeding lung, necessitating an escape to warmer climes in southern Spain and France. By the time *The Tower* appeared in February

1928, he and George had moved on to the Italian town of Rapallo, home since 1925 to Ezra Pound. Here, as Yeats recovered, awareness of his growing vulnerability to illness prompted him and George to plan major changes in their lives: he would resign from the Senate and they would give up both Thoor Ballylee and their house in Dublin's Merrion Square in preference for more modest Dublin quarters and a winter residence in Rapallo. Later that summer, after they had returned to Dublin, the Irish Free State took action on the censorship bill that Yeats had long dreaded, and this set the seal on his decision to end his term of Senate service.

For a long while thereafter, any fears of an incipient decline in the poet's physical condition seemed largely unwarranted: his health was reasonably good when he returned to Rapallo in late 1928 for his second Mediterranean winter and it stayed that way for most of the following year. Then, in early November 1929, he suffered another hemorrhage of the lung. After reaching Rapallo later that month, he fell deathly ill with Malta fever and had to make an emergency will. Once again, however, he recovered, so much so that, by the summer of 1930, he and George had gone back to Dublin and decided not to return to Rapallo for the winter of 1930–31. Before long, worries about his own health gave way to concern for Lady Gregory. Breast cancer first diagnosed several years previously closed in on her in 1931. From September to her death the following May, Yeats spent most of his time at Coole, offering what comfort he could. Lady Gregory's death meant not only the loss of his closest friend but also the demise of Coole. Robert Gregory's widow had inherited legal rights to the estate at his death, and had little interest in preserving its traditions. She auctioned the house's contents soon after her mother-in-law's death, having already sold both house and grounds to the Forestry Commission. Within ten years, the deserted house had been dismantled for building materials. As Yeats lingered in Coole's book-lined rooms and along its woodland paths during the final months of Lady Gregory's life, he knew that he was seeing the last of a friend and a place that had long offered him a refuge and symbolized his values.

Except for those weeks and months when illness prevented him, Yeats wrote prolifically between the summer of 1927 and the end of 1931. Some of what he produced was drama: in November 1930, *The Words upon the Window-Pane* appeared to great acclaim at the Abbey. This one-act work in prose depicts a séance during which the ghost of Jonathan Swift is inadvertently evoked. While convalescing from Malta fever, Yeats had immersed himself in Swift, whom his play and several poems present as a tragically defeated exemplar of an eighteenth-century Anglo-Irish caste that fostered a brief time of cultural greatness by scorning English materialism and egalitarianism in favor of idealism and hierarchy. Such thinking reflected Yeats's decades-old belief in the virtues of aristocracy as well as his more recent frustrations with the Free State's lack of consideration for its Protestant minority. The play remained unpublished until 1934, when it appeared first in a limited edition of his sister's and then as part of *Wheels and Butterflies*, a volume that collected and offered commentary on Yeats's recent plays. In addition to *The Words upon the Window-Pane*, these included *Fighting the Waves* (a prose version of *The Only Jealousy of Emer* written for performance as a ballet); *The Resurrection*, based like other Yeatsian works on the premise that Greek subjectivity yielded to objectivity when Christ assumed a physical body; and *The Cat and the Moon*, a parable about the relationship of body and soul based on the theory of lunar phases.

Though Yeats continued to compose plays and be active in Abbey affairs, most of what he wrote during the prolific period between 1927 and 1931 was lyric poetry, poetry collected first in two limited-edition volumes – *The Winding Stair* (1929) and *Words for Music Perhaps and Other Poems* (1932) – and then assembled for a larger readership in *The Winding Stair and Other Poems* (1933). This 1933 book takes *The Tower* as its point of departure. It not only follows up "Sailing to Byzantium" and "A Man Young and Old" with "Byzantium" and "A Woman Young and Old," but also alludes through its title to the cramped spiral stairway built into the actual tower's seven-foot thick walls (a feature Yeats associated with the turning gyres of *A Vision*). But *The Winding Stair and Other Poems* does not replicate *The Tower*. Instead, it offers a complement or Blakean contrary, a yin to its predecessor's yang. The central premise of *The Tower* had been that old age requires one to give up on the body and focus instead on the soul, and, though many of its poems resist or qualify this premise, most return to it in the end. By the time Yeats put together his next major collection, however, the experience of twice losing and regaining his health had renewed his appreciation for bodily existence. Thus, *The Winding Stair and Other Poems* does not portray sex and other aspects of physical life as distractions that must be renounced lest they retard the afterlife's unwinding into ghostly solitude. Instead, it depicts them as forms of necessary preparation for the purgation undergone between incarnations and thus as integral aspects of a process that takes us to permanent bliss only when all of our phases have finally run their courses.

The first poem to strike this keynote clearly is "A Dialogue of Self and Soul." Written in eight-line stanzas similar to the octaves favored in *The Tower*, "A Dialogue" begins with "My Soul" issuing a summons to transcendence that resembles the calls to soul-making heard throughout the 1928 collection. In this case, "My Soul" sings the praises not of the full moon of

Phase 15 but rather of "the star that marks the hidden pole." Here and elsewhere in the volume, the unmoving polestar (or North Star) suggests the elusive passage out of the cycle of incarnations associated with the moon and into permanently satisfying harmony with the cosmic oneness. "My Self" responds indirectly, offering an admiring description of the Japanese sword familiar from *The Tower*, an unchanging, self-mirroring blade that derives protection and adornment from being "bound and wound" with the stuff of earthly life. "My Soul" then chides "My Self" for preoccupation with "things that are / Emblematical of love and war," arguing that a being must "scorn" both the objective "earth" and its own subjective "wandering" before it can be "Deliver[ed] from the crime of death and birth." "My Self" remains undaunted: setting up Montashigi's phallic sword and its feminine windings "For emblems of the day against the tower / Emblematical of the night," it defiantly claims the right "to commit the crime once more." Hearing this, "My Soul" evokes the "fullness" that "overflows / And falls into the basin of the mind" when one ascends to that final "Heaven" where distinctions between the objective *Is* and the subjective *Ought*, the subjective *Knower* and the objective *Known* fade away. But this evocation leads to the thought that "Only the dead can be forgiven," an insight that reduces "My Soul" to stony silence and prompts four stanzas of uninterrupted contemplation from "My Self."

In these stanzas, "My Self" explains why it is "content to live it all again / And yet again" even if doing so entails pitching blindly into the impure ditches of politics and love. The permanent blessedness desired both by "My Self" and "My Soul" only "flows into the breast" when round after round of incarnation and purgation has so exhausted a being's possible forms and cravings that it is able to "cast out remorse." In other words, "My Self" consents to live repeatedly – and to endure repeated afterlives in which it "follow[s] to its source / Every event in action or in thought" – because it understands that only thus will it eventually achieve the "sweetness" that it seeks. There is no use trying to short-circuit the process by renouncing the physical world while one remains alive: "Only the dead can be forgiven." Indeed, by filling one with remorse for all that has been prematurely given up, such renunciation may do more to mar one's ghostly solitude than any worldly attachment (as we know from "Nineteen Hundred and Nineteen," "what vanishes" is loved more greatly for its very evanescence). These premises come across most clearly in lines from Yeats's first draft: "Some day at last after how many lives I cannot tell / I will laugh out suddenly or sing / Having forgiven my self at last."[18] The finished poem moves us less by developing a particular theory of reincarnation than by dramatizing the aged poet's struggle to avow a lifetime of bitter setbacks as a necessary stage in an heroic quest for redemption.

Similar dramas recur in subsequent poems, including "Blood and the Moon," "Byzantium," and "Vacillation." "Blood and the Moon" counters "A Dialogue of Self and Soul" by acknowledging how traumatic it can be to pitch into the blind man's ditch of Irish history. Yeats's dedication to *The Winding Stair and Other Poems* identifies Kevin O'Higgins's assassination as this poem's inspiration. Though its first two lines seem to follow directly from the last two lines of "A Dialogue," it quickly makes clear that Yeats has not yet been filled with the sweetness that comes from casting out remorse. Here, he offers both blessing and mockery: blessing for the "bloody, arrogant power" that "Rose out of the race" when the Anglo-Normans built such fortresses as Thoor Ballylee, and mockery for an Ireland now grown "Half dead at the top" through its betrayal of such leaders as O'Higgins. Section II elaborates by explaining that the tower symbolizes not only the poet's artistic and spiritual quest but also the "ancestral stair" trod before him by such Anglo-Irish luminaries as Jonathan Swift, Oliver Goldsmith, Edmund Burke, and George Berkeley. Yeats associated these men with the era that preceded the Rising of 1798 and the ensuing Act of Union between Ireland and Great Britain, an era when, in his view, well-bred Anglo-Irishmen possessed of their own Dublin parliament had promoted Irish cultural accomplishment. Swift, Goldsmith, Burke, and Berkeley had also opposed the materialistic worldview then spreading outward from England: Swift by raging against it in savage indignation; Goldsmith by retreating into the "honey-pot of his mind"; Burke by comparing the ideal State to a well-proportioned, hierarchical tree, indifferent to "mathematical equality"; and Berkeley by insisting that the material world existed only by means of human perceptions that ultimately originated in God. Recalling arguments familiar from "The Tower" and "Meditations in Time of Civil War," "Blood and the Moon" implies that the arrogant power of Ireland's medieval Anglo-Norman conquerors set the stage for Anglo-Ireland's eighteenth-century "magnanimity," and that modern Ireland's rejection of this heritage has precipitated its return to bloodshed. Sections III and IV enact the poet's attempt to take comfort in the thought that none of this can possibly stain "The purity of the unclouded moon." No defilement can prevent the moon's cycles from drawing us gradually toward perfection. If these cycles sometimes make us "clamour in drunken frenzy" or trap us like butterflies flitting against a moonlit window's interior, we must embrace our destiny. "[W]isdom is the property of the dead," and the living man must blindly drink his drop and wait for fate to unfold.

The fated unfolding that occurs after death provides the subject of "Byzantium," which offsets the disparagement of "sensual music" expressed in "Sailing to Byzantium" by envisioning the afterlife as an ecstatic dance suffused with violence and eros. Critics put off by its strangeness sometimes read it in the same way that the narrator of "Rosa Alchemica" interprets alchemy: as a metaphorical account of art's transforming powers. While "Byzantium" certainly concerns art's powers, it also concerns the soul's fate after death. The poem begins at midnight, a time traditionally associated with the passage between earthly and spiritual realms. As it opens, emblems of the "unpurged" hurly-burly of daily existence – the Emperor's drunken soldiery, the courtesans who walk the city, the cathedral's resonant bells – recede out of sight and hearing. Yeats calls these emblems "images" partly in response to his budding fascination with Berkeley's belief that things exist only as they are perceived by the divine mind, a belief that accorded well with his own faith in a universal spirit. In the second stanza, another sort of "image" appears: a purified "superhuman" being that has already unwound the "mummy-cloth" of its worldly experiences, a ghostly "mouth that has no moisture" but may nevertheless be summoned by such excitedly "Breathless mouths" as the poet's. This "image" then gives way to the apparition of a golden bird recalling the "bodily form" desired by the speaker of "Sailing to Byzantium." In light of Yeats's belief in art's magical powers, it comes as no surprise to learn that this bird is no mere "golden handiwork" but a "miracle" that "Can like the cocks of Hades crow / Or, by the moon embittered, scorn . . . all complexities of mire or blood." Because crowing cocks symbolize rebirth in the lore of the Golden Dawn, critics usually interpret the first of these alternatives as heralding further incarnations for the soul, and the second as auguring its final escape into bliss.

Before either of these eventualities can occur, newly dead souls must be purged of "The fury and the mire of human veins" in the euphoric dance described in stanzas four and five. Relying on the classical myth that dolphins transport souls to the afterlife, Yeats pictures wave after wave of "blood-begotten spirits" flooding the marbled pavement of a spiritual "dancing floor" where they are violently broken and refined by supernatural flames. These flames complete rather than negate the complexities they encounter. Though presumably also the shapers of the golden bird's "changeless metal," they act on mortal souls by inspiring artful movements. That these movements entail as much ecstasy as agony is everywhere evident in the poem's sensual music. Observing a pattern of Yeats's own design, each of its eight-line stanzas climaxes in a brief moment of concentrated intensity created by the trimeter rhythms of their penultimate and antepenultimate lines.

Especially toward the end, these undulations are accompanied by emphatic alliteration. The resulting voluptuousness helps to explain why the poet encountered in *The Winding Stair and Other Poems* no longer renounces his worldly attachments: instead of dreading the purgatorial unwinding such attachments necessitate, he sees it as an orgasmic dance much like the one described in "Rosa Alchemica."

"Vacillation" works toward comparable conclusions in eight associatively linked meditations. The first begins by reiterating the premise that what the body calls death, the heart experiences as "remorse," and then poses the question, "What is joy?" In response, the second section imagines a symbolic tree reconciling the "extremities" between which "Man runs his course." Half is green with physical life, half glittering with spiritual fire, and each half consumes and renews the other. Perceptions of this relationship depend on the angle of one's vision, so that sometimes one half or the other falsely seems to make up "all the scene." Anyone who finds the meeting point of these halves – an achievement symbolized by the ritual sacrifice of the ancient Greek god Attis – "May know not what he knows, but knows not grief." This conception of joy prompts the poem's third section to disparage worldly ambitions; if one is over forty, one must prepare for death, not by indiscriminately renouncing all mortal attachments, but rather by rejecting those aspects of one's psyche and life that prevent one from assuming a condition of joyful, open-eyed, self-possession. In Sections IV and V, the poet experiences a foretaste of this state before being weighed back down by remorse, something that "A Dialogue of Self and Soul" has informed us can only be cast off permanently after many incarnations. Section VI then turns to other men who, at least temporarily, hung Attis' image in the middle of the tree. Both the "great lord of Chou" and the "conqueror" joyfully accept the passing of "all things" even while savoring the "odour of the new-mown hay" or the exaltation of victory. Their examples prompt the poet to see that both sides of the tree of physical life and spiritual fire spring out of "man's blood-sodden heart" (i.e., the universal spirit); they also make him reflect that "all song" necessarily praises the process by which this tree's branches are consumed and renewed. This latter insight carries into the last two sections, where, much like "My Self" in "A Dialogue of Self and Soul," Yeats concludes that, though sainthood should be honored, he is not ready for it. As a "singer born," his "predestined part" does not lead toward such sweetness as that associated with Saint Teresa's miraculously undecayed body (and revered by such Catholic theologians as Friedrich von Hügel). Instead, it draws him after something more like the honeycomb taken by the Biblical

Samson from the side of a dead lion's body on his way to a life of desire, betrayal, anger, and bloodshed.

Like *The Tower* before it, *The Winding Stair and Other Poems* follows the lengthy and difficult works of its early stages with shorter, more accessible lyrics. According to the book's dedication, the twenty-five brief poems known as "Words for Music Perhaps" originated in a blaze of "exultant" creativity that accompanied Yeats's recovery from illness in the spring of 1929 (VP 831). Though he did not actually expect these poems to be sung, he gave them vigorous, songlike rhythms; he also endowed most with frankly erotic energies. The eleven lyrics of "A Woman Young and Old" took shape a good deal earlier, but are similar in form, mood, and theme. Perhaps the most remarkable of all these shorter poems are the seven "Crazy Jane" lyrics that open "Words for Music Perhaps." Inspired by a woman known around Coole as "Cracked Mary," these poems seem to have been partly intended as another of Yeats's protests against Irish sexual Puritanism and the Free State's official censorship. The mad wisdom of their aged heroine agrees readily with what "A Dialogue of Self and Soul," "Byzantium," and "Vacillation" suggest about the necessity of drinking one's fill from impure ditches before attempting to become a saint. Reveling in memories of her youthful sexual exploits with Jack the Journeyman, Crazy Jane defies the Bishop's disparagement of her body and its urges. In "Crazy Jane and Jack the Journeyman" she explains that – though human love is as fleeting as "a skein unwound / Between the dark and dawn" – we cannot come to permanent bliss by denying our desires. Only when love's skein has been fully wound up during life and then unwound in death can we "leap into the light lost / In [our] mother's womb," and any overzealous attempt to cut this process short only dooms our ghosts to linger in torment like the remorseful spirits who haunt such plays as *The Words upon the Window-Pane* and (later) *Purgatory*. This is why Jane declares in "Crazy Jane Talks with the Bishop" that "fair needs foul" and that "nothing can be sole or whole / That has not been rent." The daring anti-Puritanism of such statements as "Love has pitched his mansion in / The place of excrement" has made Jane an attractive figure to many later readers, including some who see her as an affirmation of the female body and its desires. But we should not let her considerable appeal blind us to the disturbing qualities of her creator's thinking. "Crazy Jane Grown Old Looks at the Dancers," for example, offers a characteristically uncanny Yeatsian vision of dancing male and female lovers on the verge of murdering each other. This apparently reflects the poet's belief that – because the masculine and feminine forces that govern the cosmos consume and renew each other like the two halves of the symbolic tree in "Vacillation" – love and sex have as much to do with pain and death as with pleasure and life. Jane's eerie vision of a love "like the lion's tooth" posits an intrinsically heterosexual cosmos with sexual violence radiating from its core.

Several other of the volume's most noteworthy poems also center on compelling female figures. At first, "In Memory of Eva Gore-Booth and Con Markievicz" may seem like little more than an eloquent, sexist requiem for the genteel traditions of Anglo-Irish womanhood. Written after Gore-Booth's death in 1926 and Markievicz's in 1927, it begins by paying tribute to the aura of truth and beauty Yeats associated with both sisters when he visited them in their youth, amid the refinements of Lissadell, their family's Sligo estate. It then attributes their ruin to their radical politics, and confesses the poet's long-frustrated desire to "recall" them to their places as upper-class Angels in the House. Addressing their ghosts directly, it concludes by asserting that "now," when death has made them shadows, they must surely know their folly. Like everyone else imagined in *The Winding Stair and Other Poems*, they have had to endure life's blindness before unwinding into death's wisdom. The fact that the poem accounts for their fate in the same terms applied to "My Self" and other masculine figures does not erase its sexist, class-conscious assumptions. But familiarity with the rest of the volume does make it easier to see that Yeats's principal concern is not to blame the Gore-Booth sisters for the demise of Anglo-Irish patriarchy. He presents them as tragic figures, piteous in life and influential in death. At the end he implores their ghosts to act as intermediaries between himself and higher powers so that he may be inspired to live through his own incarnations like a man striking match after match until time finally catches on fire. The "sages" with whom the sisters now communicate convict everyone of guilt; from their heavenly perspective, the fading glories of such estates as Lissadell are no more impressive than a "great gazebo."

Yeats could not maintain such coldly stoical attitudes when he imagined the death of Lady Gregory and the downfall of Coole Park. Both "Coole Park, 1929" and "Coole and Ballylee, 1931" suggest that – unlike Eva Gore-Booth and Constance Markievicz – Lady Gregory has done everything in her power to uphold the traditions of her class and sex. "Coole Park, 1929" presents her as a deeply rooted tree whose noble character once inspired a flock of swallow-like protégés to find "certainty" in gyring about her. "Coole and Ballylee, 1931" offers similar praises for her cultivation of "great glory." Still, both poems admit that Lady Gregory's accomplishments will ultimately prove no less ephemeral than Eva Gore-Booth's dream of "Some vague Utopia" (P 233). Coole and all it stands for will soon be "a shapeless mound," remembered only by poets and scholars (P 243). "Coole and Ballylee, 1931" relies on the same understanding of the cosmos encountered elsewhere in the volume for relief from this painful prospect. After comparing the soul in its "generated" state to the waters that flow underground from Thoor Ballylee to Coole, it suggests that, if life's waters are allowed to run their course, another, swanlike version of the soul will eventually rise out of them, unsullied by their darkness. However we may chafe against the poet's politics or religion, it is difficult to remain unmoved when his meditations are suddenly interrupted by the sound of his dying friend's "stick upon the floor." Lady Gregory's death so devastated Yeats that, during the year that followed, he wrote next to no new poetry. He recovered by pitching himself yet again into the blind man's ditch of politics and "that most fecund" ditch of love (P 236).

Blueshirts, eugenics, "lust and rage": Yeats's final works

The last six years of Yeats's life present several troubling developments. In 1933, he wrote three marching songs for the Irish Blueshirts, a quasi-fascist paramilitary movement modeled on Mussolini's Italian Blackshirts. Later, having become entangled in the pseudo-science of eugenics, he composed poems, plays, and prose tracts urging both artists and governments to counter the rise of "gangrel stocks" by promoting sexual reproduction among hereditary elites (LE 231). Meanwhile, he was also pursuing a series of extramarital affairs with women half his age. What was going on? Had Yeats suddenly become a bigoted, sex-crazed fascist? Though we must be careful not to whitewash his final years' worrying features, we also must take care not to oversimplify their complexity. During the 1930s, the turmoil created by the Great Depression convinced many people besides the poet that liberal capitalism and democracy had failed, and that only some form of fascism or communism could save the world from chaos. Before Hitler took power in Germany in 1933, the only fascist state in existence was Mussolini's Italy, where political and economic stability seemed to have been achieved with a minimum of repression, and where anti-Semitism had not yet become official policy. At this stage, those intrigued by Mussolini were no more aware that fascism would lead to the Nazi Holocaust than those attracted to Soviet communism knew that it would eventually entail Stalin's murderous purges.

As for Yeats, his flirtation with the Blueshirts had more to do with Irish conditions than with attraction to Mussolini. In 1932, the political party known as Fianna Fáil ("Soldiers of Destiny") won a majority in the Dáil. Its leader, Eamon de Valera, had sided with the anti-Treaty forces during the

Civil War, and, after being released from prison by the Free State's pro-Treaty government, had founded Fianna Fáil in 1926 as an anti-Treaty party. Fianna Fáil's electoral victory not only mandated the first change of government since the Free State's founding; it also forced the Free State's pro-Treaty establishment to yield power to a party it regarded as a rabble of unrepentant rebels responsible for, among other things, the assassination of Kevin O'Higgins. De Valera eventually proved a skillful, pragmatic leader, but in 1932 and 1933 wild rumors circulated. Some feared that Fianna Fáil was a front for diehard remnants of the anti-Treaty IRA or for Irish communism, others that its hostility to all things British would disrupt the Free State's economy and lead to further infringements of the rights of Irish Protestants. Yeats's history of anticipating apocalyptic change, his aversion to the materialism inherent in communism, and his identification with Anglo-Irish traditions made him susceptible to such rumors. When some of his conservative friends began to advocate the Blueshirts, he listened with open ears. The Blueshirts mainly consisted of disgruntled pro-Treatyite ex-servicemen and of land-owning farmers hurt financially by de Valera's confrontations with Britain. They may have numbered as many as 30,000 by July 1933, when General Eoin O'Duffy became their leader. A vocal critic of Fianna Fáil who had recently been dismissed by de Valera from his post as head of the Free State police, O'Duffy pushed the Blueshirts in the direction of Italian fascism and hinted that a *coup d'état* was coming. When he announced a March on Dublin modeled on Mussolini's infamous March on Rome, de Valera forcibly banned the Blueshirts. Afterwards, the paramilitary aspect of the movement fizzled, and most of its adherents joined the new political party known as Fine Gael ("Tribe of the Gaels"). To this day, Fine Gael and Fianna Fáil are the Republic of Ireland's two largest political parties.

Yeats's support for the Blueshirts was never much more than lukewarm. He disliked O'Duffy's zealous Catholicism and his anti-intellectual manner, and, though he disagreed with Fianna Fáil's positions, he thought de Valera an able man. His real desire was for Ireland to be governed by a cultured elite that would refine the passions of the nation's rural masses while scorning the materialism of its urban middle classes. This had been his political fantasy for more than thirty years. The main difference between his earlier contemplations of this fantasy and the anthems he wrote for the Blueshirts is that the former seem more conscious of the difficulties entailed in realizing such moonshine in the daylit modern world. His earlier works express longing for an heroic social order, lament its incompatibility with modern life, praise those who preserve it vestigially, and call on supernatural forces to hasten its return. They do not lend overt support to real-world revolutionaries intent on using violence, which is precisely what Yeats offers the Blueshirts in the songs he wrote for them. Originally known as "Three Songs to the Same Tune," these poems call on their hearers to "Justify [Ireland's] renowned generations" by "hammer[ing] . . . down" "Those fanatics" who "would undo" the Free State's achievements (i.e., Fianna Fáil and the anti-Treaty IRA) [VP 543–49]. The Blueshirts never sang them, preferring cruder anthems, and by the time the poet published them in an English periodical in February 1934, both the movement and his interest in it had begun to wane. In this initial printing, "Three Songs to the Same Tune" appeared with a note in which Yeats described his work as "half-serious exaggeration" (VP 453). He later revised the songs in ways that distanced them even further from the Blueshirts and that ultimately produced the poetic triptych known as "Three Marching Songs." In essence, he backed away as soon as it became clear that the Blueshirts' unsophisticated aims were incompatible with his vision of an aristocratic society. His brief flirtation with them confirms that he possessed such a vision and that he was willing on occasion to treat it as more than a fantasy. But it does not make him a fascist.

Yeats's interest in eugenics permeates his work more thoroughly.[19] It shows up most explicitly in the compilation of poetry, prose, and drama known as *On the Boiler*, published in September 1939, eight months after his death. Citing eugenical authorities, the prose portions of this volume argue that intelligence is hereditary and found mainly in the upper classes, who therefore deserve to rule; it also claims that modern Europe's liberal, democratic tendencies have promoted social disorder and physiological degeneration by shifting power to society's lower ranks and encouraging excessive population growth among them. Nations should put well-bred elites back in charge and limit the reproductive rights of "the unintelligent classes" (LE 232). Artists should create images of beauty and thus assist cultivated persons in recognizing appropriately noble mates, or, in Yeats's words, should give "to the sexual instinct of Europe its goal, its fixed type" (LE 249). These arguments did not suddenly crop up during the poet's final years. They represent a central consequence of his lifelong attempt to renounce the modern era's materialistic worldview – which distinguishes matter from spirit – in favor of a magical understanding that regards such categories as inseparable and that therefore perceives the supposed beauty or ugliness of a material object as an index of its spiritual status. Prior to *On the Boiler*, Yeats's attraction to these views had come across most clearly in his early story "Rosa Alchemica," in his play *The King's Threshold*, and in what *A Vision* and "The Phases of the Moon" suggest about the reshaping undergone by a being's soul and body as it moves to, through, and away from the perfection of Phase 15. Such thinking had also been latently present in all of what he had written about the noble forms and high breeding of ancient Irish heroes, Maud Gonne, and the Anglo-Irish Ascendancy. *On the Boiler* departs from Yeats's earlier considerations of matter and spirit in the same way that "Three Songs to the Same Tune" departs from his earlier writings about revolutionaries: by dismissing the self-questioning impulses that had once made him reluctant to advocate real-world policies based on his magical views. In 1901, he had opened his essay "Magic" by confessing that he "would put this belief in magic from [him] if [he] could" because it forced him "to see or to imagine, in men and women, in houses, in handicrafts, in nearly all sights and sounds, a certain evil, a certain ugliness" derived from their spiritual imperfections.[20] By 1938, such scruples had largely subsided.

Some critics have argued that *On the Boiler* preserves traces of Yeats's capacity for skeptical self-questioning by presenting itself as the frenzied rant of a mad old man. They point to its inclusion of the poem known as "Why should not Old Men be Mad?" and to its title's allusion to a "mad ship's carpenter" who once railed at passersby in Sligo from atop an old rusty boiler (LE 220). The problem with this view is that the volume's prose adopts a perfectly straight-faced manner to explain what "recent statistics" and "intelligence tests" reveal about the decline of "better stocks" and the rise of the "stupider and less healthy" (LE 224, 231, 229). The poet's defenders take up firmer ground when they remind us that, in his day, eugenics had not yet been linked to genocidal anti-Semitism by the Nazis. Though many of Yeats's friends and associates hated Jews, no trace of anti-Semitism surfaces in his work. *On the Boiler* does express distaste for Ireland's Catholic bourgeoisie, but even in this it stops short of naked tribal prejudice: instead of claiming that Catholics are naturally inferior, it attributes their supposed failings to the seventeenth-century defeats that forced Catholic aristocrats out of Ireland, and suggests that "history will soon fill the gap" (LE 242).

Why did Yeats embrace such extreme manifestations of his views in the middle 1930s? And why did he not more loudly denounce European fascism after its character had become clearer? The answer to the second question lies mainly in what the poet's visionary system had taught him about the inevitability and tragic beauty of epoch-changing violence. It also had to do with an Irish nationalist's profound reluctance to take sides against Britain's rivals. The first question speaks to the effects of chronic illness and the inexorable approach of death. Though the poet enjoyed relatively good health during the first half of the decade, the lung congestion that had first troubled him in 1927 returned with other serious ailments in 1935 and 1936. Afterwards, his condition remained precarious and his temperament grew more volatile: a sense that time was short made him less afraid of offending others. He had also come to regard the expression of highly charged political feeling as a means of spurring himself out of the creative slumps he sometimes suffered in the aftermath of Lady Gregory's death. Thus, during his last six years, he not only wrote songs for the Blueshirts and advocated eugenics in *On the Boiler.* He also produced strident panegyrics praising Charles Stewart Parnell; ballads denouncing the accusers of the Irish patriot Roger Casement; and such vehemently anti-British poems as "The Curse of Cromwell." His aggressiveness tallied with what *The Winding Stair and Other Poems* had suggested about the need to plunge into the world and thereby drown the desires that would otherwise plague one's afterlife with remorse.

Yeats's application of this conviction did not limit itself to politics. In 1934, at the age of sixty-eight, he underwent the "Steinach operation." This involved nothing more exotic than a vasectomy, thought at the time to restore sexual potency and slow the effects of age by stimulating the production and retention of male hormone. Such claims made the procedure a medical fad in the twenties and thirties and, though science has since discredited them, Yeats believed himself powerfully affected. Before the operation, he seems to have experienced a lengthy period of diminished libido and sexual impotence that he associated with creative incapacity. Afterwards, he convinced himself that both his sexual and creative energies had been reinvigorated. These new energies did not impel him in the direction of his wife. Since the cessation of George's automatic writing, she and Yeats had drifted apart; she remained a friend and dutiful caregiver, but no longer played the part of a spiritually inspiring lover. She spent much of the poet's last half-decade tending the extensive gardens at Riversdale – the suburban Dublin house they had acquired in 1932 – while he devoted his healthy weeks and months to romantic adventures and creative projects that took him to England or to warmer, Mediterranean climes. Within six months of the Steinach operation he was searching for new love with the same recklessness he had displayed in 1917 when he proposed to George on the heels of Iseult Gonne's rejection. The first of his infatuations began in London in October 1934 and centered on a beautiful, 27-year-old, manic-depressive actress and poet known as Margot Ruddock. Though the overtly erotic phase of their relationship was brief, Ruddock remained a force in Yeats's life for several years to come, most notoriously when, in the midst of a manic episode, she turned up unexpectedly at a villa he and George had rented in Majorca, fled from there to Barcelona, jumped out a window, broke her knee-cap, hid in the hold of a ship, and obliged the Yeatses to rescue her from the local authorities.

Two months after meeting Ruddock, Yeats became enamored of a second young English beauty by the name of Ethel Mannin. Mannin was a 34-year-old novelist and journalist known for feminist and Marxist views. Next came Dorothy Wellesley, a somewhat older English poet and aristocrat whom he met in 1935 and whose estate in rural Sussex provided a much-frequented retreat. Finally, in 1937, he encountered Edith Shackleton Heald, a well-known journalist then entering her mid-fifties. Biographers generally agree that these liaisons entailed little sexual contact: apparently, the Steinach procedure revived Yeats's libido and eagerness for romance more than his physical capabilities. He seems to have had at least one sexual experience with both Ruddock and Mannin, and to have been more repeatedly intimate with Heald. Wellesley, by contrast, quickly informed him of her lesbianism and made clear that their relationship would go no further than passionate friendship. These details have provoked mixed reactions from feminist critics. On the one hand, Yeats's treatment of George manifests disappointing assumptions about the subordinate status of a wife. On the other, his friendships with Ruddock and her successors reflect his lifelong fascination with accomplished women; they also reflect his willingness to respond affirmingly to female sexuality, and to act as a mentor to aspiring female writers. There is no question that these relationships affected his writing greatly. He not only composed several poems that obviously refer to Ruddock or Wellesley (including "Sweet Dancer," "A Crazed Girl," "Man and the Echo," and "To Dorothy Wellesley"). He also suffused his work with sexual subject matter, frequently dramatizing himself as a "wild old wicked man" spurred into song by "lust and rage" (P 310 and 312). Some of this work is dissatisfying in ways that recall the limitations of "Three Songs to the Same Tune" or *On the Boiler*: it seems forced rather than deeply felt, as if Yeats is using exaggerated ribaldry to make up for declining artistic and sexual powers. Yet if the output of his final years does not always match the standards set by *The Tower* and *The Winding Stair and Other Poems*, much of what he produced is as inventive and powerful as anything he ever wrote.

Few have sought to demonstrate this claim by instancing the drama and poetry published in *The King of the Great Clock Tower, Commentaries and Poems* (1934) and then repeated, with additions and revisions, in *A Full Moon in March* (1935). *The King of the Great Clock Tower* gives dramatic form to the motif of the severed, singing head encountered in the story "The Binding of the Hair." Yeats wrote it during a "barren" period in the hope that he "might be forced to make lyrics for its imaginary people" (VP 1309). He reworked the same materials for *A Full Moon in March*, intending to create a vehicle for Margot Ruddock's acting. This intention remained unfulfilled, and neither play pleased him greatly. The poems he published with them include the songs he wrote for the Blueshirts, the more intricate political poem known as "Parnell's Funeral," and a sequence of "Supernatural Songs." "Parnell's Funeral" presents its hero as having made an epoch-changing sacrifice and condemns both de Valera and O'Duffy for pandering to the mob instead of following his example.[21] The "Supernatural Songs," by contrast, center on a persona called Ribh (pronounced "Reeve"), who, like Crazy Jane, expresses audacious views about religion and sex. Yeats's notes describe him as an early Irish Christian – a contemporary of St. Patrick's – whose half-pagan version of Christianity avoids the condemnation of bodily desires typical of modern orthodoxy. In "Ribh at the Tomb of Baile and Aillinn," he reads his "holy book" in the magical light emitted from the tomb of two pagan lovers. In "Ribh denounces Patrick," he criticizes his rival for failing to see similarities between sexual and divine love. The sequence's most acclaimed poetry occurs in its final lyric, the Shakespearean sonnet "Meru." Alluding to a Himalayan mountain considered sacred in Hindu lore, "Meru" reflects Yeats's interest in parallels between ancient Indian sages and early Irish Christians like Ribh.[22] It asserts that "Civilisation is hooped together" by the shared delusions that allow any culture's inhabitants to rest content with the status quo. It then suggests that, eventually, the "semblance of peace" sustained by such "manifold illusion" must yield to the impulse to "come / Into the desolation of reality." This impulse motivates – and perhaps, in some magical way, is assisted by – such "Hermits" as those "upon Mount Meru or Everest." In a "Commentary" attached to "Parnell's Funeral," Yeats claims that a similar "passion for reality" infused Irish art when the collapse of Parnellism exposed the manifold illusions of late-nineteenth-century Ireland (VP 835).

Yeats's final two poetic collections, *New Poems* (1938) and the posthumously published *Last Poems and Two Plays* (1939), offer a wider array of important works. "The Gyres" begins *New Poems* by declaring that, for those who understand history's cycles, the appropriate response to such "Irrational streams of blood" as those beginning to flow in Europe in the late 1930s is to "laugh in tragic joy." By the collection's end, however, "The Municipal Gallery Re-visited" has demonstrated that memories of the poet's dead friends can still weigh him down "in despair that time may bring / Approved patterns of women or of men / But not that selfsame excellence again." In the intervening poems, his pursuit of the mask of "tragic joy" gradually gives way to fascination with "lust and rage" (P 312). The overall effect recalls *Responsibilities*, where we witness the poet's agonizing struggle to move through postures of public anger toward the sweet mask of secret exultation. Here, this struggle yields at least one unquestioned masterpiece, "Lapis Lazuli," written in July 1936. By this point, Mussolini had invaded Ethiopia, Hitler had remilitarized Germany, and Spain had begun its descent into civil strife. The English circles Yeats frequented during his trips to London and to Wellesley's country estate were buzzing with alarm at the prospect of war. Hence the poem's opening passage, which attributes to "hysterical women" the view that desperate times have made the arts irrelevant, and that, "if nothing drastic is done," German aeroplanes and zeppelins will drop their bombs "Until the town lie beaten flat." Readers familiar with "The Gyres," which precedes "Lapis Lazuli" in *New Poems*, know that Yeats regards such attitudes as hysterical not only because they privilege physical action over artistic creation but also because they fail to recognize the inevitability of violence. That history unfolds through a succession of violent conflicts is deftly underscored by the poem's reference to "King Billy," which fuses allusions to England's King William III, conqueror of seventeenth-century Ireland, and Kaiser Wilhelm, German emperor during World War I.[23]

The poem's second section at once derides and dignifies the anxious inhabitants of late-thirties England. The would-be Hamlets and Ophelias of the present are merely strutting actors performing history's cyclical melodrama. And yet, if they could master themselves – if they could unite their ordinary selves with such tragic masks as those imagined by Shakespeare – they would attain a state of completion, of "Gaiety transfiguring all that dread." In such a state, everything that "men have aimed at, found and lost" achieves fulfillment, and this allows the "Black out" that accompanies life's final curtain to summon "Heaven blazing into the head." The stunning terseness of the poet's language suggests that he experiences a foretaste of this transformation even as he speaks, and the poem's remainder is equally dramatic. The third section sympathizes with the human and artistic casualties of "Old civilisations put to the sword" by describing them in loving detail; thus, instead of simply announcing that "All things fall and are built again / And those that build them again are gay," it enacts the poet's attempt to wear the mask of his stoical convictions. The fourth and fifth sections contemplate the eighteenth-century Chinese carving in lapis lazuli that Yeats received as a gift and that inspired the poem's title. Here, he quickly begins to offer more than mere description. First, he interprets the carving in emblematic and narrative terms, reading its "long-legged bird" as "A symbol of longevity" and asserting that one of its human figures is "doubtless a serving-man." As his imagination begins to heat up, he transforms "Every discolouration of the stone / Every accidental crack or dent" into "a watercourse or an avalanche, / Or lofty slope" leading to the "little half-way house" that is "doubtless" sweetened by "plum or cherry-branch." By the end he resembles the speaker of Keats's "Ode on a Grecian Urn," "Delight[ing] to imagine" scenes suggested by – but not actually on – the object before his eyes. He thus presents himself in the act of becoming one of those who build things again imaginatively and are thereby redeemed by tragic joy. His concluding vision makes clear that those who achieve this state do not blithely turn from the suffering of the world to enter an escapist reverie (as supposed by the "hysterical women"). Instead, they "stare" on "the tragic scene," allowing art's "mournful melodies" to enlarge their perceptions to the point that "Their eyes mid many wrinkles, their eyes, / Their ancient, glittering eyes, are gay."

Last Poems and Two Plays features comparably significant poems and a comparably suggestive arrangement. As published in the limited edition issued by Yeats's sister in July 1939, six months after his death, it begins with "Under Ben Bulben" and ends with the two plays *The Death of Cuchulain* and *Purgatory.* In 1940, the trade edition known as *Last Poems & Plays* added the contents of *New Poems* as well as three poems printed in *On the Boiler*; it also made "Under Ben Bulben" the collection's final lyric. This scheme subsequently informed all major editions of Yeats's collected *Poems* until the 1980s, by which time it had become clear that the poet's original designs for *New Poems* and *Last Poems and Two Plays* better reflected his intentions. Mainly because of their bearing on "Under Ben Bulben," these matters are crucial. When Yeats placed this poem first in *Last Poems and Two Plays* he established a pattern familiar from earlier collections in which a strongly worded opening statement – such as "Sailing to Byzantium" or "The Gyres" – precedes a series of poems that play against it in various ways. By making "Under Ben Bulben" the final lyric of *Last Poems & Plays,* the poet's literary executors converted it from an opening statement to a concluding credo.

One can see why the poem seemed like a fitting finale, since it ends by describing Yeats's grave and unveiling his chosen epitaph. But as stirring as its conclusion may be, its earlier passages include some of the most unpalatable lines the poet ever penned. His most satisfying poems brilliantly exemplify the distinction often made by writing teachers between "telling" and "showing." Instead of simply telling us what their author believes, they show us what it feels like to be buffeted by contending visions. "Under Ben Bulben," by contrast, begins by evoking sources of inspiration ranging from ancient Christian "Sages" to Shelley's "Witch of Atlas" to Ireland's "superhuman" Sidhe, and then proceeds to tell us "the gist of what they mean." In doing so it not only reiterates Yeats's belief that, impelled by the "human mind," a being reincarnates many times, moving between union with other beings and perfected individual existence. It also describes this process in overtly racial terms as a movement "Between [man's] two eternities, / That of race and that of soul." Section III follows up this emphasis on race by presenting the Irish people as endowed by their violent history with an intuitive knowledge of Yeats's conception of the mask. Such nationalists as those influenced by John Mitchel's *Jail Journal* (1854) instinctively understand that the highest function of words is to hasten the arrival of that violently passionate, heroic condition achieved after "all words are said," a condition in which a man "completes his partial mind," laughs in tragic joy, and suddenly sees how "he can accomplish fate / Know his work or choose his mate."

The last of these implications – that part of art's purpose is eugenical – forms the core of Sections IV and V. In Section IV, Yeats instructs modern artists to "Bring the soul of man to God" by making "him fill the cradles right." Like ancient Egyptian and Greek sculptors, and like Michelangelo – whose Sistine Chapel's "half-awakened Adam / Can disturb globe-trotting Madam / Till her bowels are in heat" – modern artists must serve the "purpose set / Before the secret working mind: / Profane perfection of mankind." After relating how later European artists gradually lost sight of this goal, Yeats spends Section V asking Ireland's present and future poets to safeguard his vision of the nation's racial identity:

> Irish poets learn your trade
> Sing whatever is well made,
> Scorn the sort now growing up
> All out of shape from toe to top,
> Their unremembering hearts and heads
> Base-born products of base beds.
> Sing the peasantry, and then
> Hard-riding country gentlemen,
> The holiness of monks, and after
> Porter-drinkers' randy laughter;
> Sing the lords and ladies gay
> That were beaten into the clay
> Through seven heroic centuries;
> Cast your mind on other days
> That we in coming days may be
> Still the indomitable Irishry.

By this point, the race-centered aesthetics first encountered in "Rosa Alchemica" and *The King's Threshold* has been espoused more unreservedly than in any of Yeats's other poems. He makes little attempt to evoke multifaceted reactions to his impulses. Instead, he uses emphatic rhythms and rhymes to cajole his readers into accepting the preposterous notion that art's purpose is to scorn "Base-born products of base beds." The only thing that prevents "Under Ben Bulben" from being just as repellent as *On the Boiler* is the fact that it doesn't call on the State to enforce its eugenical imperatives.

The poem thus provides a very disquieting conclusion for Yeats's *Last Poems*. As the first of these poems, however, it initiates a sequence that better reflects his capacity for complex emotion and self-critical thought. This is not to suggest that the rest of *Last Poems and Two Plays* retracts "Under Ben Bulben": "The Statues" claims that Europe "put down / All Asiatic vague immensities" when the forms created by ancient Greek sculptors taught European women what to look for in a mate, while *Purgatory* focuses on a man who kills his son after concluding that their line has been polluted by base blood. Instead of retracting its opening statement, *Last Poems and Two Plays* forces it to stand in tension with works more committed to dramatic complexity. "The Black Tower," for example, portrays a group of ancient warriors who would rather sacrifice themselves to a fleeting ideal than parley with their opponents. Whether they represent admirably stalwart heroes or self-defeating fanatics is left for the reader to judge. "Cuchulain Comforted" envisions a similarly mysterious scenario, in which the hero's ghost joins a troop of sweetly singing spirits who in life were "Convicted cowards." This apparently reflects Yeats's belief that, after the dead unwind their earthly lives, they enter a second ghostly state in which they encounter the opposite of all they have been before. Like the earlier lyric "Paudeen," "Cuchulain Comforted" reminds us that, for all his snobbery, the poet believes in a cosmos where everything seeks its contrary and all beings periodically emit "a sweet crystalline cry" (P 110).

Yeats's self-critical side stands out even more sharply in "Man and the Echo" and "The Circus Animals' Desertion." "Man and the Echo" begins with Man shouting frantic questions into an oracular cleft on the side of Knocknarea, in County Sligo. Did he contribute to the deaths of the 1916 rebels by writing such incendiary plays as *Cathleen ni Houlihan*? Was he responsible for Margot Ruddock's mania? Could he have prevented the ruin of Coole after Lady Gregory's death? The fact that Echo answers by repeating Man's last four words implies continued awareness on Yeats's part that communications from the spirit world may be nothing more than solipsistic self-mirrorings. Man himself seems sure that the instruction to "Lie down and die" comes from the great beyond, but he doesn't propose to obey. Instead, he multiplies the poem's ironies by arguing with the oracle. In his view, an old man should not seek death until his spiritual intellect has fully woken him from the torpor of bodily experience, thus enabling him to understand and judge himself, dismiss what he has been, and sink without regret "at last into the night." That Man remains painfully distant from this condition is implicit not only in his remorseful opening questions but also in his final supplication. When Echo confirms only that "night" must fall, Man pleads for reassurance:

> O rocky voice
> Shall we in that great night rejoice?
> What do we know but that we face
> One another in this place?

In these and the following lines – in which the cries of a rabbit struck by a hawk or owl distract his stoical thoughts – Man indirectly admits that pursuing the "spiritual intellect's great work" may have cut him off from the only reality he assuredly faces, the reality of the suffering world around him. The poem's drama centers on the paradoxical possibility that, in making this admission, he advances the process of waking up to that "one clear view" of himself that eventually will allow him to stand "in judgment on his soul."

"The Circus Animals' Desertion" stages a similar confession. Here, the poet acknowledges his lifelong tendency to substitute art for life. In doing so he makes a hesitant but real attempt at being "satisfied with [his] heart." To be satisfied with one's heart – to lie down in it despite its foulness, to stop imagining alternatives to it – is to arrive at something very like the strangely joyful, remorse-free state of self-knowledge, self-judgment, and self-dismissal recommended by many of Yeats's later poems. Indeed, "The Circus Animals' Desertion" carefully follows the formula outlined in "Man and the Echo": it arranges Yeats's life in one clear view, stands in judgment on that life, dismisses it, and begins the final descent back into the primal point of origin, "the foul rag and bone shop of the heart." One of the poem's superb ironies is that the poet only acknowledges his art's limitations after his creativity seems to have failed him; another is that in disclosing these limitations he finds renewed artistic purpose. Are his creative difficulties and broken humanity tokens of failure? Or are they the long-awaited signs that he has exhausted everything he was meant to do and be, and thus is ready to act on the advice of "Vacillation" and "come / Proud, open-eyed and laughing to the tomb"?

Purgatory provides another example of the horrible splendor of Yeats's last works. Performed at the Abbey in August 1938 and then printed both in *Last Poems and Two Plays* and *On the Boiler*, it displays his views about breeding at their most appalling. At the same time, however, it vividly dramatizes the dangers of mistaking the brightness of the moon for the prosaic light of day. It focuses on an old man whose Anglo-Irish mother ruined the cultured, aristocratic house into which she was born by marrying a drunken stable-man. Soon afterward, she died in childbirth, leaving her son – the old man – to be raised by his wastrel of a father, who eventually set fire to the house. Now, after long years of impoverished wandering, the old man has returned to his ruined birthplace in company with his own son, and together they witness the ghosts of his parents reenacting events from their wedding night. The old man explains this phenomenon in terms familiar from *The Dreaming of the Bones* and *The Words upon the Window-Pane*: his mother's spirit is in purgatory, where she must relive her transgression again and again until its effects have dissipated. To the extent that she has sinned against herself, "There is no help but in [herself] / And in the mercy of God" (lines 40–41). To the extent that her sin has been against others, "others may bring help / For when the consequence is at an end / The dream must end" (lines 37–39). Assuming that his mother's transgression has been of this latter sort, the old man stabs his son, wielding the same knife he has earlier admitted to having used as a sixteen-year-old to kill his drunken father. But his assumption proves terribly wrong: his mother's ghost remains imprisoned by "remorse," and he must confess himself "Twice a murderer and all for nothing" (lines 222 and 217).

The old man's veneration of the Ascendancy, his revulsion for the base-born, and his willingness to embrace violence reflect positions straightfor-wardly adopted by Yeats in the prose portions of *On the Boiler*. And yet, in the play, the old man comes across as someone whose attempt to remake the spiritual world by acting brutally in the material one has magnified disaster. In this respect he differs from those Yeatsian heroes who, like the Happy Shepherd or the sages in "Lapis Lazuli," know that "Words alone are certain good" and hence withdraw from the realm of physical action (P 7). From the opening curtain, the play's austere setting, starkly beautiful poetry, and ra-pidly developing plot establish the aura of classical tragedy. The old man – and through him, to some extent, the playwright himself – comes to seem a tragic figure, driven by fate and instinct to extremities of transgression and suffering.

Death

Yeats continued writing almost to the moment of his death. In October 1938 he left Ireland for the final time, journeying first to England, and then, accompanied by George, to Cap Martin in the south of France. Here, in December, strong in mind but frail in body, he completed *The Death of*

Cuchulain, a last dramatic depiction of his longtime alter ego in which the hero bravely faces his end, confident that his soul "is about to sing" (line 183). On January 21 he finished his last poem, "The Black Tower." Two days later, he suffered a sudden flare-up of the chronic lung and heart ailments that had long sapped his strength. After weakening for several days, he died peacefully on the afternoon of January 28, aged seventy-three years old. Foreseeing that his death would prompt calls for an extravagant Dublin funeral, he had instructed George to bury him temporarily in France and then later remove his body to Drumcliff in County Sligo. She accordingly arranged for a temporary grave in nearby Roquebrune. Though she initially planned to move the body before the year was out, the onset of World War II in September forced a lengthy delay. Finally, in 1948, Yeats was laid to rest under his beloved Ben Bulben in the yard of the small Protestant church where his great-grandfather had been Rector. By this time, the academic study of his works – the subject of the present book's brief concluding chapter – was already well underway.

Chapter 4

Yeats's critics

Bibliographies, scholarly editions, and biographies   *115*
Critical studies   *118*

The words of a dead man / Are modified in the guts of the living.
W. H. Auden, "In Memory of W. B. Yeats"

K. P. S. Jochum's *W. B. Yeats: A Classified Bibliography of Criticism* (1990) lists over 10,000 items, and thousands more have appeared since its compilation. The present chapter offers suggestions for getting started with this material. It begins by considering such basic resources as bibliographies, scholarly editions, and biographies. It then outlines the major critical trends from the 1930s to the present.

Bibliographies, scholarly editions, and biographies

One first needs to know what Yeats wrote. Allan Wade's *A Bibliography of the Writings of W. B. Yeats* (1968) documents the poet's books as well as his contributions to periodicals and to books assembled by others. It also catalogs early studies of his work, and provides information about translations, radio broadcasts, and his sister's press. The 1978 edition of Jochum's *Classified Bibliography* lists a number of publications by Yeats that surfaced subsequent to Wade's inventory, and additional updates appear in *Yeats: An Annual of Critical and Textual Studies.* For an account of the books owned by the poet, see Edward O'Shea's *A Descriptive Catalog of W. B. Yeats's Library* (1985).

Next comes the question of which editions to read. Yeats's revisions make this a complex matter, especially in the case of his poems. The two best current trade editions – Richard J. Finneran's *The Poems, Revised* (1989) and A. Norman Jeffares's *Yeats's Poems* (1989) – reflect different interpretations of revisions undertaken in the 1930s. Yeats spent much of 1931 and 1932 correcting proofs for a multi-volume Edition de Luxe of his collected works

115

that, for economic reasons, never reached the public. Instead, his publisher brought out a one-volume edition of his poetry followed by a similar collection of his plays. Though *The Collected Poems of W. B. Yeats* (1933) turned out to be the last collected edition of the poetry to appear during the poet's lifetime, he never definitively clarified whether he intended it to supersede his work on the Edition de Luxe, from which it differed in many ways. Finneran regards *The Collected Poems* as a permanent revision; Jeffares contends that it constituted a temporary and inferior substitute for the unpublished Edition de Luxe. The two editors thus produce two quite different editions, distinguished most notably by different orderings of the poems. Finneran follows *The Collected Poems* – and later editions deriving from it – in placing the longer narrative poems in a separate section at the end. Jeffares maintains the traditions of the Edition de Luxe, which interweave the longer poems with the shorter lyrics. One edition opens with "Crossways" and plays up Yeats's lyric talents; the other begins with "The Wanderings of Oisin" and stresses his role as heroic Ireland's modern bard. Both editions reflect diligent scholarship, but neither is beyond question. Anyone interested in the poetry's arrangement or in the finer points of its wording and punctuation should carefully study their differences.[1]

No matter what one concludes about current trade editions, one should not rely solely on the revised versions of Yeats's works authorized in the 1930s. Students of the poet's development must also consult earlier versions or risk the absurdity of drawing conclusions about his initial phases from texts established later. Early texts may also shed light on later versions, or manifest their own aesthetic charms. A number of scholarly resources document the evolution of Yeats's texts. *The Variorum Edition of the Poems* (ed. Peter Allt and Russell K. Alspach, 1966) and *The Variorum Edition of the Plays* (ed. Russell K. Alspach, 1966) record all published versions of the poems and plays to appear during their author's lifetime. They also chart the changing arrangements of his poetic collections, and detail his notes, prefaces, and dedications. For access to pre-publication drafts one must turn to the ongoing series known as the Cornell Yeats. Each volume in this series treats a different play or poetic collection, printing photographs of manuscripts and typescripts on the left-hand pages with typographic transcriptions on the right.[2] Together, the Cornell Yeats and the two *Variorum* editions trace the history of Yeats's poems and plays from their earliest surviving drafts through their various published forms. Other editions focus on variant texts of the prose. These include *The Secret Rose, Stories by W. B. Yeats: A Variorum Edition* (1992) and *Yeats's "Vision" Papers* (1992 and 2001); they also include *Memoirs* (1972), which prints a rough draft of the poet's autobiography and the journal he began in 1908.[3] The best trade editions of the plays and prose appear in the ongoing series known as *The Collected Works of W. B. Yeats.*[4] Many libraries also offer access to *The W. B. Yeats Collection* (1999), an online electronic archive of the revised versions of the major works, plus the 1925 edition of *A Vision.*

Yeats's biographers have created similarly important resources. The poet saw his own autobiographical writings more as occasions for remaking himself than as strictly accurate chronicles, and many scholars have investigated the relationship between his self-presentation and the life he actually lived. R. F. Foster's highly acclaimed, two-volume biography, *W. B. Yeats: A Life* (1997 and 2003), provides the most comprehensive and evenhanded account. Foster proceeds chronologically, and, though his analysis is perceptive, he refrains from imposing any single, overarching interpretation. He thus concentrates more on the spiritual, emotional, and political contexts that influenced Yeats than on explication of his writings. Those who prefer to begin with a briefer study featuring more attention to the poet's works will be well served by Terence Brown's *The Life of W. B. Yeats: A Critical Biography* (1999). Other useful biographies focus on particular aspects of Yeats's life or on members of his family. John Harwood's *Olivia Shakespear and W. B. Yeats* (1989) sheds light on the poet's relationships with women and on his nineties work. Brenda Maddox's *Yeats's Ghosts* (1999) – titled *George's Ghosts* in the British edition – describes the occult occurrences associated with Yeats's marriage, but is marred by a tendency to sensationalize matters. A more scholarly treatment of the marriage appears in Ann Saddlemyer's *Becoming George: The Life of Mrs. W. B. Yeats* (2002). William M. Murphy's *Prodigal Father: The Life of John Butler Yeats* (1978) provides an informative account of the poet's father. Many biographical commentaries have been published in *Yeats Annual* and *Yeats: An Annual of Critical and Textual Studies*; of these, Deirdre Toomey's analyses of Yeats's relationship with Maud Gonne and with his mother are particularly valuable.[5] In addition to these comparatively recent inquiries, two early biographies remain notable milestones in the evolution of Yeats studies: Joseph Hone's *W. B. Yeats, 1865–1939* (1942) and A. Norman Jeffares's *W. B. Yeats: Man and Poet* (1949). An even more significant early study is Richard Ellmann's *Yeats: The Man and the Masks* (1948). Synthesizing biography and criticism, it concentrates on the poet's struggle to unify his identity, emphasizing his occult studies and the influence of his father. More than fifty years after publication, it remains a must-read for serious students.

Serious students will also wish to consider letters, reviews, and the memoirs of Yeats's contemporaries. Three superbly edited and annotated installments of *The Collected Letters of W. B. Yeats* – covering the poet's earliest years up through 1904 – have thus far been issued, and more are on the way.[6] *The Letters of W. B. Yeats* (ed. Allan Wade, 1954) and other collections offer further selections from his correspondence, and *Letters to W. B. Yeats* (ed. Richard J. Finneran, George Mills Harper, and William M. Murphy, 2 vols., 1977) supplements these resources.[7] The most extensive listing of reviews appears in Jochum's *Classified Bibliography* (with subsequent updates in *Yeats: An Annual of Critical and Textual Studies*). A. Norman Jeffares's *W. B. Yeats: The Critical Heritage* (1977) prints an extensive selection of reviews and other contemporary press accounts, as does David Pierce's *W. B. Yeats: Critical Assessments* (2000). George Moore's *Hail and Farewell* (3 vols., 1911–14) sketches the most famous of the many Yeatsian portraits to appear in memoirs by contemporaries: it delineates a brilliant satirical caricature, not a lifelike rendering. Maud Gonne's *A Servant of the Queen* (1938) says comparatively little about the poet, but is useful in understanding how Gonne saw herself. Lady Gregory's published diaries and autobiographies contain much that pertains to Yeats.[8] For a sampling of additional recollections by such figures as Sean O'Casey and Frank O'Connor, see E. H. Mikhail's *W. B. Yeats: Interviews and Recollections* (2 vols., 1977).

Critical studies

Even before Yeats's death, assessments of his work were beginning to exceed the bounds of routine literary journalism. The first book-length study appeared in 1904: Horatio Sheafe Krans's *William Butler Yeats and the Irish Literary Revival*. Still, serious critical interest did not become widespread until the 1930s and 1940s. During this period, such so-called "Thirties poets" as W. H. Auden and Louis MacNeice measured Yeats against their own secular and left-leaning views, while the American "New Critics" and their British contemporaries also appraised his achievement. Auden's marvelous elegy "In Memory of W. B. Yeats" (1939) constitutes one of the most influential pieces of Yeats criticism ever published. By advancing the perceptive (though oversimplified) suggestion that Yeats's "gift" for dramatizing powerful emotions "survived" his "silly" thinking, it opened an approach followed by numerous subsequent analysts. Auden's essay "The Public Vs. The Late Mr. William Butler Yeats" (1939) makes a more particularized case against the poet's "feudal mentality" and belief in "mumbo-jumbo" before reaching similar conclusions.[9] MacNeice also balances skepticism and sympathy, but takes Yeats's convictions more seriously. In *The Poetry of W. B. Yeats* (1941), he argues that his fellow Irishman's interest in the matter of Ireland gradually forced him to synthesize his Romantic and esoteric fantasies with keen attention to everyday life. Like both Auden and MacNeice, the New Critics weighed Yeats's off-putting politics and religion against the greatness of his artistry. A few passed negative judgments: Yvor Winters concluded that he failed to meet the moral and aesthetic standards of great literature (as defined in terms of such values as rationality).[10] But most preferred to emphasize the poet's artistry, often by using formalist "close reading" to analyze particular poems in isolation from historical contexts. Though this sometimes resulted in absurdly secularized and depoliticized depictions, the ablest of the New Critics were more flexible than recent caricatures let on. James Hall's and Martin Steinmann's *The Permanence of Yeats* (1950) provides a good way to gain familiarity with New Critical perspectives. It collects essays written during the thirties and forties by such contributors as Cleanth Brooks, R. P. Blackmur, John Crowe Ransom, Allen Tate, and F. R. Leavis.

Most of the New Critics formulated their judgments at a time when little if any specialist work on Yeats's biography, revisions, or occult beliefs had yet been published. This situation improved significantly after World War II, when such pioneering Yeats experts as Richard Ellmann, T. R. Henn, and Thomas Parkinson came on the scene. Ellmann is remembered not only for *Yeats: The Man and the Masks* but also for *The Identity of Yeats* (1954), which focuses on the poetry's thematic and stylistic development. Countering the tendency to assume that Yeats attained greatness as a modern poet by breaking radically with his early Romanticism, *The Identity* argues for coherent patterns of thought and mood underlying the evolution of his diction, imagery, and symbolism. In Ellmann's view, Yeats forged a cohesive artistic identity not by expressing a system of unchanging beliefs, but by repeatedly re-engaging a nexus of unresolvable conflicts. Together, Ellmann's two books convinced many critics that the poet's esoteric convictions were too coherent and profound to be dismissed as mumbo-jumbo. Henn's *The Lonely Tower* (1950) strengthened this conviction by rooting *A Vision* and other Yeatsian works in the traditions of western philosophy, mysticism, literature, and painting. An Irishman, Henn also emphasized Yeats's responses to the Easter Rising and its aftermath. Parkinson emphasized composition and revision. In *W. B. Yeats, Self-Critic* (1951), he analyzed revisions of the early poems to demonstrate the effects on the poet's lyric manner of his involvement in the theatre. According to Parkinson, playwriting taught Yeats to value dramatic conflict and thus tempered his attraction to cloudy reverie. Parkinson also stressed Yeats's commitment to dramatic conflict in his study of the composition, symbolism, and prosody of *The Later Poetry* (1964).

As the 1940s gave way to the fifties, sixties, and seventies, critics began to rethink Yeats's affiliation with the traditions of nineteenth-century British literature. This trend occurred in conjunction with a more general reassessment of literary modernism's relationship to Romantic writing. Following the lead of T. S. Eliot, the New Critics and their contemporaries had typically associated modernism with a rejection of Romantic precedents. As champions of modernism who wished to bolster its prestige by bringing Yeats into its ranks, they tended to underestimate his Romanticism while overstating his debt to the French symbolist influences valued by Eliot and his admirers. (Allen Tate exemplifies the first aspect of this tendency, Edmund Wilson the second.)[11] In 1947, Northrop Frye's influential "Yeats and the Language of Symbolism" called attention to the poet's Romantic inheritance.[12] Soon after, Graham Hough published *The Last Romantics* (1949), which set Yeats in the context of such Victorian figures as John Ruskin, D. G. Rossetti, William Morris, and Walter Pater. One of the subsequent works Frye's essay helped to inspire was Hazard Adams's *Blake and Yeats: The Contrary Vision* (1955). Adams concerns himself less with Blake's influence on Yeats than with comparing the two figures. In his view, Yeats found it more difficult to transcend the fallen world by visionary means, and many of his poems succeed artistically by dramatizing doubts and failures. Yeats's attitudes toward Shelley received attention in two important studies published in 1970, Harold Bloom's *Yeats* and George Bornstein's *Yeats and Shelley*. Bloom's provocative book tests the theories he later elaborated in *The Anxiety of Influence* (1973), reading Yeats's oeuvre as a series of creative "swerves" away from Romantic writers, Shelley and Blake in particular. Bornstein offers a more carefully delineated account of Yeats's readings and misreadings of Shelley. According to him, Yeats began as a devotee but grew less sympathetic after 1903, when he began to react against (and exaggerate) Shelley's ethereality. Bornstein's second book, *Transformations of Romanticism in Yeats, Eliot, and Stevens* (1976), placed Yeats in both Romantic and modernist contexts.[13] Others have augmented Hough's interest in late-nineteenth-century influences, including Frank Kermode in *Romantic Image* (1957) and Ian Fletcher in *W. B. Yeats and His Contemporaries* (1987).[14]

Meanwhile, critics were also considering a range of additional issues. Curtis Bradford's *Yeats at Work* (1965) extended Parkinson's inquiries into the textual histories of Yeats's writings, as did Jon Stallworthy's *Between the Lines: Yeats's Poetry in the Making* (1963) and *Vision and Revision in Yeats's "Last Poems"* (1969). Before the onset of the Cornell Yeats, critics who lacked direct access to the poet's manuscripts relied on these books for information about his compositional practices. In 1964, Edward Engelberg published *The Vast Design: Patterns in W. B. Yeats's Aesthetic*, which analyzes the poet's writings about art and artists in order to chart his development of a coherent theory of art. According to Engelberg, this theory increasingly emphasized the coming together of such opposing qualities as lyrical stillness and dramatic action. Also appearing in 1964 was Thomas R. Whitaker's *Swan and Shadow: Yeats's Dialogue with History*, which argues "that history was for Yeats a mysterious interlocutor, sometimes a bright reflection of the poet's self, sometimes a shadowy force opposed to that self."[15] Embracing both positions allowed Yeats to view history from a God's-eye perspective while also experiencing it dramatically; he thereby created fuller forms of selfhood and art than either stance permitted singly. Other important contributions came from Phillip L. Marcus, George Mills Harper, and James Olney. Marcus's *Yeats and the Beginning of the Irish Renaissance* (1970) gives a detailed account of the poet's activities and contemporaries in the 1890s. Three books by (or edited by) Harper – *Yeats's Golden Dawn* (1974), *Yeats and the Occult* (1976), and *The Making of Yeats's "A Vision": A Study of the Automatic Script* (2 vols., 1987) – put the study of Yeats's occultism on a more solid scholarly footing than had previously been achieved; the last of these offers a day-by-day description and explication of Yeats's visionary sessions with George.[16] Olney's *The Rhizome and the Flower: The Perennial Philosophy – Yeats and Jung* (1980) attributes parallels between Yeats and Carl Jung to sources in Plato, Platonic tradition, and such pre-Socratic philosophers as Pythagoras, Parmenides, Heraclitus, and Empedocles.

Yeats's plays received comparatively little consideration prior to the sixties and seventies. F. A. C. Wilson's *W. B. Yeats and Tradition* (1958) and Helen Vendler's *Yeats's "Vision" and the Later Plays* (1963) scrutinized the drama while concentrating mainly on its expression of Yeats's esoteric interests. (Vendler develops the provocative argument that *A Vision* can be read less as a statement of belief than as an exercise in literary history and poetic theory.) The specifically dramatic qualities of Yeats's plays attracted greater attention in David R. Clark's *W. B. Yeats and the Theatre of Desolate Reality* (1965) and Leonard Nathan's *The Tragic Drama of William Butler Yeats* (1965). Clark argues that *Deirdre, The Dreaming of the Bones, The Words upon the Window-Pane,* and *Purgatory* center on moments of intense perception; Nathan's more wide-ranging study describes Yeats's plays as dramatizations of the conflict between spiritual and physical realities. The mid-1970s saw a spate of additional books on Yeats's drama, including two by critics who had mounted productions of his plays. James W. Flannery's *W. B. Yeats and the Idea of a Theatre* (1976) focuses on the evolution of Yeats's theatrical theories during the early years of the Abbey and on his difficulties in actually staging the sorts of productions he had in mind; it also emphasizes his debts to such continental playwrights as Maeterlinck and to the English set-designer, Gordon Craig. Liam Miller's *The Noble Drama of W. B. Yeats* (1977) offers a fact-filled account of Yeats's theatre work, and features copious illustrations. Other useful books from this era include Richard Taylor's *The Drama of W. B. Yeats: Irish Myth and the Japanese Nō* (1976) and Katharine Worth's *The Irish Drama of Europe from Yeats to Beckett* (1978). Worth's book makes a strong case for Yeatsian influence on Samuel Beckett and Harold Pinter, among others. A more recent contribution to our understanding of Yeats's theatrical career is Adrian Frazier's *Behind the Scenes: Yeats, Horniman, and the Struggle for the Abbey Theatre* (1990).

By the early 1980s, the poet's politics had taken center stage. Prior to this point, the two most important considerations of Yeats's relationship to Irish history and politics had been Donald T. Torchiana's *W. B. Yeats and Georgian Ireland* (1966) and Conor Cruise O'Brien's "Passion and Cunning: An Essay on the Politics of W. B. Yeats" (1965).[17] Torchiana shows how Yeats's idealization of the eighteenth-century Protestant Ascendancy developed out of his disillusionment with nineteenth- and twentieth-century Ireland. He explores the poet's affiliation with Lady Gregory and with such figures as Swift, Burke, Berkeley, and Goldsmith.[18] O'Brien offers a far less sympathetic account of Yeats's politics; minimizing the sincerity of the poet's Irish nationalism, he charges Yeats with class prejudice, anti-Catholicism and thorough-going fascism. O'Brien's essay shocked many Yeatsians at the time of its first publication, which occurred amid celebrations of the poet's centenary. But during the next two decades, as newly skeptical forms of historicist criticism began to emerge, discussions of Yeats in particular – and of modernism and Irish culture in general – became more attentive to political matters. The eighties witnessed a series of books on Yeats's politics by such critics as Elizabeth Cullingford and Paul Scott Stanfield. Cullingford's *Yeats, Ireland and Fascism* (1981) answers O'Brien's critique by charting the evolution of Yeats's politics and by stressing the complexity of his views. Emphasizing the influence of John O'Leary's individualist nationalism and William Morris's socialism as well as the tentativeness of the poet's attraction to the Blueshirts, she concludes that, basically, Yeats espoused "an aristocratic liberalism that combined love of individual freedom with respect for the ties of the organic social group."[19] Stanfield's *Yeats and Politics in the 1930s* (1988) uncovers additional details about Yeats's final decade and offers an illuminating account of his views of de Valera.

Meanwhile, other politically minded critics were placing Yeats in the context of revisionist histories of modernism and Irish literature. Cairns Craig's *Yeats, Eliot, Pound, and the Politics of Poetry* (1981) argues that all three of its subjects regarded art as incompatible with democracy, while Michael North's *The Political Aesthetic of Yeats, Eliot, and Pound* (1991) considers parallels between Yeats's "cultural nationalism," Eliot's "conservatism," and Pound's "fascism." North's book draws on critiques developed in the seventies and eighties by Irish critics whose proximity to Northern Ireland's violent "Troubles" made them acutely mistrustful of the poet's anti-Catholic, pro-Ascendancy leanings. These included W. J. McCormack, Richard Kearney, Declan Kiberd, and above all Seamus Deane. McCormack debunked Yeats's idealizations of the Anglo-Irish Ascendancy; Kearney reproved him for valorizing a nationalist mythos of blood sacrifice; Kiberd argued that he had subjected modern Ireland to debilitating nostalgia.[20] Deane's writings – as exemplified by "Heroic Styles: The Tradition of an Idea" (1984) and *Celtic Revivals* (1985) – accused Yeats and other Anglo-Irish contributors to the Irish Literary Revival of being "literary Unionists" who shored up the decaying fortunes of their privileged class by writing texts that "[transferred] the blame for the drastic condition of the country from the Ascendancy to the Catholic middle classes or to their English counterparts."[21] The hostility expressed by Deane and other revisionists began to dissipate somewhat after Edward W. Said's lecture on "Yeats and Decolonization" at the annual Yeats International Summer School in Sligo in 1986, a lecture subsequently published in *Culture and Imperialism* (1993). Said reminded his listeners that writers in many recently decolonized countries regarded Yeats as an imperfect but inspiring model of resistance to colonial oppression. One of the most influential works to appear in the wake of Said's intervention was Kiberd's *Inventing Ireland* (1995), which develops an impressively nuanced application of "postcolonial theory" to Yeats and other nineteenth- and twentieth-century Irish writers.[22] The applicability of such theory to Yeats continues to be debated, as in Jahan Ramazani's "Is Yeats a Postcolonial Poet?" (1998) and the collection edited by Deborah Fleming entitled *W. B. Yeats and Postcolonialism* (2001).[23] Jonathan Allison's *Yeats's Political Identities* (1996) offers an introduction to the earlier revisionist debate by bringing together excerpts from the work of O'Brien, Cullingford, Deane, and others; it includes a useful annotated bibliography describing additional discussions of Yeats's politics.

It took a surprisingly long time for discussions of Yeats's politics to incorporate feminist assessments of his attitudes about gender and sex. Gloria C. Kline's *The Last Courtly Lover* established a starting point in 1983 by overviewing his relationships with women and by investigating his pre-occupation with feminine archetypes from the traditions of courtly love.[24] A more thorough-going breakthrough came with Elizabeth Cullingford's *Gender and History in Yeats's Love Poetry* (1993). Balancing skepticism with appreciation, Cullingford shows how the women in Yeats's life and the sexual politics of his era conditioned his adaptations of love poetry's sexist conventions. She stresses his friendships with assertive women and his tendency to identify with femininity, and she relates these biographical phenomena to such contexts as the emancipation of women, the decolonization of Ireland, and the censorious sexual Puritanism of the Irish Free State. Cullingford's book was followed by Marjorie Howes's *Yeats's Nations: Gender, Class, and Irishness* (1996) and Deirdre Toomey's edited collection, *Yeats and Women* (1997).[25] Howes's book uses feminist and postcolonial theory to examine how issues of gender and class affected Yeats's changing conceptions of Irishness; she takes up some of the same questions as Cullingford, but focuses on different texts, including *The Countess Cathleen*, such "Big House" poems as "Ancestral Houses," and *Purgatory*. Highlights from Toomey's collection include her own essays on Yeats's relationships with Maud Gonne and with his mother; they also include two essays by James Pethica on Lady Gregory's material support for the poet and her part in writing *Cathleen ni Houlihan*. Vicki Mahaffey's *States of Desire* (1998) makes another noteworthy contribution; it argues that Wilde, Yeats, and Joyce conducted verbal experiments designed to undermine authoritarian understandings of such constructs as nationality, class, gender, and sexual preference.

Another long-term trend in Yeats studies involves examining the poet's books as integral units inhabiting significant physical forms. Hugh Kenner began this trend in his 1955 essay, "The Sacred Book of the Arts," which describes the thematic and imagistic links between the poems of volumes like *The Tower* as constituting carefully arranged dramatic progressions.[26] According to Kenner, Yeats "didn't accumulate poems, he wrote books" (14). John Unterecker applied Kenner's approach to Yeats's entire collected *Poems* in *A Reader's Guide to William Butler Yeats* (1959), as did Hazard Adams in *The Book of Yeats's Poems* (1990). Unterecker offers an introductory, poem-by-poem account; Adams's more theoretically sophisticated analysis reads the *Poems* as Yeats's attempt to construct a fictive version of his life story. Several other critics have produced in-depth studies of one or more of Yeats's books. Allen R. Grossman's *Poetic Knowledge in the Early Yeats* (1969) elucidates the mythic structure of *The Wind Among the Reeds*, while Steven Putzel's *Reconstructing Yeats* (1986) treats both *The Wind Among the Reeds* and *The Secret Rose*. David Young's *Troubled Mirror* (1987) focuses on

The Tower. More recently, critics have connected the study of Yeats's books to assessments of his politics and to ongoing debates about the status of his texts' various versions. Building on George Bornstein's essay "What Is the Text of a Poem by Yeats?" (1993), David Holdeman's *Much Labouring: The Texts and Authors of Yeats's First Modernist Books* (1997) examines the verbal and physical texts of several books from the poet's middle period, arguing that their modernism, nationalism, and gender politics were conditioned by Yeats's revisions and interactions with publishers.[27] Bornstein's *Material Modernism* (2001) shows how the physical embodiments of various modernist works attached political and other connotations to them; his two chapters on Yeats focus on "When You are Old," "September 1913," and *The Tower.* Yug Mohit Chaudhry's *Yeats, the Irish Literary Revival and the Politics of Print* (2001) analyzes periodical printings of the early work. He offers a less sympathetic account than either Holdeman or Bornstein, objecting in particular to Bornstein's claim that "September 1913" implied solidarity with striking workers when printed amid coverage of the strike in the *Irish Times.*

Though many additional studies merit discussion, only a few more can be mentioned here. The two most noteworthy examinations of the poet's interest in folklore are Mary Helen Thuente's *W. B. Yeats and Irish Folklore* (1980) and Frank Kinahan's *Yeats, Folklore, and Occultism* (1988). Giorgio Melchiori's *The Whole Mystery of Art* (1960) traces pictorial (and other) sources for such poems as "Leda and the Swan," while Elizabeth Bergmann Loizeaux's *Yeats and the Visual Arts* (1986) correlates Yeats's development with changes in his thinking about painting and sculpture. In different ways, both Wayne K. Chapman's *Yeats and English Renaissance Literature* (1991) and David Pierce's *Yeats's Worlds* (1995) stress English influences; the latter provides a beautifully illustrated overview of the poet's life and work that also considers Irish contexts. Daniel T. O'Hara's *Tragic Knowledge* (1981) applies the theories of Paul Ricoeur to Yeats's autobiography, while Paul de Man's deconstructive approach exemplifies itself in *The Rhetoric of Romanticism* (1984).[28] Douglas Archibald's *Yeats* (1983), Phillip L. Marcus's *Yeats and Artistic Power* (1992), and Michael J. Sidnell's *Yeats's Poetry and Poetics* (1996) offer wide-ranging, insightful commentary. Several recent books, including Steven Matthews's *Yeats as Precursor* (1999), address the poet's impact on other writers, a matter previously taken up in Terence Diggory's *Yeats and American Poetry* (1983).

Readers interested in learning more about Yeats's critics should begin by consulting the relevant chapters in Richard J. Finneran's *Anglo-Irish Literature: A Review of Research* (1976) and *Recent Research on Anglo-Irish Writers* (1983).

They should then press on to David Pierce's *W. B. Yeats: A Guide through the Critical Maze* (1989) and *W. B. Yeats: Critical Assessments* (2000). They should also examine the essays and reviews in *Yeats Annual* and *Yeats: An Annual of Critical and Textual Studies*. Though the vast quantity of extant scholarship may make it seem like nothing remains to be said, the critical conversation continues. Writing about Yeats has become an important way for people interested in literature and culture to reflect on the modern world, and the need for fresh assessments of his work seems unlikely to diminish soon.

Notes

1 Early Yeats

1. Pronunciations provided in this book are approximate. For precise phonetic equivalents, see "Appendix Five: Pronunciation," in *Yeats's Poems* (Macmillan, 1989), ed. A. Norman Jeffares.
2. The resources for making such comparisons are discussed in Chapter 4.
3. *The Complete Poetry and Prose of William Blake*, ed. David V. Erdman (Doubleday, 1988), 565. *Shelley's Poetry and Prose*, ed. Donald H. Reiman and Sharon B. Powers (Norton, 1977), 93.
4. See *The Field Day Anthology of Irish Writing*, vol. II, ed. Seamus Deane, Andrew Carpenter, and Jonathan Williams (Field Day Publications, 1991), 28–29 and 51–52.
5. Anon., *The Freeman's Journal* (February 1, 1889), 2.
6. *Pall Mall Gazette* (July 12, 1889), 3.
7. *The Collected Letters of W. B. Yeats, Volume I: 1865–1895*, ed. John Kelly and Eric Domville (Clarendon, 1986), 30.
8. Yeats initially preferred the spelling "Kathleen," but later opted for "Cathleen."
9. James Joyce, *Ulysses*, ed. Hans Walter Gabler (Random House, 1986), 403.
10. *The Complete Poetry and Prose of William Blake*, 1. For Blake's "universal Poetic Genius," Yeats preferred such terms as "Universal Mind," "great mind," "great memory," "anima mundi" ("soul of the world"), and "spiritus mundi" ("spirit of the world").
11. Ibid., 34.
12. *The Academy* 42:1065 (October 1, 1892), 278–79.
13. "Aedh" is an identically pronounced, variant spelling of "Aodh."
14. *The Collected Letters of W. B. Yeats, Volume II: 1896–1900*, ed. Warwick Gould, John Kelly, and Deirdre Toomey (Clarendon, 1997), 424.
15. *Ulysses*, 475.
16. *The Saturday Review* (May 6, 1899), 553–54.
17. *The Collected Letters, Volume II*, 320.

2 Middle Yeats

1. *19th Century British Minor Poets* (Delacorte, 1966), 16.
2. "Baile" is pronounced "BOLL-ya."
3. *The Collected Letters of W. B. Yeats, Volume III: 1901–1904*, ed. John Kelly and Ronald Schuchard (Clarendon, 1994), 167.
4. Ibid., 303.
5. The oath and several details mentioned below are drawn from revised versions of the play.
6. A spurious offshoot of evolutionary theory, the eugenics movement sought to safeguard the bloodlines of Anglo-Saxon and Nordic "races" by preventing interbreeding with blacks, Jews, the Irish, and the peoples of southern and eastern Europe; it also sought to limit the reproductive rights of criminals and of the mentally and physically handicapped. Between 1910 and 1930 it enjoyed considerable success, particularly in the United States, where it inspired laws restricting interracial marriage and immigration. Yeats's most notorious consideration of these matters occurs in *On the Boiler* (1939; discussed in Chapter 3).
7. *The Collected Works of W. B. Yeats, Volume VIII: The Irish Dramatic Movement*, ed. Mary FitzGerald and Richard J. Finneran (Scribner, 2003), 27.
8. See Chapter 3, 72–73.
9. "Aillinn" is pronounced "ALL-yin."
10. *Selected Prose of T. S. Eliot*, ed. Frank Kermode (Harcourt, 1975), 177.
11. Ibid., 251.
12. *Essays and Introductions* (Collier, 1968), 271 and 272. *Discoveries* should be compared with the poet's first major critical collection, *Ideas of Good and Evil* (1903), where such essays as "Magic" and "The Symbolism of Poetry" sum up his early beliefs about the universal mind and its evocation through symbols.
13. *A Portrait of the Artist as a Young Man*, ed. R. B. Kershner (Bedford, 1983), 187.
14. *Selected Prose of T. S. Eliot*, 38.
15. See, for example, the statement in Wilde's "The Critic as Artist" (1890) that "Man is least himself when he talks in his own person. Give him a mask, and he will tell you the truth" (*Collins Complete Works of Oscar Wilde* [HarperCollins, 1999], 1142). Nietzsche employs mask metaphors in such works as *Beyond Good and Evil* (1886), where he writes that "Everything deep loves a mask" (trans. Marion Faber [Oxford University Press, 1998], 38).
16. *Memoirs: Autobiography – First Draft: Journal*, ed. Denis Donoghue (Macmillan, 1972), 137–38 and 142.
17. "The Later Yeats," *Poetry* (Chicago), 4:2 (May 1914), 64–69.
18. Ibid.
19. *Selected Prose of T. S. Eliot*, 251.
20. The volume originally followed "The Grey Rock" with "The Two Kings," a second mythological poem that some versions of Yeats's oeuvre position outside of *Responsibilities*.

3 Late Yeats

1. Robartes appears in many early works, including "Rosa Alchemica"; for Aherne, see "The Tables of the Law."
2. One accessible starting point is Yeats's introduction to *A Vision* (1937). Another is *The Trembling of the Veil* (1922), a section of the poet's *Autobiographies* written while he was first developing his new theories.
3. Yeats ultimately wrote five Cuchulain plays. Arranged in the order by which they tell Cuchulain's story, these are *At the Hawk's Well* (1917), *The Green Helmet* (1910), *On Baile's Strand* (1904), *The Only Jealousy of Emer* (1919), and *The Death of Cuchulain* (1939).
4. *Essays and Introductions*, 225.
5. *The Collected Works of W. B. Yeats, Volume X: Later Articles and Reviews*, ed. Colton Johnson (Scribner, 2000), 173.
6. *The Senate Speeches of W. B. Yeats*, ed. Donald R. Pearce (Indiana University Press, 1960), 99.
7. Norreys Jephson O'Conor, "A New Yeats Collection," *Bookman* (September 1924), 91.
8. *Literary Essays of Ezra Pound* (New Directions, 1968), 3.
9. These were *Seven Poems and a Fragment* (1922), *The Cat and the Moon and Certain Poems* (1924), and *October Blast* (1927). *The Tower* also included one poem not in any of these books, "Colonus' Praise."
10. *A Vision* (1937; Collier, 1966), 279. For the 1925 version of *A Vision*, see *A Critical Edition of Yeats's "A Vision" (1925)*, ed. George Mills Harper and Walter Kelly Hood (Macmillan, 1978).
11. Ibid., 279–80.
12. See the end of Yeats's play *The Resurrection* (1931). This formulation – derived from Heraclitus – also occurs in both versions of *A Vision* and in *On the Boiler* (1938).
13. For Yeats's story "Red Hanrahan" (1903), see SR.
14. Edmund Burke (1729–97), Dublin-born statesman and political thinker. Henry Grattan (1746–1820), leader of the Irish Parliament prior to the Act of Union (1800) between Great Britain and Ireland.
15. Section IV refers to "seven years ago," i.e. 1912, when the third Home Rule bill first passed the House of Commons.
16. For such octaves, see the second part of "The Tower," the final part of "Meditations," and "Two Songs from a Play." For the ten-line stanza, see the second part of "Meditations," the second and third parts of "Nineteen Hundred and Nineteen," and "All Souls' Night."
17. *Nation & Athenaeum*, (April 21, 1928), 81.
18. See *The Winding Stair (1929): Manuscript Materials by W. B. Yeats*, ed. David R. Clark (Cornell University Press, 1995), 43.
19. For a definition of eugenics, see Chapter 2, note 6.

20. *Essays and Introductions*, 28.
21. Some versions of Yeats's *Poems* present these lyrics under the heading of "From *A Full Moon in March.*" Others use the rubric "Parnell's Funeral and Other Poems." Yeats died before he could incorporate these poems into a collected edition and thereby establish his preference.
22. This interest derived from Yeats's recent friendship with Shri Purohit Swami, with whom he translated *The Ten Principal Upanishads* (1937).
23. An anonymous ballad on "The Battle of the Boyne" in *Irish Minstrelsy*, ed. H. Halliday Sparling (Walter Scott, 1888) tells how "King William threw his bomb-balls in."

4 Yeats's critics

1. Finneran explains his views in *Editing Yeats's Poems: A Reconsideration* (St. Martin's Press, 1990). Warwick Gould defends Jeffares's position in an appendix to *Yeats's Poems*.
2. Published by Cornell University Press, the Cornell Yeats includes at present: Alison Armstrong, ed., *The Herne's Egg* (1993); George Bornstein, ed., *The Early Poetry, Volume I: "Mosada" and "The Island of Statues"* (1987) and *The Early Poetry, Volume II: "The Wanderings of Oisin" and Other Early Poems to 1895* (1994); Wayne K. Chapman, ed., *"The Dreaming of the Bones" and "Calvary"* (2003); David R. Clark, ed., *"Parnell's Funeral and Other Poems" from "A Full Moon in March"* (2003), *The Winding Stair (1929)* (1995), and *Words for Music Perhaps and Other Poems* (1999); Jared Curtis, ed., *The Land of Heart's Desire* (2002); Mary FitzGerald, ed., *The Words Upon the Window Pane* (2002); David Holdeman, ed., *"In the Seven Woods" and "The Green Helmet and Other Poems"* (2002); Carolyn Holdsworth, ed., *The Wind Among the Reeds* (1993); Phillip L. Marcus, ed., *The Death of Cuchulain* (1982); J. C. C. Mays and Stephen Parrish, eds., *New Poems* (2000); William H. O'Donnell, ed., *Responsibilities* (2003); Thomas Parkinson, ed., with Anne Brannen, *Michael Robartes and the Dancer* (1994); Stephen Parrish, ed., *The Wild Swans at Coole* (1994); James Pethica, ed., *Last Poems* (1997); Catherine Phillips, ed., *The Hour-Glass* (1994); Virginia Bartholome Rohan, ed., *Deirdre* (2004); Michael J. Sidnell and Wayne K. Chapman, eds., *The Countess Cathleen* (1999); Sandra F. Siegel, ed., *Purgatory* (1986); and Steven Winnett, ed., *"The Only Jealousy of Emer" and "Fighting the Waves"* (2004).
3. Warwick Gould, Phillip L. Marcus, and Michael J. Sidnell are the editors for *The Secret Rose, Stories by W. B. Yeats: A Variorum Edition* (Macmillan, 1992). The four volumes of *Yeats's "Vision" Papers* are edited by Steve L. Adams, Barbara J. Frieling, and Sandra L. Sprayberry (vols. I–II, University of Iowa Press, 1992), Robert A. Martinich and Margaret Mills Harper (vol. III, University of Iowa Press, 1992), and George Mills Harper and Margaret Mills Harper (vol. IV,

Palgrave, 2001). Denis Donoghue is the editor of *Memoirs: Autobiography – First Draft: Journal* (Macmillan, 1972).

4. Published by Scribner and Macmillan, *The Collected Works of W. B. Yeats* thus far includes: *Vol. I: The Poems, Revised*, ed. Richard J. Finneran (1989); *Vol. II: The Plays*, ed. David R. Clark and Rosalind E. Clark (2001); *Vol. III: Autobiographies*, ed. William H. O'Donnell and Douglas N. Archibald (1999); *Vol. V: Later Essays*, ed. William H. O'Donnell (1994); *Vol. VI: Prefaces and Introductions*, ed. William H. O'Donnell (1989); *Vol. VII: Letters to the New Island*, ed. George Bornstein and Hugh Witemeyer (1989); *Vol. VIII: The Irish Dramatic Movement*, ed. Mary FitzGerald and Richard J. Finneran (2003); *Vol. IX: Early Articles and Reviews*, ed. John P. Frayne and Madeleine Marchaterre (2004); *Vol. X: Later Articles and Reviews*, ed. Colton Johnson (2000); and *Vol. XII: John Sherman and Dhoya*, ed. Richard J. Finneran (1991).

5. Despite their similar titles, *Yeats: An Annual of Critical and Textual Studies* and *Yeats Annual* are two different publications. Deirdre Toomey's essays on Maud Gonne and on Yeats's mother originally appeared in *Yeats Annual* 9 (1992) and *Yeats Annual* 10 (1993); both were subsequently reprinted in *Yeats and Women*, ed. Toomey (Macmillan, 1997). Another useful source of biographical information is John Kelly's *A W. B. Yeats Chronology* (Palgrave, 2003).

6. These are edited by John Kelly and Eric Domville (*Volume I: 1865–1895* [1986]); Warwick Gould, John Kelly, and Deirdre Toomey (*Volume II: 1896–1900* [1997]); and John Kelly and Ronald Schuchard (*Volume III: 1901–1904* [1994]). All three volumes are published by Clarendon Press.

7. Further editions of Yeats's correspondence include: Ursula Bridge, ed., *W. B. Yeats and T. Sturge Moore: Their Correspondence, 1901–1937* (Oxford University Press, 1953); Richard J. Finneran, ed., *The Correspondence of Robert Bridges and W. B. Yeats* (Macmillan, 1977); Roger McHugh, ed., *"Ah, Sweet Dancer": W. B. Yeats/ Margot Ruddock, A Correspondence* (Macmillan, 1970); Ann Saddlemyer, ed., *Theatre Business: The Correspondence of the First Abbey Theatre Directors: William Butler Yeats, Lady Gregory, and J. M. Synge* (Pennsylvania State University Press, 1982); Anna MacBride White and A. Norman Jeffares, eds., *The Gonne-Yeats Letters, 1893–1938* (Norton, 1993); and Dorothy Wellesley, ed., *Letters on Poetry from W. B. Yeats to Dorothy Wellesley* (1940; intro. Kathleen Raine, Oxford University Press, 1964).

8. See *Lady Gregory's Diaries, 1892–1902*, ed. James Pethica (Oxford University Press, 1996); *Lady Gregory's Journals*, 2 vols., ed. Daniel J. Murphy (Colin Smythe, 1978 and 1987); *Our Irish Theatre: A Chapter of Autobiography* (1913; intro. Roger McHugh, Colin Smythe, 1972); and *Seventy Years: Being the Autobiography of Lady Gregory*, ed. Colin Smythe (Macmillan, 1976).

9. For Auden's poem, "In Memory of W. B. Yeats," see *W. H. Auden, Collected Poems*, ed. Edward Mendelson (Random House, 1976), 197–98; for his essay, "The Public Vs. The Late Mr. William Butler Yeats," see *Partisan Review* 6 (Spring 1939), 46–51.

10. *The Poetry of W. B. Yeats* (Swallow, 1960).

11. See Allen Tate, "Yeats's Romanticism: Notes and Suggestions," *The Southern Review* 7:3 (Winter 1942), 591–600 (rpt. in *The Permanence of Yeats: Selected Criticism*, ed. James Hall and Martin Steinmann [Macmillan, 1950]). See also Edmund Wilson, *Axel's Castle: A Study in the Imaginative Literature of 1870–1930* (Scribner, 1931).

12. Northrop Frye, "Yeats and the Language of Symbolism," *University of Toronto Quarterly* 17:1 (October 1947), 1–17.

13. Other studies of Yeats and modernism include Daniel Albright's *Quantum Poetics: Yeats, Pound, Eliot, and the Science of Modernism* (Cambridge University Press, 1997), Donald J. Childs's *Modernist Eugenics: Woolf, Eliot, Yeats, and the Culture of Degeneration* (Cambridge University Press, 2001), James Longenbach's *Stone Cottage: Pound, Yeats, and Modernism* (Oxford University Press, 1988), and C. K. Stead's *The New Poetic: Yeats to Eliot* (Hutchinson University Library, 1964). See also the studies by Craig, North, and Mahaffey mentioned below.

14. Nietzsche's influence receives extensive treatment in Otto Bohlmann's *Yeats and Nietzsche* (Barnes and Noble, 1982) and in Frances Nesbitt Oppel's *Mask and Tragedy: Yeats and Nietzsche, 1902–1910* (University Press of Virginia, 1987).

15. Thomas R. Whitaker, *Swan and Shadow: Yeats's Dialogue with History* (University of North Carolina Press, 1964), 4.

16. For additional analysis of Yeats's occult beliefs and *A Vision*, see Kathleen Raine's *Yeats the Initiate* (Dolmen, 1986) and Hazard Adams's *The Book of Yeats's Vision* (University of Michigan Press, 1995).

17. O'Brien's essay appeared in *In Excited Reverie: A Centenary Tribute to William Butler Yeats, 1865–1939*, ed. A. Norman Jeffares and K. G. W. Cross (Macmillan, 1965), 207–78.

18. See also Daniel A. Harris's *Yeats: Coole Park and Ballylee* (Johns Hopkins University Press, 1974).

19. Elizabeth Butler Cullingford, *Yeats, Ireland and Fascism* (New York University Press, 1981), 235.

20. See W. J. McCormack, *Ascendancy and Tradition in Anglo-Irish Literary History from 1789 to 1939* (Clarendon Press, 1985); Richard Kearney, "Myth and Terror," *Crane Bag* 2:1–2 (1978), 125–39; and Declan Kiberd, "The War against the Past," in *The Uses of the Past: Essays on Irish Culture*, ed. Audrey S. Eyler and Robert F. Garratt (University of Delaware Press, 1988), 24–54.

21. "Heroic Styles: The Tradition of an Idea" as reprinted in *Ireland's Field Day*, ed. Seamus Deane et al. (Hutchinson, 1985), 48.

22. For another important treatment of some of the same themes, see G. J. Watson's *Irish Identity and the Literary Revival* (1979; Catholic University of America Press, 1994).

23. Jahan Ramazani, "Is Yeats a Postcolonial Poet?" *Raritan* 17:3 (Winter 1998), 64–89. See also Deborah Fleming's *"A man who does not exist": The Irish Peasant in the Work of W. B. Yeats and J. M. Synge* (University of Michigan Press, 1995).

24. For another study emphasizing feminine archetypes, see Patrick J. Keane's *Terrible Beauty: Yeats, Joyce, Ireland, and the Myth of the Devouring Female* (University of Missouri Press, 1988).

25. Many of the essays in *Yeats and Women* are reprinted from *Yeats Annual* 9 (1992), edited by Toomey and devoted to the topic of "Yeats and Women."

26. Hugh Kenner, "The Sacred Book of the Arts," *Irish Writing* 31 (1955), 24–35. Rpt. in his *Gnomon: Essays on Contemporary Literature* (Obolensky, 1958), 9–29.

27. For Bornstein's essay, see *Palimpsest: Editorial Theory in the Humanities*, ed. Bornstein and Ralph G. Williams (University of Michigan Press, 1993), 167–93.

28. For a broader sample of theoretical approaches, see Leonard Orr, ed., *Yeats and Postmodernism* (Syracuse University Press, 1991).

Guide to further reading

The following selection lists a number of critical and biographical studies that would make especially good starting points for students who wish to read more about Yeats. For discussion of these and other studies – and of such important resources as critical editions of the poet's writings – see Chapter 4.

Adams, Hazard. *Blake and Yeats: The Contrary Vision.* Cornell University Press, 1955. Compares Yeats to one of his most important precursors.

    The Book of Yeats's Poems. Florida State University Press, 1990. Reads the collected *Poems* as Yeats's attempt to construct a fictive version of his life story.

Albright, Daniel. *Quantum Poetics: Yeats, Pound, Eliot, and the Science of Modernism.* Cambridge University Press, 1997. Considers how modernist poetry was influenced by modern physics.

Allison, Jonathan, ed. *Yeats's Political Identities.* University of Michigan Press, 1996. Collects various important critical discussions of Yeats's politics.

Archibald, Douglas. *Yeats.* Syracuse University Press, 1983. A wide-ranging survey of the poet's career; includes valuable accounts of many major poems.

Bloom, Harold. *Yeats.* Oxford University Press, 1970. Reads Yeats's oeuvre as a series of creative "swerves" away from Romantic writers, especially Blake and Shelley.

Bornstein, George. *Yeats and Shelley.* University of Chicago Press, 1970. A carefully delineated account of Yeats's readings and misreadings of Shelley.

Brown, Terence. *The Life of W. B. Yeats: A Critical Biography.* Blackwell, 1999. A good option for those in need of a briefer biography than Foster's.

Childs, Donald J. *Modernist Eugenics: Woolf, Eliot, Yeats, and the Culture of Degeneration.* Cambridge University Press, 2001. Describes eugenics as a pervasive influence on early-twentieth-century culture; includes a lengthy chapter on Yeats.

Cullingford, Elizabeth Butler. *Gender and History in Yeats's Love Poetry.* Cambridge University Press, 1993. The first full-length feminist study of Yeats.

    Yeats, Ireland and Fascism. New York University Press, 1981. Charts the evolution of Yeats's politics, emphasizing the influence of John O'Leary and William Morris.

Deane, Seamus. *Celtic Revivals: Essays in Modern Irish Literature, 1880–1980.* Faber and Faber, 1985. Includes "Yeats and the Idea of Revolution."

Donoghue, Denis. *William Butler Yeats.* Viking, 1971. A valuable introduction by one of Ireland's best-known critics; emphasizes Nietzsche's influence.

Ellmann, Richard. *The Identity of Yeats.* Oxford University Press, 1954. An early and influential exploration of the patterns of thought and mood underlying the evolution of Yeats's diction, imagery, and symbolism.

Yeats: The Man and the Masks. 1948. Norton, 1979. A seminal early study. Focuses on the poet's struggle to unify his identity, emphasizing his occult studies and the influence of his father.

Engelberg, Edward. *The Vast Design: Patterns in W. B. Yeats's Aesthetic.* University of Toronto Press, 1964. Analyzes Yeats's writings about art and artists in order to chart his development of a coherent theory of art.

Flannery, James W. *W. B. Yeats and the Idea of a Theatre: The Early Abbey Theatre in Theory and Practice.* Yale University Press, 1976. Focuses on Yeats's theatrical theories during the early years of the Abbey Theatre and on his difficulties in actually staging the sorts of productions he had in mind.

Fletcher, Ian. *W. B. Yeats and His Contemporaries.* St. Martin's, 1987. Stresses late-nineteenth-century influences.

Foster, R. F. *W. B. Yeats: A Life, Volume I: The Apprentice Mage, 1865–1914,* and *Volume II: The Arch-Poet, 1915–1939.* Oxford University Press, 1997 and 2003. The most comprehensive, reliable, and even-handed biography.

Harwood, John. *Olivia Shakespear and W. B. Yeats: After Long Silence.* St. Martin's, 1989. Sheds light on the poet's relationships with women and on his nineties work.

Harper, George Mills. *Yeats's Golden Dawn.* Macmillan, 1974. A detailed account of Yeats's involvement in the internal affairs of the Order of the Golden Dawn.

Harper, George Mills, ed. *Yeats and the Occult.* Macmillan, 1976. Collects informative scholarly essays by various hands as well as several important texts by Yeats himself.

Howes, Marjorie. *Yeats's Nations: Gender, Class, and Irishness.* Cambridge University Press, 1996. Employs feminist and postcolonial theory to examine how issues of gender and class affected Yeats's changing conceptions of Irishness.

Kiberd, Declan. *Inventing Ireland: The Literature of the Modern Nation.* Harvard University Press, 1995. A sweeping, influential application of postcolonial theory to modern Irish literature; includes several chapters on Yeats.

Loizeaux, Elizabeth Bergmann. *Yeats and the Visual Arts.* Rutgers University Press, 1986. Correlates the poet's development with changes in his thinking about painting and sculpture.

Longenbach, James. *Stone Cottage: Pound, Yeats, and Modernism.* Oxford University Press, 1988. The most thorough treatment of Yeats's relationship with Pound.

MacNeice, Louis. *The Poetry of W. B. Yeats.* 1941. Oxford University Press, 1969. An important early study. Argues that Yeats's interest in Irish realities gradually forced him to synthesize his Romantic and esoteric fantasies with keen attention to everyday life.

Marcus, Phillip L. *Yeats and the Beginning of the Irish Renaissance.* Cornell University Press, 1970. A detailed account of the poet's activities and contemporaries in the 1890s.

Miller, Liam. *The Noble Drama of W. B. Yeats.* Dolmen, 1977. A fact-filled account of Yeats's theatre work, featuring copious illustrations.

Olney, James. *The Rhizome and the Flower: The Perennial Philosophy – Yeats and Jung.* University of California Press, 1980. Attributes parallels between Yeats and Jung to sources in Plato, Platonic tradition, and pre-Socratic philosophy.

Parkinson, Thomas. *W. B. Yeats, Self Critic: A Study of His Early Verse.* University of California Press, 1951. Analyzes revisions of the early poems to demonstrate the effects on the poet's lyric manner of his involvement in the theatre.

W. B. Yeats: The Later Poetry. University of California Press, 1964. Examines the composition, symbolism, and prosody of the later poetry, stressing Yeats's commitment to dramatic conflict.

Pierce, David. *Yeats's Worlds: Ireland, England and the Poetic Imagination.* Yale University Press, 1995. A beautifully illustrated overview of the poet's life and work that considers both Irish and English contexts.

Thuente, Mary Helen. *W. B. Yeats and Irish Folklore.* Gill and Macmillan, 1980. The best book on its topic.

Toomey, Deirdre, ed. *Yeats and Women.* Macmillan, 1997. Partly rpt. from *Yeats and Women: Yeats Annual No. 9,* 1992. Collects important essays on Yeats's relationships with his mother, Maud Gonne, Lady Gregory, and others.

Torchiana, Donald T. *W. B. Yeats and Georgian Ireland.* Northwestern University Press, 1966. Shows how Yeats's idealization of the eighteenth-century Ascendancy developed out of his disillusionment with nineteenth- and twentieth-century Ireland.

Unterecker, John. *A Reader's Guide to William Butler Yeats.* Noonday, 1959. An important early attempt to read Yeats's collected *Poems* as a carefully arranged oeuvre.

Vendler, Helen. *Yeats's "Vision" and the Later Plays.* Harvard University Press, 1963. Explores the later plays in relation to Yeats's esoteric interests, arguing that *A Vision* can be read as an exercise in literary history and poetic theory.

Watson, G. J. *Irish Identity and the Literary Revival: Synge, Yeats, Joyce and O'Casey.* 1979. Catholic University of America Press, 1994. A path-breaking account of Irish identity in the work of four important writers.

Whitaker, Thomas R. *Swan and Shadow: Yeats's Dialogue with History.* University of North Carolina Press, 1964. Discusses Yeats's conceptions of history.

Index

The entry for "Yeats, William Butler" includes references to his works and nothing more. Entries concerning his attitudes or experiences – such as the ones for "afterlife" or "illnesses" – are interspersed throughout the main body of this index.

Achebe, Chinua, 77
Adams, Hazard, 120, 124, 132 n. 16
Adams, Steve L., 130 n. 3
AE, *see* Russell, George
afterlife, reincarnation, *or* lunar phases: in "Shepherd and Goatherd" and "The Phases of the Moon," 68–70; and dancer symbolism, 76; and *The Tower*, 81; and "Nineteen Hundred and Nineteen," 88; and "Among School Children," 91; and *The Cat and the Moon*, 94; and "A Dialogue of Self and Soul," 94–96; and "Blood and the Moon," 96; and "Byzantium," 97–98; and "Crazy Jane and Jack the Journeyman," 99; and "In Memory of Eva Gore-Booth and Con Markievicz," 100; and *On the Boiler*, 103; and Yeats's late aggressiveness, 105; and "Under Ben Bulben," 109; and "Cuchulain Comforted," 111; and *Purgatory*, 112–13
aisling, 31, 41
Albright, Daniel, 132 n. 13
Allingham, William, 12
Allison, Jonathan, 123

Allt, Peter, 116
Alspach, Russell K., 116
Anglo-Irish War, *see* War of Independence
Anglo-Irish, *see* Catholics *or* Catholicism, Protestants *or* Protestantism
Archibald, Douglas, 125, 131 n. 4
aristocracy: and *The Countess Cathleen*, 15; and Lady Gregory, 38–39; and *On Baile's Strand*, 43–44; and *The King's Threshold*, 44–45; and masks, 53; and *The Green Helmet*, 55; and *The Green Helmet and Other Poems*, 57; and "To a Wealthy Man ...," 60; and Noh drama, 72, 73; and the Gore-Booth sisters, 74–75; and "The Second Coming," 77; and "The Tower," 85; and "Ancestral Houses," 85; and the Blueshirts, 102; and *Purgatory*, 112–13; discussed by Yeats's critics, 122, 123; *see also* Catholics *or* Catholicism, Protestants *or* Protestantism *and* eugenics
Aristotle, 90
Armstrong, Alison, 130 n. 2
Auden, W. H., 36, 118, 119

Beardsley, Aubrey, 24, 67
Beardsley, Mabel, 67
Beckett, Samuel, 122
Berkeley, George, 96, 97, 122
Blackmur, R. P., 119
Blake, William, 6, 8, 12, 17–18, 25,
    62, 120
Blavatsky, Madame Helena
    Petrovna, 5, 18
Bloom, Harold, 120
Blueshirts, 102–03, 105, 107, 122
Bohlmann, Otto, 132 n. 14
Bornstein, George, 120, 125, 130 n. 2,
    131 n. 4
Bradford, Curtis, 120
Brannen, Anne, 130 n. 2
Bridge, Ursula, 131 n. 7
Bridges, Robert, 131 n. 7
Brooks, Cleanth, 119
Brown, Terence, 117
Browning, Robert, 30
Buddhism *or* Buddha, 5, 69, 70
Burke, Edmund, 85, 96, 122

Cabala *or* Cabalism, 18, 43, 69
Casement, Roger, 105
Castiglione, Baldassare, 60
Catholics *or* Catholicism, Protestants
    or Protestantism (or the
    Anglo-Irish): and Yeats's family
    background, 4; and his aversion
    to orthodox religious institutions,
    5; his attitudes shaped by Lady
    Gregory and the hostile Dublin
    reception of his early plays,
    38–39; and *The Green Helmet*, 55;
    and the "Introductory Rhymes"
    for *Responsibilities*, 59–60; and
    "September 1913," 60; and the
    Gore-Booth sisters, 74–75; and
    the Free State's treatment of
    Protestants, 79–80; and "The
    Tower," 85; and "Among School
    Children," 90–91; and Yeats's
    interest in Swift, 93–94; and

"Blood and the Moon," 96;
    and the Blueshirts, 102; and
    Purgatory, 112–13; *see also*
    aristocracy *and* eugenics
Chapman, Wayne K., 125, 130 n. 2
Chaudhry, Yug Mohit, 125
Childs, Donald J., 132 n. 13
Christ, 71, 77, 78, 94
Civil War, 64, 78–79, 81, 85, 88
Clark, David R., 121, 130 n. 2,
    131 n. 4
Clark, Rosalind E., 131 n. 4
class politics, *see* aristocracy
Coole Park, *see* Gregory, Lady Augusta
Craig, Cairns, 123
Craig, Gordon, 46, 122
Cullingford, Elizabeth Butler, 122, 123,
    124, 125
Cunard, Lady Emerald, 72
Curtis, Jared, 130 n. 2

Dante Alighieri, 67
Darwin, Charles, 1
Davis, Thomas, 5, 10, 11, 21
de Man, Paul, 125
de Valera, Eamon, 101–02, 107, 122
Deane, Seamus, 123
Descartes, René, 70
Dickinson, Mabel, 55, 75
Digges, Dudley, 40
Diggory, Terence, 125
Domville, Eric, 131 n. 6
Donoghue, Denis, 131 n. 3
Dowson, Ernest, 24

Easter Rising: breaks out, 63–64, 65;
    includes Maud Gonne's husband
    among its executed leaders, 64,
    65; its impact on Yeats's work, 66,
    67, 71; influences his attitude
    about World War I, 68; and *The
    Dreaming of the Bones*, 71; and
    Michael Robartes and the Dancer,
    73, 82; discussed by
    T. R. Henn, 119; *see also* "Easter,

1916" *and* "On a Political
Prisoner"

Eliot, T. S.: describes Yeats as
adumbrating Joyce, 48; praises *In
the Seven Woods*, 49, 59; his
modernist conception of the self
compared to Yeats's, 54; praises
the "Introductory Rhymes" to
Responsibilities, 59; attends
performance of *At the Hawk's
Well*, 72; his modernism
compared to Yeats's, 80, 81, 88,
123; influences the New
Critics, 120

Ellis, Edwin, 18

Ellmann, Richard, 117, 119

Emmet, Robert, 26, 60

Empedocles, 121

Engelberg, Edward, 121

eugenics, 29, 45, 101, 103, 104, 105,
110–11, 112–13, 128 n. 6,
132 n. 13

fascism, *see* Blueshirts

Fay, Frank *and* Fay, Willie, 40,
46, 47

Finneran, Richard J., 115, 116,
118, 125, 131 n. 4, 131 n. 4,
131 n. 7

Fitzgerald, Edward, 60

FitzGerald, Mary, 130 n. 2, 131 n. 4

Flannery, James W., 121–22

Fleming, Deborah, 123, 132 n. 23

Fletcher, Ian, 120

Foster, R. F., 117

Frayne, John P., 131 n. 4

Frazier, Adrian, 122

Free State: established, 64; Yeats
supports it during the Civil War,
but later questions its tendency to
make Catholic doctrine into law,
78–80; and "The Tower," 85; and
"Leda and the Swan," 89; passes
censorship bill, 93; and Yeats's
views on Swift, 94; and the "Crazy

Jane" poems, 99; and the
Blueshirts, 102, 103; discussed by
Elizabeth Cullingford, 124

Freud, Sigmund *or* Freudian theory,
26, 32, 81

Frieling, Barbara J., 130 n. 3

Frye, Northrop, 120

gender *or* sex *or* the body: and Maud
Gonne and *The Countess
Cathleen*, 13–16; and Olivia
Shakespear, Maud Gonne, *The
Secret Rose*, and *The Wind Among
the Reeds*, 23–35; Yeats idealizes
revised feminine archetype in *On
Baile's Strand* and "The Old Age
of Queen Maeve," 36–37; Yeats's
middle work becomes more
"masculine," 41, 52; and *Cathleen
ni Houlihan* 41, 42; and *On Baile's
Strand* and *The King's Threshold*,
42–45; and "In the Seven Woods,"
48; and "The Old Age of Queen
Maeve," 48; and "Adam's Curse,"
49; and "Old Memory," "Never
give all the Heart," and "O do not
Love Too Long," 51–52; and *The
Green Helmet*, 55; and the
"Introductory Rhymes" to
Responsibilities, 59–60; and "The
Phases of the Moon," 69–70;
Yeats's censuring of
"opinionated" women and "On a
Political Prisoner," "Michael
Robartes and the Dancer,"
"Solomon and the Witch," and
"A Prayer for My Daughter,"
75–77; his opposition to the Free
State's sexual Puritanism, 80; and
"Sailing to Byzantium" and
"The Tower," 83; and "Leda and
the Swan" and "Among School
Children," 89–91; and "A
Man Young and Old," 91–92; and
The Winding Stair and Other

Poems, 94; and the Crazy Jane poems and "In Memory of Eva Gore-Booth and Con Markievicz," 99–100; and Yeats's late infatuations, 105–06; and "Supernatural Songs," 107; discussed by Yeats's critics, 123–24; *see also* eugenics

Golden Dawn, 18–19, 37, 40, 43, 51, 64, 65, 97, 121

Goldsmith, Oliver, 96, 122

Gonne, Iseult, 34, 55, 64, 67, 68, 71, 75, 105

Gonne, Maud: Yeats's earliest responses to, 12–17; and "The Rose," 19; his fixation with her prevents him from pursuing other women, 24; and his liaison with Olivia Shakespear, 25, 26; and *The Wind Among the Reeds*, 31, 33; she confesses her affair with Millevoye, 33–35; her marriage's effect on him, 36–37, 39, 41, 51, 52, 54; her responses to his theatrical work, 38, 40, 61; plays title role in *Cathleen ni Houlihan*, 41; and *The King's Threshold*, 42, 44, 46; after her marriage falls apart, she and Yeats resume their spiritual union and conduct a brief sexual affair, 55; and "Friends," 62; Yeats proposes after MacBride's death, 64; and *The Wild Swans at Coole*, 68; and *The Only Jealousy of Emer*, 71; and Yeats's attraction to less uncontrollable women, 75; sides with anti-Treaty forces during the Civil War, 79; and "The Tower," 84; and "Among School Children," 90; and "A Man Young and Old," 91; and Yeats's eugenical views, 104; as author of *A Servant of the Queen*, 118; discussed by Deirdre Toomey,

124; her correspondence with Yeats, 131 n. 7; mentioned, 37, 58, 66

Gore-Booth, Eva, 74–75, 100

Gould, Warwick, 130 n. 1, 130 n. 3, 131 n. 6

Grattan, Henry, 85

Gregory, Lady Augusta: helps found the Irish National Theatre and has lasting impact on Yeats's politics, 37–38; supports him during controversy over Synge's *In the Shadow of the Glen*, 40; helps direct National Theatre Society, 40, 79; co-authors *Cathleen ni Houlihan*, 41–42; and "In the Seven Woods," 47, 48; and the Lane pictures controversy, 60; and "To a Friend whose Work has come to Nothing," 61; and "Friends," 62; and her son's death, 68; as an emblem of Anglo-Irish traditions, 75; her death and the downfall of Coole Park, 93, 100–01, 105, 111; her diaries, autobiographies, and correspondence, 118, 131 n. 7; discussed by Yeats's critics, 122, 124

Gregory, Major Robert, 68, 93

Grossman, Allen R., 124

gyres (or other references to historical cycles): and George Yeats's automatic writing, 71; and *Calvary*, 71; and "The Second Coming," 77–78; and the impact of *A Vision* on *The Tower*, 81; and Yeats's conception of Byzantium, 82; and "I see Phantoms of Hatred …," 87; and "Nineteen Hundred and Nineteen," 88; and "Leda and the Swan," 89; and "Among School Children," 91; and *The Resurrection*, 94; and *The Winding Stair and Other Poems*,

94; and "Blood and the Moon,"
96; and "The Gyres," 107, 108;
and "Lapis Lazuli," 108

Hall, James, 119
Harper, George Mills, 118, 121,
130 n. 3
Harper, Margaret Mills, 130 n. 3
Harris, Daniel A., 132 n. 18
Harwood, John, 117
Heald, Edith Shackleton, 106
Henn, T. R., 119
Heraclitus, 121, 129 n. 12
Hinduism, 5, 69, 107
history, *see* gyres
Hitler, Adolf, 101, 108
Holdeman, David, 125, 130 n. 2
Holdsworth, Carolyn, 130 n. 2
Hone, Joseph, 117
Horniman, Annie, 40, 47, 122
Hough, Graham, 120
Howes, Marjorie, 124
Hügel, Friedrich, Baron von, 98
Hyde, Douglas, 40

Ibsen, Henrik, 46
illnesses, 92–93, 94, 104–05, 114
Irish Civil War, *see* Civil War
Irish Free State, *see* Free State
Irish War of Independence, *see* War of
Independence
Ito, Michio, 72

Jeffares, A. Norman, 115, 116, 117,
118, 131 n. 7
Jochum, K. P. S., 115, 118
Johnson, Colton, 131 n. 4
Johnson, Lionel, 22, 23, 24, 25
Joyce, James, 16, 32, 48, 54, 80, 81, 124
Jung, Carl, 121

Keane, Patrick J., 133 n. 24
Kearney, Richard, 123
Keats, John, 30, 31, 67, 91, 109
Kelly, John, 131 n. 5, 131 n. 6

Kenner, Hugh, 124
Kermode, Frank, 120
Kiberd, Declan, 123
Kinahan, Frank, 125
Kline, Gloria C., 123
Krans, Horatio Sheafe, 118

Land War, 38
Lane, Sir Hugh, 60, 61
Leavis, F. R., 119
Logue, Cardinal Michael, 39
Loizeaux, Elizabeth Bergmann, 125
Longenbach, James, 132 n. 13

MacBride, Major John, 37, 39, 42, 55,
64, 73
MacDonagh, Thomas, 73
Macleod, Fiona, *see* Sharp, William
MacNeice, Louis, 118–19
MacSwiney, Terence, 44
Maddox, Brenda, 117
Maeterlinck, Maurice, 46, 122
Mahaffey, Vicki, 124
Mangan, James, 10, 11, 19
Mannin, Ethel 106
Marchaterre, Madeleine, 131 n. 4
Marcus, Phillip L., 121, 125, 130 n. 2,
130 n. 3
Markievicz, Constance (née
Gore-Booth), 73, 74–75, 100
Martinich, Robert A., 130 n. 3
Martyn, Edward, 37, 39, 40
masks *or* "the mask": and modernist
conceptions of the self, 53–54, 81;
and *The Green Helmet*, 55; and
*The Green Helmet and Other
Poems*, 56–57; and
Responsibilities, 59, 60, 61; and
"Ego Dominus Tuus," 67; and
"In Memory of Major Robert
Gregory," 68; and "The Phases of
the Moon," 69; and *At the Hawk's
Well*, 73; and "Sailing to
Byzantium," 82; and "Among
School Children," 90; and *New*

Poems, 107; and "Lapis Lazuli," 108; and "Under Ben Bulben," 110; Yeats's thinking influenced by Wilde and Nietzsche, 128 n. 15; mentioned, 76
Mathers, MacGregor, 18
Matthews, Steven, 125
Mays, J. C. C., 130 n. 2
McCormack, W. J., 123
McHugh, Roger, 131 n. 7
Melchiori, Giorgio, 125
Michelangelo Buonarroti, 110
Mikhail, E. H., 118
Mill, John Stuart, 1
Miller, Liam, 122
Millevoye, Lucien, 13, 34, 36
Mitchel, John, 110
modernism *or* modern poetry: 49, 53–54, 58, 80–81, 88, 120, 123, 132 n. 13
Moore, George, 118
Moore, T. Sturge, 131 n. 7
Morris, William, 6, 12, 25, 30, 120, 122
Murphy, Daniel J., 131 n. 8
Murphy, William M., 117, 118
Mussolini, Benito, 101, 102, 108

Nathan, Leonard, 121
Nietzsche, Friedrich, 54, 69, 128 n. 15, 132 n. 14
Noh drama, 47, 72–73, 122
North, Michael, 123
Northern Ireland, 41, 64, 78, 79, 123

O'Brien, Conor Cruise, 122, 123
O'Casey, Sean, 80, 118
O'Connor, Frank, 118
O'Donnell, Frank Hugh, 39
O'Donnell, William H., 130 n. 2, 131 n. 4
O'Duffy, General Eoin, 102, 107
O'Hara, Daniel T., 125
O'Higgins, Kevin, 92, 96, 102
O'Leary, John, 5–6, 10, 60, 122
O'Shea, Edward, 115

O'Shea, Katharine, 17
Olney, James, 121
Oppel, Frances Nesbitt, 132 n. 14
Order of the Golden Dawn, *see* Golden Dawn
Orr, Leonard, 133 n. 28

Parkinson, Thomas, 119–20, 130 n. 2
Parmenides, 121
Parnell, Charles Stewart, 6, 17, 34, 60, 105, 107
Parrish, Stephen, 130 n. 2
Pater, Walter, 120
Pearse, Patrick, 73
Pethica, James, 124, 130 n. 2, 131 n. 8
phases of the moon, *see* afterlife
Phillips, Catherine, 130 n. 2
Picasso, Pablo, 80, 81
Pierce, David, 118, 125, 126
Pinter, Harold, 122
Plato, 70, 83, 84, 90, 121
Plotinus, 84
Poe, Edgar Allan, 27
Pollexfen, William, 4, 60
Pound, Ezra: his modernist conception of the self compared to Yeats's, 54; reviews *Responsibilities*, 58; introduces Yeats to Noh drama, 72; attends performance of *At the Hawk's Well*, 72; his modernism compared to Yeats's, 81, 88, 123; the Yeatses join him in Rapallo, 93; mentioned, 58, 59
Pre-Raphaelites, 6, 30
Protestants *or* Protestantism: *see* Catholics *or* Catholicism, Protestants *or* Protestantism
Purohit Swami, Shri, 130 n. 22
Putzel, Steven, 124
Pythagoras, 70, 121

Quinn, Maire, 40

Raine, Kathleen, 132 n. 16
Ramazani, Jahan, 123

Ransom, John Crowe, 119
reception: of *The Wanderings of Oisin
    and Other Poems*, 12; of *The
    Countess Kathleen and Various
    Legends and Lyrics*, 22–23; of *The
    Secret Rose* and *The Wind Among
    the Reeds*, 33; hostile reactions to
    the Irish Literary Theatre, 38,
    40–41; of *Responsibilities and
    Other Poems*, 58–59; of *Later
    Poems*, 80; of *The Tower*, 92
reincarnation, *see* afterlife
revisions: of *The Wanderings of Oisin
    and Other Poems*, 7; of *The
    Countess Cathleen*, 15–16; of *The
    Wind Among the Reeds*, 30; of *The
    King's Threshold*, 44; of Yeats's
    oeuvre between 1904 and 1908,
    51–52; of *The Wild Swans at
    Coole*, 68; of "A Man Young and
    Old," 92; of "Three Songs to the
    Same Tune," 103; of *New Poems*
    and *Last Poems and Two Plays*
    into *Last Poems & Plays*, 109; as
    interpreted by Yeats's editors
    and critics, 115–17, 120, 121, 125
Rhymers Club, 24
Rhys, Ernest, 23
Ricoeur, Paul, 125
Rohan, Virginia Bartholome, 130 n. 2
Romanticism, 6, 8, 12, 20–21, 49,
    53–54, 81, 120
Rosicrucianism, 18
Rossetti, Christina, 12
Rossetti, Dante Gabriel, 25, 30, 120
Rousseau, Jean-Jacques, 53
Ruddock, Margot, 105–06, 111,
    131 n. 7
Ruskin, John, 6, 120
Russell, George, 5, 23
Russian Revolution, 77, 78

Saddlemyer, Ann, 117, 131 n. 7
Said, Edward W., 123
Savoy magazine, 24–25, 26, 27, 30, 89

Schoenberg, Arnold, 80
Schuchard, Ronald, 131 n. 6
Senate, Yeats's service in the, 79–80,
    89, 93
sex, *see* gender
Shakespear, Olivia: her sexual affair
    with Yeats, 25, 26, 34; and "The
    Binding of the Hair," 27; and
    The Wind Among the Reeds, 31,
    32–33; resumes friendship with
    Yeats, 58; and "Friends," 62; Yeats
    meets George through
    Shakespear's social circle, 63–64,
    65; mentioned, 55
Shakespeare, William, 108
Sharp, William, 23
Shaw, George Bernard, 23, 46
Shelley, Percy Bysshe, 6, 8, 31, 109, 120
Sidnell, Michael J., 125, 130 n. 2,
    130 n. 3
Siegel, Sandra F., 130 n. 2
Smithers, Leonard, 24
Smythe, Colin, 131 n. 8
Sophocles, 92
Spenser, Edmund, 45, 91
Sprayberry, Sandra L., 130 n. 3
Stalin, Joseph, 101
Stallworthy, Jon, 120
Stanfield, Paul Scott, 122
Stead, C. K., 132 n. 13
Stein, Gertrude, 80
Steinach operation, 105, 106
Steinmann, Martin, 119
Swift, Jonathan, 93–94, 96, 122
symbols *or* symbolism: compared to
    magical spells, 5, 8, 18–19;
    used more sparingly in Yeats's
    middle works, 46, 47, 48, 52;
    compared to masks, 53, 82;
    Yeats's views summed up in "The
    Symbolism of Poetry," 128 n. 12;
    mentioned, 61
Symons, Arthur, 24, 33, 37
Synge, John Millington, 40–41, 42, 44,
    54–55, 60, 131 n. 7

Tate, Allen, 119, 120
Taylor, Richard, 122
Theosophy, 5, 8, 11, 18, 69
Thoor Ballylee, 71, 78, 86, 88, 93, 96
Thoreau, Henry David, 21
Thuente, Mary Helen, 125
Tone, Theobald Wolfe, 26, 60
Toomey, Deirdre, 117, 124, 131 n. 6
Torchiana, Donald T., 122
Tynan, Katharine, 14

Unterecker, John, 124

Vendler, Helen, 121

Wade, Allan, 115, 118
War of Independence, 44, 64, 71, 73, 78, 81, 88
Watson, G. J., 132 n. 22
Wellesley, Dorothy, 106, 108, 131 n. 7
Whitaker, Thomas R., 121
White, Anna MacBride, 131 n. 7
Wilde, Oscar, 12, 24, 54, 124, 128 n. 15
Wilson, Edmund, 120
Wilson, F. A. C., 121
Winnett, Steven, 130 n. 2
Winters, Yvor, 119
Witemeyer, Hugh, 131 n. 4
Woolf, Virginia, 80, 81, 92
Wordsworth, William, 12, 21, 53
World War I: suspends implementation of Irish Home Rule, 63; Yeats's ambivalence about, 68; and "The Second Coming," 77, 78, 81; and modernism, 81; and "Nineteen Hundred and Nineteen," 88; and "Lapis Lazuli," 108; mentioned, 64
Worth, Katharine, 122

Yeats, Anne Butler, 71, 79
Yeats: An Annual of Critical and Textual Studies, 115, 117, 118, 126
Yeats Annual, 117, 126

Yeats, Elizabeth Corbet ("Lolly"), 58, 66, 81, 94, 109
Yeats, Georgie ("George," née Hyde Lees): marries Yeats and begins experiments with automatic writing, 65; and "Shepherd and Goatherd," 68; and "The Phases of the Moon," 69; and "The Double Vision of Michael Robartes," 70; George's automatic writing shifts to historical matters, 71; and *The Only Jealousy of Emer*, 71; and Yeats's attraction to women less uncontrollable than Gonne, 75; and "The Second Coming," 78; is nearly shot during the Civil War, 79; and "The Tower," 84; goes to Rapallo with Yeats, 93; returns with Yeats from Rapallo to Dublin, 93; drifts apart from Yeats after the automatic writing ceases, 105–06; accompanies Yeats to Cap Martin, 113; has him buried in France, 114; mentioned, 68, 82
Yeats, Jack Butler, 3
Yeats, John Butler, 1, 2–3, 4, 5, 6, 14
Yeats, Michael Butler, 71
Yeats, Susan Mary (née Pollexfen), 2, 4, 14, 26, 37, 124
Yeats, William Butler
  single poems or poetic sequences:
  "Adam's Curse," 48, 49–50, 51
  "All Souls' Night," 81, 92
  "All Things can tempt Me," 57
  "Among School Children," 89–91, 92
  "Ancestral Houses," 85–86, 124
  "Another Song of a Fool," 70
  "Arrow, The," 48
  "At Galway Races," 57
  "Baile and Aillinn," 48
  "Beggar to Beggar cried," 62
  "Black Tower, The," 111, 114

"Blood and the Moon," 96
"Brown Penny," 57
"Byzantium," 68, 94, 96, 97–98, 99
"Cap and Bells, The," 32
"Circus Animals' Desertion, The,"
  111, 112
"Closing Rhyme" ["While I,
  from that reed-throated
  whisperer"], 59, 60, 63
"Coat, A," 63
"Cold Heaven, The," 62
"Colonus' Praise," 129 n. 9
"Coole and Ballylee, 1931,"
  100–01
"Coole Park, 1929," 100
"Crazed Girl, A," 106
"Crazy Jane and Jack the
  Journeyman," 99
"Crazy Jane Grown Old Looks at
  the Dancers," 99–100
"Crazy Jane Talks with the
  Bishop," 99
"Cuchulain Comforted," 111
"Cuchulain's Fight with the
  Sea," 21
"Curse of Cromwell, The," 105
"Dialogue of Self and Soul, A,"
  94–96, 98, 99, 101
"Dolls, The," 62–63
"Double Vision of Michael
  Robartes, The," 70, 76
"Easter, 1916," 73–74, 75, 77
"Ego Dominus Tuus," 67
"Everlasting Voices, The," 31
"Fascination of What's Difficult,
  The," 56, 59
"Fergus and the Druid," 21
"Fiddler of Dooney, The," 33
"First Love," 91
"Fisherman, The," 67
"Folly of being Comforted, The,"
  48, 49
"Friends," 62, 63
"From 'Oedipus at Colonus,'" 92
"Grey Rock, The," 60, 128 n. 20

"Gyres, The," 107, 108, 109
"Happy Townland, The," 48
"He bids his Beloved be at
  Peace," 31
"He gives his Beloved certain
  Rhymes," 27, 32
"He mourns for the Change that
  has come upon Him and his
  Beloved, and longs for the End
  of the World," 32
"He tells of the Perfect
  Beauty," 33
"He wishes for the Cloths of
  Heaven," 33
"He wishes his Beloved were
  Dead," 29–30, 32
"His Dream," 56
"Hosting of the Sidhe, The," 30
"Hour before Dawn, The," 62
"Human Dignity," 91
"I see Phantoms of Hatred and of
  the Heart's Fullness and of the
  Coming Emptiness," 87, 89
"In Memory of Eva Gore-Booth
  and Con Markievicz," 100
"In Memory of Major Robert
  Gregory," 68, 85
"In the Seven Woods," 47–48,
  49, 85
"Indian to his Love, The," 9
"Indian upon God, The," 9
"Into the Twilight," 32
"Introductory Rhymes"
  ["Pardon, old fathers, if you
  still remain"], 59–60
"Irish Airman foresees his Death,
  An," 68
"Lake Isle of Innisfree, The,"
  21–22, 77
"Lapis Lazuli," 108–09, 113
"Leaders of the Crowd, The," 75
"Leda and the Swan," 81,
  89–90, 125
"Lines written in Dejection,"
  67–68

Yeats, William Butler (cont.)
"Living Beauty, The," 68
"Lover mourns for the Loss of
Love, The," 31
"Madness of King Goll, The,"
9–11, 12, 15
"Magi, The," 62
"Man and the Echo," 106, 111–12
"Man Young and Old, A," 89,
91–92, 94
"Mask, The," 56, 57
"Meditations in Time of Civil
War," 85–88, 89, 91, 92, 96
"Memory," 68
"Men improve with the
Years," 67–68
"Mermaid, The," 91
"Meru," 107
"Michael Robartes and the
Dancer," 76, 77
"Municipal Gallery Re-visited,
The" 107
"My Descendants," 86
"My House," 86
"My Table," 86, 90
"Never give all the
Heart," 51–52, 54
"Nineteen Hundred and
Nineteen," 88–89, 91, 92, 95
"No Second Troy," 59
"O do not Love Too Long,"
51–52, 54
"Old Age of Queen Maeve, The,"
36, 48, 52
"Old Memory," 51–52
"On a Political Prisoner,"
74–75, 77
"On being asked for a War
Poem," 68
"On Woman," 75
"Parnell's Funeral," 107
"Paudeen," 61, 63, 111
"Phases of the Moon,
The," 69–70, 103
"Poet to His Beloved, A," 32

"Prayer for my Daughter,
A," 76–77, 82
"Presences," 68
"Realists, The," 62
"Red Hanrahan's Song about
Ireland," 48
"Ribh at the Tomb of Baile and
Aillinn," 107
"Ribh denounces Patrick," 107
"Road at My Door, The," 87
"Rose of Battle, The," 19
"Rose of Peace, The," 19
"Rose of the World, The," 19, 21
"Rose Tree, The," 73
"Running to Paradise," 62
"Sad Shepherd, The," 9
"Sailing to Byzantium," 81,
82–83, 90, 91, 92, 94, 97, 109
"Saint and the Hunchback,
The," 70
"Second Coming, The," 71,
77–78, 81
"Secret Rose, The," 35, 46
"September 1913," 60–61, 125
"Shepherd and Goatherd,"
68–69
"Sixteen Dead Men," 73
"Solomon and the Witch," 76
"Song, A," 68
"Song from 'The Player Queen,'
A," 62
"Song of the Happy Shepherd,
The," 7–9, 10, 12, 20, 113
"Song of Wandering Aengus,
The," 31
"Spur, The," 106, 107
"Stare's Nest by My Window,
The," 87
"Statues, The," 111
"Stolen Child, The," 11–12, 30
"Supernatural Songs," 107
"Sweet Dancer," 106
"These are the Clouds," 57, 85
"Three Beggars, The," 61, 62
"Three Hermits, The," 61

"Three Marching Songs," *see*
  "Three Songs to the Same
  Tune"
"Three Songs to the Same Tune,"
  103, 104, 106
"To a Child dancing in the
  Wind," 62
"To a Friend whose Work has
  come to Nothing," 61
"To a Wealthy Man who
  promised a second
  Subscription to the Dublin
  Municipal Gallery if it were
  proved the People wanted
  Pictures," 60
"To a Young Beauty," 68
"To a Young Girl," 68
"To Dorothy Wellesley," 106
"To Ireland in the Coming
  Times," 20–21
"To the Rose upon the Rood of
  Time," 19, 20, 21, 22, 26
"Tower, The," 83–85, 92, 96
"Two Kings, The," 128 n. 20
"Two Songs of a Fool," 70
"Two Years Later," 62
"Under Ben Bulben," 109–111
"Upon a Dying Lady," 67
"Upon a House shaken by the
  Land Agitation," 57
"Vacillation," 96, 98–99, 112
"Valley of the Black Pig,
  The," 32
"Wanderings of Oisin, The," 7,
  9–10, 11, 12, 14, 15, 83
"When You are Old," 125
"Why should not Old Men be
  Mad?," 104
"Wild Old Wicked Man,
  The," 106
"Wild Swans at Coole, The," 67
"Woman Young and Old, A,"
  94, 99
"Words for Music Perhaps," 99
"Words," 56

plays:
  At the Hawk's Well, 71–73, 84, 92,
    129 n. 3
  Calvary, 71, 78
  Cat and the Moon, The, 94
  Cathleen ni Houlihan, 41–42, 43,
    111, 124
  Countess Cathleen, The, 15–16,
    37, 38, 39, 40, 54, 124
  Death of Cuchulain, The, 109, 113,
    129 n. 3
  Deirdre, 51, 121
  Dreaming of the Bones, The, 71,
    73, 113, 121
  Fighting the Waves, 94
  Full Moon in March, A, 106
  Green Helmet, The, 54–55,
    129 n. 3
  Hour-Glass, The, 42, 47
  *King of the Great Clock Tower,
    The*, 106
  King's Threshold, The, 42, 44–45,
    46, 47, 51, 103, 110
  *Land of Heart's Desire,
    The*, 22–23
  On Baile's Strand, 36, 42–44, 46,
    47, 48, 51, 52, 55, 71, 129 n. 3
  Only Jealousy of Emer, The, 71, 72,
    94, 129 n. 3
  Pot of Broth, The, 42
  Purgatory, 68, 99, 109, 111,
    112–13, 121, 124
  Resurrection, The, 94
  *Words upon the Window-Pane,
    The*, 93–94, 99, 113, 121
volumes of poems and/or plays:
  *Cat and the Moon and Certain
    Poems, The*, 129 n. 9
  *Countess Kathleen and Various
    Legends and Lyrics, The*, 15,
    19, 22
  "Crossways," 7–12
  Four Plays for Dancers, 71–73
  Full Moon in March, A, 106–07,
    130 n. 21

Yeats, William Butler (cont.)
  Green Helmet and Other Poems,
    The, 56–58, 59
  In the Seven Woods, 47–50, 51–52,
    54, 58, 59
  King of the Great Clock Tower,
    Commentaries and Poems, The,
    106–07
  Last Poems & Plays (1940),
    109
  Last Poems and Two Plays (1939),
    107, 109–113
  Michael Robartes and the Dancer,
    71, 73–78, 80, 81
  New Poems, 107–09
  October Blast, 129 n. 9
  "Parnell's Funeral and Other
    Poems," 129 n. 21
  Responsibilities and Other Poems,
    58–63, 64, 66–67, 107,
    130 n. 20
  "Rose, The," 19–22, 48, 59
  Seven Poems and a Fragment,
    129 n. 9
  Tower, The, 81–92, 94, 95, 99, 106,
    124, 125
  Wanderings of Oisin and Other
    Poems, The, 7, 9, 12
  Wheels and Butterflies, 94
  Wild Swans at Coole,
    The, 66–70, 75
  Wind Among the Reeds, The, 23,
    24, 25, 26, 27, 29–33, 35, 47,
    48, 58, 59, 80, 124
  Winding Stair and Other Poems,
    The (1933), 94–101, 105, 106
  Winding Stair, The (1929), 94
  Words for Music Perhaps and
    Other Poems, 94
  collected editions:
  Collected Poems of W. B. Yeats, The
    (1933), 116
  Collected Works in Verse and
    Prose, 51, 52
  Later Poems, 80, 92

  Poems (1895), 7, 19, 22, 23, 51, 80
  Poems, 1899–1905, 51
  other works (e.g., fiction,
    autobiographical and critical
    writings, folklore collections,
    occult treatises):
  "Adoration of the Magi,
    The," 27
  "Binding of the Hair, The,"
    26–27, 32, 106
  Celtic Twilight, The, 23
  "Certain Noble Plays of
    Japan," 72
  "Death of Synge, The," 53
  Discoveries, 52–53
  "Estrangement," 53
  Fairy and Folk Tales of the Irish
    Peasantry, 11
  Ideas of Good and Evil, 128 n. 12
  Irish Fairy Tales, 11
  John Sherman, 14, 15
  "Magic," 104, 128 n. 12
  On the Boiler, 103–04, 105, 106,
    109, 111, 112, 113
  Per Amica Silentia Lunae, 53
  Reveries over Childhood and
    Youth, 58, 59, 63, 64
  "Rosa Alchemica," 27–29, 31, 33,
    44, 56, 97, 98, 103, 110
  Secret Rose, The, 23, 25, 26–29, 30,
    33, 58, 124
  Stories of Red Hanrahan, 27
  "Symbolism of Poetry, The,"
    128 n. 12
  "Tables of the Law, The," 27
  Ten Principal Upanishads, The,
    130 n. 22
  Trembling of the Veil, The, 80,
    129 n. 2
  Vision, A, 65, 69, 78, 81, 82, 88,
    89, 92, 94, 103, 119, 121,
    129 n. 2, 132 n. 16; *see also*
    afterlife
Yellow Book, 24, 25
Young, David, 124